IS IT A LOST CAUSE?

Is It a Lost Cause?

HAVING THE HEART OF GOD
FOR THE CHURCH'S CHILDREN

Marva J. Dawn

William B. Eerdmans Publishing Company
Grand Rapids, Michigan / Cambridge, U.K.

Library of Congress Cataloging-in-Publication Data

Dawn, Marva J.

Is it a lost cause? having the heart of God for the church's children/

Marva J. Dawn

p.   cm.

Includes bibliographical references.

ISBN 0-8028-4373-5 (pbk: alk. paper)

1. Church work with children — United States.

2. Christian education of children — United States.

3. Christianity and culture — United States.

4. United States — Church history — 20th century.

I. Title.

BR526.D37 1997

261.8'3423 — dc21   97-17548

CIP

Unless otherwise noted, Scripture quotations are from the New Revised Standard Version of the Bible, copyright © 1989 by the Division of Christian Education of the National Council of the Churches of Christ in the U.S.A., and used by permission.

The author and publisher wish to thank the individuals and publishers listed on page 256 for permission to use the listed materials in this book.

This book is dedicated

to children everywhere,
who deserve to be treasured
because they are the beloved of God
and who need to be mentored and guided and formed
because they are children,

and especially
to my godchildren —
Heidi (and Tim),
Katie,
Joy Marva,
Martha,
Zachary and Rachel,

and particularly in memory of
Joshua Critchett (1979-1997),
beloved godson of strong faith,
whose tragic death, we pray,
will also be a means somehow
of glorifying God.

Contents

CONTENTS

PART TWO
Having God's Heart for Our Children
in a Contrary World

CHAPTER 1

Prologue: This Is Not the Book I Started to Write

Or, Can You Find a Good Roofer Anywhere These Days?

Bless all those who nurture children,
sharing knowledge, showing love,
who by faithful words and actions
lead young lives to God above!
Bless all those whose voice and presence,
deep devotion, dignity,
motivate the church to rev'rence,
guiding Christ's community!

Jesus taught both by example and
with words of lasting worth;
Christ has given ways to sample
hints of heaven here on earth!
In the same way Christian teachers
model true humanity,
demonstrating in their witness
glimpses of eternity!

PROLOGUE

Bless these lives of dedication —
days and seasons, weeks and years,
spent in serving congregations,
spreading joys and soothing tears!
Bless these lives so firmly planted
in the grace the Savior brings,
flourishing as God has granted,
soaring high on Spirit wings!

John A. Dalles (1993, modified 1994)
Tune: Hymn to Joy, Ludwig van Beethoven (1824)[1]

The new roof on our study addition was still leaking after two months and in spite of various efforts by its builder to fix it. Meanwhile, he kept telling us that the problem was the roof on the rest of the house, which he would fix for a reasonable price. We called two other roofers to get bids to compare — and to our enormous surprise both of them said that the old roof was just fine. Then they showed us everything faulty about the new roof; it had been built entirely wrong! When we confronted the first builder with the evidence, he argued and accused and lied and lambasted.

---

1. I have been immensely formed by hymns, which "pray twice" with both their melody and their deep words; consequently, all of the chapters and parts in this book begin with a hymn, new or old, that captures well some of my emphases. This one begins the book, of course, because my major goal here is to pray for God's blessings on all who work with children as their parents, pastors, youth directors, and teachers and to encourage them to recognize the importance of their words and care and modeling. Because poetry and music are excellent tools to reinforce lessons learned or to stimulate new avenues for thinking, I pray that you will not skip over these songs but will contemplate them carefully. I hope especially that you will read these aloud — or, if possible, sing them (you can find the melodies in a hymnbook if you don't know them already) — in order that their sound can also heighten the enrichment. This hymn is sung to the well-known melody of the last movement of Beethhoven's 9th Symphony, the setting of the hymn "Joyful, Joyful, We Adore You." All of the hymns printed are from *The Moravian Book of Worship* (Bethlehem, PA: Moravian Church in America, 1995).

Can you find a good roofer anywhere these days — one who is a craftsman with his work, who is totally competent, honest, and trustworthy? Throughout our society — in government, commerce, social services, construction — we are desperate for persons of integrity, people of moral character, individuals who work hard and well, people who make us glad to be alive with them. How can these virtues be formed?

Of course, I'm not so much worried about builders in this book — though the hassles with them have prevented me from writing this in a study with enough space to work without losing notes, pieces of research, my temper, or time. I am concerned about what causes people, such as builders, to develop certain kinds of character, particular attitudes toward life, specific priorities that influence how they work and relate and think. My experiences over thirty years of working with thousands of young people in churches and schools, convocations and camps make me especially troubled about children in Christian families, members of the Church, residents of God's household. How are our children being formed? Do they know themselves primarily as citizens of the kingdom of God? Do we and our offspring look, act, talk, and think like people who are shaped by the narratives of our faith, by God's Revelation?

As I revise this introduction, our roof has been rebuilt by a young man whose honesty and skill are lauded by those who know him well. We were impressed because he refused to use certain slightly inferior techniques and materials, answered our questions thoroughly and courteously, and hired minority men to be his helpers. He was recommended to us by a contractor who is known for his faithful participation in the Church. Other workers have not been so diligent and skillful, with the remarkable exception of the cabinet builder. One day, as we talked together about faith and ethics and ministry, he said, "You know, we can get so busy with our work and other stuff that we forget that we are here on earth for just one reason." When I look at the cabinets his company built, I can tell that he cares about glorifying God with excellent craftsmanship.

In our region of the state of Washington there is a community of Finnish Apostolic Lutherans. They are very devout Christians, a bit set apart from the world in their refusal usually to own television sets, in their strong commitment to families, in their kindness to everyone, and in their diligent labor. All the teachers I know who have Apostolic Lutherans in their classrooms are supremely grateful because, in contrast to the typical U.S.[2] student, these children are usually careful and thorough workers, courteous youngsters, willing and gracious helpers, students who are eager to learn.

On our wedding anniversary the year I had cancer, a man who is an Apostolic Lutheran came to investigate for the power company why our radio was so full of static. As he explored our electrical problems, we chatted about why music was so helpful when I felt so ill from chemotherapy — and about faith. As he was leaving I thanked him profusely for solving our problems (caused, he discovered, by the doorbell motor) and ended with "I hope you have a wonderful day." He replied, "I already have." That gentle man brought me healing both with his good work to restore my music and with his gracious character.

What do certain groups, like the Apostolic Lutherans, do to cause their children to grow up with such integrity and faith? Is it possible to nurture children and develop adults so profoundly without retreating into an isolation that would keep us from ministering to the world around us? Obviously the answer is Yes, since the Apostolic Lutherans and the cabinet builder are highly respected in this region.

But why is it not happening more often? Why do we find ourselves trusting the work of others less and less? Why do we worry about the habits of the children in my husband's fifth grade class and wonder what will become of them in the future? Most important for my purposes here, why do I encounter lots of teenagers at church youth convocations who don't have the fog-

---

2. I write "the typical U.S. student" instead of "the typical American student" here because I think Christians should avoid the imperialism of calling ourselves "Americans," since the United States is only one part of the whole hemisphere, and most of us are immigrants from other lands. This is especially important because the true Americans, the natives of South and North America, continue to be oppressed in many places, such as Guatemala and areas in Mexico.

giest notion of what it means to believe and live as a Christian? Why do the Church's young people make the same choices as the rest of the world about their sexuality, their use of money and time, their attitudes toward work, their flippancy and cynicism?

Wait! Your impulse might be to get away from these questions as fast as possible, but they reveal a formidable problem. Why do so many of the youth in our churches not really understand why their faith is important, what it means, who they are in light of it, how we live because we believe?

On my way to writing a book about ethics and moral formation I realized that it needed a prelude — not a soft flute or violin wooing us to contemplation, but a piercing trumpet blast to wake us up. Our increasingly postmodern[3] world is, usually unconsciously, desperate for the gifts of the Christian faith, and what are our churches doing in response? Individuals without a home yearn for community; people without a story seek a framework for understanding; "boomers" who have rejected moral authority search for a reference point; "busters" without motivation long for meaning beyond the next entertainment; teenagers pursue love and ache for it to last; children crave attention and a reason to care about anything. Are our churches hospitable enough to enfold them all in God's Way and Truth and Life? Most of all, are we raising our own children to live the substance and presence of faith — and to pass God's love and their faith on to their friends, neighbors, and peers at school? Or are we letting them be sucked into the behavior patterns, the attitudes, the meaninglessness, and the despair of the world around them?

---

3. Those elements of postmodernism that are important for our discussion in these pages will be elaborated as we go along, but especially in Chapter 2. At first glance, some of the word choices and descriptions in this book might seem unnecessary and/or too difficult. Please bear with me through my explanations. I am convinced that members of the Church must understand thoroughly these aspects of our contemporary times, so that we use the right resources to counteract them — especially for our children's sake!

We Are Not In Charge Anymore

Is the raising of genuinely *Christian* children a lost cause in our post-Christian society? My claim in this book is that it is not — if we wake up. I am not so presumptuous as to think that my little efforts here will make much difference, but I pray that at least some parents or pastors will realize from reading this book that the task is larger than we had previously acknowledged. In fact, it is a mortal combat with the principalities and powers.

I suppose some readers might wince when I use the words *principalities and powers* because that biblical notion has been reduced in our times to contorted stories of little demons flying around and spewing sulfur (in such novels as Frank Peretti's *This Present Darkness*). Contrarily, I use the phrase as the Bible does to signify societal forces, cultural directions, and social institutions that contradict the purposes of God. These powers will be displayed in the second part of this book, but don't worry: we won't get bogged down in technical details. A complete exegetical and sociological description of the powers is not necessary here.[4]

What is necessary is a wake-up call — for the Church to realize that we are not in charge anymore. In the past children were formed with Christian values more easily because the society around us supported Christian beliefs, ethics, and rites. The dominant culture never has to worry about character formation because its principles and morals are easily imbibed.

But Christianity is no longer the dominant culture in the United States. If we want our children to grow up with Christian convictions, capacities, and choices, we must much more deliberately nurture the faith and its concomitant lifestyle.

This book is a prelude, then, to a fuller exposition of trinitarian biblical ethics.[5] This overture is an attempt to rouse parents, congre-

---

4. For a more thorough explication, see Marva J. Dawn, "The Concept of 'the Principalities and Powers' in the Works of Jacques Ellul" (Ph.D. dissertation, University of Notre Dame, 1992).

5. My future book on ethics, sketched before this one was written, is tentatively called *For Mercy's Sake: An Easter Ethic of Biblical Formation* (forthcoming from Eerdmans).

gations, and church leaders to *see* what is happening in our culture and therefore to our children and to suggest some means by which we can *counteract* the principalities and powers. Let us together be more deliberate in *thinking Christianly* about raising children.

Why Is Another Book Necessary?

I am not so smug as to think my purpose here is unique. There certainly are many others issuing this call extremely well.[6] You might wonder, then, why this book is necessary. Why do I have to write it?

It is an urgency, a passion, the old Jeremiah problem that the Word is fire in my bones and I am weary of holding it in. I watch too many young people at a loss for who they are. I observe too many children who have no way to know that they are the beloved of God. I am tired of seeing the boys and girls in my husband's classroom bored with life and uninterested in learning. I counsel too many youths who have made serious mistakes because no one ever told them that God has a better idea concerning their sexuality — or their money, or their time, or their goals. I notice youngsters at grocery stores who in their insatiable craving for instant gratification are headed for trouble, kids in elementary school who lash out in violence they learned from television, teenagers at youth convocations who hate themselves, students at colleges and universities who try to drown their pain in destructive entertainments. I meet too

---

6. Though not all dealing specifically with children, but laying groundwork in understanding the Christian community, some of the best are Rodney Clapp, *A Peculiar People: The Church as Culture in a Post-Christian Society* (Downers Grove, IL: InterVarsity Press, 1996), and *Families at the Crossroads: Beyond Traditional and Modern Options* (Downers Grove, IL: InterVarsity Press, 1993); Stanley Hauerwas and William H. Willimon, *Resident Aliens* (Nashville: Abingdon, 1989); George R. Hunsberger and Craig Van Gelder, eds., *The Church Between Gospel and Culture: The Emerging Mission in North America* (Grand Rapids: Eerdmans, 1996); Chris William Erdman, *Beyond Chaos: Living the Christian Family in a World Like Ours* (Grand Rapids: Eerdmans, 1996); and especially Dorothy C. Bass, ed., *Practicing Our Faith: A Way of Life for a Searching People* (San Francisco: Jossey-Bass, 1997).

many pastors and parents struggling by themselves to raise children in faith. I cry with too many teachers and counselors who despair over the immense problems of the children for whom they serve. I encounter too many churches who are doing things in their Sunday schools, youth groups, and worship services that trivialize God and trivialize the young people. I listen to too many teenagers begging for more depth, for a God worth loving and a Christianity worth pursuing. All these are too many cries and needs for me not to try to do something. And the issues are so important that every attempt to wake up churches contributes a little.

My inability to have children of my own because of physical handicaps makes me more concerned for all children. My husband and I worry deeply about the overwhelming percentage of children in his classroom who are violent, unfocused, uninterested in learning, bored with or alienated from the world, profoundly angry, or suffering from the abuse or negligence of one parent or two or four. Seeing the wonderful things happening in the lives of my godchildren and Myron's nieces and nephews convinces us that there are other options. It is indeed possible to raise Christian children in this post-Christian world — if Christian communities and parents can really be the Church.

In this book we will examine some parenting and mentoring habits that are necessary for producing godly and faith-full children, as well as forces in our culture that harm our children and oppose our efforts. Research about culture and the principalities and powers underlies my analyses, but the most important basis for my perceptions has been the undergirding of a lifelong reading of the biblical narratives.

Let us explore together, then, what it can mean to raise children who are deeply rooted in the Christian faith and life, who are formed by God's Word and community to live as his[7] people.

---

7. Out of my concern to reach the widest audience possible, I have chosen to refer to God with the pronouns *he, his,* and *him,* which I have always understood as gender-neutral — and yet personal — when used in connection with God. I apologize to anyone who might be offended by my word choices and pray that you will accept my decision to use our inadequate language as carefully as possible to speak to the widest audience. Certainly God is neither masculine nor feminine, but more than all our words can ever connote.

Let us ask questions of ourselves to stir us up for love and good works and for living out biblical visions of the Church, visions of a people being formed by Scripture and worshiping in Spirit and in Truth, visions of pastors and parents with the heart of God for the children of the Christian community. These visions are described not to cause despair because we cannot attain them but to point to the direction we must pursue to raise our children in faith. Feel free to reject whatever might not fit your situation (after you've thought about it seriously first in case it really does) and hang on to whatever strikes you as truth, whatever might help to change the world. Let's not ask God for anything small. He wants to use us for his world-transforming purposes. May we be awakened to how we can be agents of his rehabilitating justice, holiness, and love.

Acknowledgments

I have titled this section clearly in case you want to skip this part — but if you find this book helpful, please join me in thanking God for all the persons who have influenced it. I can't name them all because this book is rooted in my whole life. My parents, who are superb Lutheran educators, first influenced my awareness of Christianity as countercultural. They taught me how wonderful it is to be weird and to celebrate the Joy of devoting your life to serving God. After them came numerous teachers and authors, humble parents and bold pastors, articulate children and angry youth, confused collegians and steadfast students, earnest teenagers in loving families, admonishing friends, and stimulating theologians who have incited my thought.

I am especially grateful to the good people at Eerdmans Publishing, who let me explore what burns within me, and I'm particularly thankful for my gentle and skillful editor, Jennifer Hoffman. My husband, Myron, lets me visit his elementary school classroom and, by sharing his burdens for his students, prevents me from becoming an academic ivory-towerite. How he can still hug me after my fits over the state of the Church or the pain of the culture is beyond me. He supports me in my efforts to change the world even though he knows it can't entirely be done yet.

For further reflection, discussion, transformation, and practice:

I do not envision my comments in this book as definitive answers or solutions to the problems of raising *Christian* children in our post-Christian world. Rather, please consider this book's observations as suggestive guidelines and introductory starting points for your own thinking and, even more important, for your discussion with other members of the community of faith. In these postmodern times the Church must recognize that wisdom for life is best gained in a community of learners. Furthermore, it is considerably more important that this book be not only elaborated but also put into practice in congregations and families. Consequently, with each chapter I am including questions for further reflection and discussion beyond the points set forth here to contemplate in connection with readers' own lives, families, and communities. I pray that you will be inspired to work seriously on issues posed in this book with other Christians — other members of your congregational community, your spouse, other parents in your neighborhood — so that no one is left trying to raise children in the faith alone.

1. In which dimension of social life have I noticed the greatest lack of moral character? What are the results? How does it affect me? our world?

2. Are there any groups of people from whom I have noticed excellent results in the raising of their children? What are their secrets? What can I learn from them?

3. What is my understanding of the biblical notion of "the principalities and powers"?

4. Was the description of "the powers" given above consistent with what I read in the Scriptures?

5. What evidences do I see that prove that Christianity is no longer the dominant culture? What difference does that make?

6. Is my congregation doing a thorough job of raising its children to be Christian? Why or why not?

7. With which other people could I study this book so that we can work together to put its lessons into practice?

PART ONE

Learning the Heart of God

We are called to be God's people,
showing by our lives his grace,
one in heart and one in spirit, sign of hope for all the race.
Let us show how he has changed us, and remade us as his own,
let us share our life together as we shall around his throne.

We are called to be God's servants, working in his world today;
taking his own task upon us, all his sacred words obey.
Let us rise, then, to his summons, dedicate to him our all,
that we may be faithful servants, quick to answer now his call.

We are called to be God's prophets,
speaking for the truth and right,
standing firm for godly justice, bringing evil things to light.
Let us seek the courage needed, our high calling to fulfill,
that the world may know the blessing
of the doing of God's will.

Thomas A. Jackson (1973), alt.
Tune: Austrian Hymn, Franz Joseph Haydn (1797)

CHAPTER 2

The Heart of the World

I heard the voice of Jesus say, "Come unto me and rest;
Lay down, O weary one, lay down your head upon my breast."
I came to Jesus as I was, so weary, worn and sad;
I found in him a resting place, and he has made me glad.

I heard the voice of Jesus say, "Behold, I freely give
the living water; thirsty one, stoop down and drink and live."
I came to Jesus, and I drank of that life-giving stream;
my thirst was quenched, my soul revived, and now I live in him.

I heard the voice of Jesus say, "I am this dark world's Light;
look unto me, your morn shall rise, and all your day be bright."
I looked to Jesus, and I found in him my Star, my Sun;
and in that Light of life I'll walk, till trav'ling days are done.

Horatius Bonar (1846), alt.
Tune: Three Mode Melody, Thomas Tallis (1561)[1]

---

1. This yearning hymn by Horatius Bonar, which lays the groundwork for what will follow in this chapter, is sung to the tune "Three Mode Melody" by Thomas Tallis (1561), which is the beautiful theme on which Ralph Vaughn Williams composed his magnificent symphonic "Fantasia on a Theme by Thomas Tallis." This song always stirs up in me a deeper awareness of the great longings, the *Sehnsucht*, that this chapter will describe, that only Jesus can fill. Our great

In what kind of world are the Church's children growing up? If we recognize that many of its dimensions are destructive to Christian growth, are we left helpless before the onslaught? Is it possible to change the world? Is it possible to protect our children from it?

Almost fifty years ago, theologian H. Richard Niebuhr characterized different Christian denominations by their understanding of how their faith directed them to deal with the culture. Some church bodies that retreat from the world see Christ primarily as "*against* Culture." Others accommodate in response to a "Christ *of* Culture," while others synthesize with the culture because Christ is *above* it. Lutherans were primarily cast by Niebuhr as those who perceive "Christ and Culture *in Paradox*," while Calvinists understand Christ as "the *Transformer* of Culture."[2]

It seems to me that for raising our children we need most of those attitudes — with the possible exception of the Christ *of* culture, which has tended throughout history to mean identifying Christ with only one's own culture in a way disdainful of others'. It is my intention here not to elaborate or critique Niebuhr's typology, though the latter is certainly necessary, but only to emphasize its usefulness in cautioning us to think carefully about our relationship with various aspects of the society around us if we want to raise children who are formed as Christians. In the present time Christian churches and parents need to be more deliberate about distinguishing those aspects of our culture to highlight and cherish; other elements should be rejected outright; some can be transformed. All must be tested against the narratives of the Scriptures, which reveal to us God's designs for life and growth.

We will be able to think more thoroughly about this process of discernment if we first consider carefully the nature of our world and then various dimensions in the character of the Church under

---

compassion for the world around us arises from our recognition of both our own profound yearnings and also the rest, water of life, and light that can be received only from God. Similarly, to raise our children in the faith we must be aware of their deep longings and point them to the only One sufficient to satisfy them.

2. See H. Richard Niebuhr, *Christ and Culture* (New York: Harper and Row, 1951).

the Lordship of Christ. You might wonder if we are ever going to get to practical suggestions for parenting and pastoring, but what I want to suggest pragmatically won't make much sense if we don't first really comprehend the heart of the world and the heart of the issues. It seems to me that much of the poor child-raising I observe arises because pastors and parents, churches and communities don't understand what they are up against in their endeavor to form Christian character in young people.

I am employing the word *heart* in this grounding section of the book in a much broader sense than our customary English metaphorical usage, wherein it signifies primarily emotions. When the word *heart* is used in both Testaments of the Bible, it refers instead to the will, one's deliberate intentions, one's inner core. Feelings might be included, but only as a caboose, with the mind and spirit being the engine of will.[3] People in the society that surrounds churches depend to an inordinate extent on their feelings; their heart or core is less deliberate and more easily (subconsciously) influenced than we will want ours to be in the Church. If we want to raise Christian children, we will want to base our judgments and decisions more on a will formed by the gospel. Thus, after this chapter through the rest of this book, the denotation of the word *heart* will become more disciplined and intentional as we progress from what surrounds our churches to what should be inside our churches for the purpose of nurturing godly offspring.

I use the word *world* here not in opposition to the Church, but as surrounding it. I do not intend to set up hostility between the world and God's people. The hostility is between the Christian community and the principalities or powers of evil. The world is the victim of the powers, without the resources of the Church to combat them. Four significant aspects of the world's weariness, thirstiness, and darkness (as in the hymn above) are important to recognize at this point. (All of Part Two elaborates on the issues of our society raised here.)

---

3. When an accentuation of feelings is intended, the First Testament Hebrew uses instead the word for "kidneys" and the Greek New Testament says "bowels."

17

1. The Source of the World's Pain

Before we can consider how best to nurture the Church's children in a life of faith, we must understand the forces that pull them away from it. At root, our neighbors — and we ourselves — are driven by a profound, unquenchable yearning, and we all try various methods to deal with it. This burning longing, this powerful thirst, in its essence is a yearning for God and is part of what it means to have been created in God's image. The early church father Saint Augustine recognized this weariness when he wrote, "Oh, Lord, Thou hast made us for Thyself, and our heart is restless until it rests in Thee."

C. S. Lewis's insightful treatment of this restlessness formed the subject for my M.A. thesis in English literature. His perceptions continue to enlighten my observations and to ground my mentoring — but, most of all, his discernment critiques me for my various idolatries.

Lewis named this human ache *Sehnsucht*, a fitting German term that we will continue to employ here to signify this pressing, restless longing for fulfillment that nothing can satisfy more than temporarily. Long ago I tried to capture its essence in a song (now lost). At that time I visited a nursing home every week and sang for the patients, one of whom understood only German (so I'd make up simple German songs when I ran out of the few I knew). One day I tested my song with her to see if the melody matched the words — and was gratified when she immediately responded, "Ah, *Sehnsucht!*"

"Exactly," I thought, falsely proud of my congruent composing, until she continued, "Ist das nicht ein 'cowboy' lied?" Was it not a cowboy tune, my song about longing for God? How frustrating — until I realized the truth of what she asked. Country and western music is so evocative because it taps into the haunting *Sehnsucht* that afflicts us all, and even as the cowboy rides off into the sunset we know that his yearning will never be stilled.

Lewis pointed out that human beings try to handle this hunger in three different ways. The first method he called "the fool's way." This person imagines that if she can reach a particular goal, she will be fulfilled. She dedicates herself to achieving it and focuses her energies and resources on that goal.

When she reaches it, however, she discovers that it doesn't satisfy her for long. After a while, a new goal must be conceived and achieved, but that fulfillment, too, will be fleeting. Consequently, her life consists in jumping from one inadequate goal to another.

The second method used for dealing with one's *Sehnsucht* Lewis named the "sensible person's way." This individual recognizes that the yearning cannot be stilled, so he tries instead to push it under — often in unwise ways. Lewis's term *sensible* perhaps is no longer appropriate, since many in our present culture never let the *Sehnsucht* infiltrate their consciousness because they are already "amusing themselves to death."[4]

This insensibility can never be successful either, for the stabbing longing always threatens to surface. One's attempts to repress it must constantly be renewed.

Lewis brilliantly proposed a third way. He said that if we have this intense longing and (#1) nothing in the world can satisfy it, and (#2) nothing in the world can push it under, then (#3) we must be made for another world! To recognize that *Sehnsucht* is our God-created longing for our true home in God is to find the roots of the longing itself.

We who are biblically formed know — from Ecclesiastes, for example — the vanity of trying to satisfy or repress one's yearning for God. We want to enable the children of the Christian community, and to remember ourselves, to resist the world's false methods of stilling the hunger. However, at the threshold of the twenty-first century, several factors in U.S. society escalate the fool's and sensible person's ways, aggravate the yearning, and accentuate the despair of its unquenchableness.[5] For these reasons Christians need

4. The significance of this phrase by Neil Postman will be explored in Chapter 9 below. See his *Amusing Ourselves to Death: Public Discourse in the Age of Show Business* (New York: Viking Penguin, 1985).

5. For a devotional approach to these issues, see also Marva J. Dawn, "The Cry of Human *Sehnsucht*," chapter 6 of *To Walk and Not Faint: A Month of Meditations on Isaiah 40* (Grand Rapids: Eerdmans, 1997). Throughout this book I will be making reference to other writings of mine. Be assured that I do this not to make money (for all the royalties of my Eerdmans books are given away), but because I want to encourage readers of this volume to explore more deeply the issues raised.

to be much more vigilant in nurturing Christian responses in our young people and much more discerning and compassionate in dealing with our neighbors.

2. *The Principalities and Powers*

There are a variety of inadequate goals by which persons in our culture try to appease or repress their spiritual hunger. These idolatries often begin with genuine concern for things that are important, but the devotion gets out of hand and usurps the place of the one true God. Worshipers don't often consciously claim their gods or recognize that they are worshiping them. The result is that those idolatries exert a power over them that continues to escalate. Thus, though we know, as the apostle Paul says, that "no idol in the world really exists" and that "there is no God but one" (1 Cor. 8:4), yet "there may be so-called gods in heaven or earth — as in fact there are many gods and many lords" (v. 5). What doesn't really exist except in our granting it such authority does indeed become a god and thus functions as one of the powers in our lives.

The very nature of the principalities and powers is that they were created for good (Col. 1:16), and they don't become gods if we keep them in their rightful place; but they share in the fallenness of all creation (Rom. 8:19-22) and consequently always overstep their bounds. For example, why does money have such control over so many people? At root it is a spiritual problem, the god Mammon transgressing the limits of its proper sphere.

The Bible does not define the essence or being of the powers, but it does demonstrate that Christ has triumphed over them (Rom. 8:38-39; 1 Cor. 15:25-26; Col. 2:14-15; 1 Pet. 3:22). Distinct from angels and demons, the principalities are referred to both in supernatural ways (Eph. 3:10 and 6:12) and in connection with human beings (1 Cor. 2:8). Integrating all these aspects, we discover that powers of evil turn human beings, institutions, laws, rulers, cultural elements, or authorities away from their God-given roles into functioning for harm. God's creative purposes are thwarted when we acquiesce in evil's uses of deception, division,

20

accusation, destruction, power, or Mammon.[6] Thus, we must do battle against these forces of darkness (Eph. 6:10-18) and expose them, even as Christ did (Col. 2:15), which is one of my goals in this book. Though exactly what the powers are in biblical terms remains mysterious, we can recognize their functions and, in the Christian community, deliberately expose and oppose their influence on our life.

What makes the battle so intense in the present world is that so much of life is becoming ambiguous, chaotic, fearsome, unmoored. Consequently, people cling more desperately to whatever idolatries seem to them capable of freeing them from pain, confusion, weariness, or meaninglessness. The powers function to twist such things as efficiency, money, or fame into the gods of our lives, and thus God's designs for good are distorted, corrupted, and deflected into contrary purposes. Our neighbors in the world (and we, in spite of knowing better) wind up with ultimate concerns that are trite, violent, enslaving, or flimsy. These goals will never ultimately satisfy or repress our deepest longing; they will never alleviate our aching bone-weariness, satiate our galling thirst, or pierce our bitter darkness.

In Part Two we will explore aspects of our contemporary culture that display individuals' efforts to achieve some fulfillment for, or to repress, the deep yearning within them. Since our intense longing for God cannot be quenched or assuaged by any human means, we want to equip all members of the Church, especially its children, to resist the entrapment of these hopeless efforts.

"Principalities and powers" language is helpful because it reminds us that these efforts to satisfy or repress our longing are idolatrous and doomed to failure, that we need spiritual weapons to deal with what enslaves us. We need to think about the powers of evil with repentance, for we all must acknowledge how easily

---

6. Jacques Ellul identifies these six as the functions of the principalities and powers in *The Subversion of Christianity*, trans. Geoffrey W. Bromiley (Grand Rapids: Eerdmans, 1986), pp. 174-90. I don't agree with the way Ellul limits the powers to these six functions, but certainly these half dozen cover the primary methods of evil.

21

they turn us away from living as followers of Christ. Especially we can't expect our children to resist the gods of the world unless we equip them — and ourselves — with knowledge of, and trust in, a true God who is strong enough to be worth turning to, away from what fascinates their peers.

3. Postmodernism

The fool's way and the sensible person's way, techniques of goal-chasing and repression, are accentuated in the present world by the growing postmodern despair.[7] The term *postmodernism* is used in a wide variety of ways and covers a wide variety of ideas. In university history departments, postmodernism leads to revisionist accounts of events and an ever-increasing fracturing of society into victim groups demanding their own stories. Postmodernist philosophers absolutize the relativity of truth, stress playfulness, and speak in random aphorisms. English teachers and visual artists who accept postmodern theories claim that there is no meaning in texts or paintings except what the reader or viewer brings to them.

We could list all kinds of manifestations of postmodern thinking, but my concern here is for how postmodern notions — often without our awareness — have hit the streets, our homes, and our children and lead to a rejection of truth, authority, meaning, and hope. The philosophy rightfully spurns many modern myths, but offers nothing to take their place. Instead, we are bombarded by — and young people especially believe — postmodern slogans such as these:

7. For an interesting collection of disparate views on a Christian approach to postmodernism, see Timothy R. Phillips and Dennis L. Okholm, eds., *Christian Apologetics in the Postmodern World* (Downers Grove, IL: InterVarsity Press, 1995). See also Diogenes Allen, *Christian Belief in a Postmodern World: The Full Wealth of Conviction* (Louisville: Westminster/John Knox Press, 1989), and Timothy R. Phillips and Dennis L. Okholm, eds., *The Nature of Confession: Evangelicals and Postliberals in Conversation* (Downers Grove, IL: InterVarsity Press, 1996).

- the Enlightenment project is a bust — there is no such thing as progress;
- life has no meaning — it's just a game;
- you are the only one who cares about you;
- no story is universally true;
- there is no such thing as truth except what you create for yourself;
- every claim to truth is a power play;
- therefore, everything must be mistrusted (or deconstructed, the philosophers say);
- there is no order — all is random;
- you only go around once, so do it with gusto.

Postmodernism's tenets are rapidly spreading throughout the world and have entered every major aspect of contemporary life, including the sciences. Recently at a small college on the West Coast, a guest lecturer insisted that Newtonian physics (emphasizing such natural principles as the law of gravity) was simply the product of European white male oppression and should therefore be replaced by an openness to other perspectives. A female professor, after trying unsuccessfully to get him to see reason, satirically responded that perhaps, then, this lecturer should demonstrate non-Newtonian physics by jumping *up* from the edge of a twenty-story building!

What is the result when even the law of gravity is discarded because any claim to truth is seen as oppressive, when people insist that truth cannot be known? We have to reckon with the effects of such postmodern thinking on our children and on the average person, on the attitudes of those to whom the Church seeks to minister. Many of our children's friends and our neighbors have no reference point, no guiding standard by which to assess life; many others concoct their own "spirituality" by intermingling whatever appeals to them.

The Roots of the Postmodern Condition

We can best understand this present postmodern condition by tracing its roots in three particular themes of the premodern and modern worlds. This is not to be reductionistic about the complexities of postmodernity, but it will be especially helpful for our purposes here to focus simply on each epoch's understanding of God, authority, and truth.

In the premodern world, everyone believed in some sort of god. It is critical for understanding the massive changes in our world to recognize that, prior to the European Age of Enlightenment which ushered in the modern epoch, all cultures were focused on a god, on the recognition of some superior supernatural force. Moreover, in premodernity those who knew the most about the cultures' gods functioned as the society's authorities. They taught the laypeople what needed to be done to worship or appease the gods, so they were the agents who passed on the truth. Truth was understood as absolute because it came from the god, and it was reliably transmitted by the shaman, priest, or witch doctor.

The development of science and reason in the modern world moved the focus of cultures from the supernatural to the natural. The locus of authority shifted from persons who passed on the Truth of God to the scientific method, which objectively discovered the truths of the natural world. Because many people had only had a "god of the gaps" (that is, a god to whom anything not otherwise understood was attributed) before the onslaught of scientific disproof, they thought they had decreasing need for the God of the Bible (although the first scientists were, generally, faithful Christians). With the intensifying ascent of technology, human beings progressively thought that they could control their own futures, that with just the right technological fix they could solve all their problems. With increasing scientific insights and technological power and improved economics and communications to combat ignorance, superstition, natural forces, and poverty in a never-ceasing spiral of progress, the modern spirit insisted that everything would get better and better — that we could remove the obstacles in the world with enough scientific discovery and technological fixes. Human beings insisted on their autonomy, and all truth — except for truth that could be scientifically, "objectively" determined — became relative. Now God was no longer absolute, and religion was relegated to the private sphere.

Because this modern world of science and technology was built on shaky foundations, without adequate checks on who controlled the power, the postmodern spirit was really inevitable. The euphoria of the myth of progress began to give way to the despair and hopelessness of grave anxiety as the twentieth century unfolded with disastrous world wars, severe economic depressions, the violence of Hitler and horror of Auschwitz, the world-changing terror of Hiroshima, the assassinations of leaders and massive betrayals by the government in the United States, environmental destruction and the relentless dread of the Cold War, the present frenzy of ethnic cleansing and tribalism, economic chaos in the face of massive global joblessness, the emptiness and ennui of entertainment that keeps dramatically escalating in violence and immorality, the obvious loss of any moral consensus or commitment to the common good.

Through all these graphic contradictions to "progress" the move to postmodernism escalates into spirals of despair and hopelessness. The poor outlook for jobs leaves young people without any reason to learn, even as their entertainments deprive them of the brain space or skills to do so.[8] We might as well "amuse ourselves to death." One very visible indicator of postmodern anomie is the immense proliferation of gambling casinos and lotteries. In the United States, minority peoples, the handicapped, and other marginalized folk who did not share in the economic pie were perhaps the first postmodernists, and their resultant rage has sometimes erupted into violent catastrophe and alienated rejection of the society's common story.

Most important of all, the failure of the hyped-up promises of science and technology accentuates the loss of truth already inherent in modernist relativizing and in the rejection of authoritative structures or persons with moral authority. Consequently, the major characteristic of the postmodern condition is the repudiation of any truth that claims to be absolute or truly true. "Christianity might be true for you, but not for me," our children used to say with modernist relativity — but now they are learning in their schools and from the media that any claim to truth is merely a means to hide an oppressive will to power. The result is

8. See Jane M. Healy, *Endangered Minds: Why Our Children Don't Think* (New York: Simon and Schuster, 1990), and Chapter 10 below.

a malaise of meaninglessness, the inability to trust anything or anyone, an indifference to any standards for evaluative judgment, the loss of any core of character around which to construct one's life.

Postmodernists recognize that science has degenerated into a scientism that needs to be deconstructed. In the postmodernists' view, technicism and economism are also idols, as are the grand narratives of truth, justice, freedom, and beauty. All these gods must be debunked; their proponents must be unmasked as the oppressive authorities that they are, using these narratives merely to gain power. Deconstruction leads to a playful or haphazard use of forms, a loss of meaning, a rejection of any fixed point of reference. Postmodern art uses a mixture of different methods and modes ironically juxtaposed; postmodern literature uses amalgamations of style, genre, and even typeface in the printing.[9] Channel surfing with the remote control illustrates the postmodern condition: from a distance the viewer experiences not a plot but merely disconnected images and smatterings of feelings.

As many scholars have noticed, postmodernism has moved young people from the alienation of the 1960s to the schizophrenia or multiphrenia (a legion of selves with no constant core of character) of the 1990s.[10] Having no larger story in which to place themselves, youth don't know who they are. Constantly shifting their image of themselves to fit in with the fads and fashions of the times, adolescents especially lack a nucleus of identity, a personality that has been formed by moral authority and mentoring models. Furthermore, since they have no sense of themselves, they are unable to make commitments to another person in marriage or friendship or to a job, a vision, a vocation. Their subconscious cry often becomes, "Keep entertaining me, so that I don't have to face the absence of my self."

Though the philosophers use words like *random, playfulness,*

9. See especially Philip Sampson, "The Rise of Post-modernity," in *Faith and Modernity,* ed. Philip Sampson, Vinay Samuel, and Chris Sugden (Oxford: Regnum Books, 1994), pp. 29-57.

10. See, for example, Louis A. Sass, *Madness and Modernism: Insanity in the Light of Modern Art, Literature, and Thought* (New York: BasicBooks, 1992).

and *banter* to describe their assessment of and approach to post-modern life, the effects on young people seem more like catastrophe, confusion, and chaos. Without authorities in the post-modern world to guide the formation of their moral character, children today lack basic resources of principled disposition to know how to find joy in what is beautiful, to have compassion for those who suffer, to develop goals for their work and lives. Distorted by the entertainment mentality of their parents, juveniles have little desire to learn, insufficient conscience calling them to civility and propriety, hardly any sense of meaning and purpose in life, no belief that there is any truth except for what they create for themselves.[11]

When people cannot satisfy that deep, restless yearning (which is rooted in their need for God), postmodernism tells them only to push it under with whatever appeals to them. Sadly, those means are usually destructive, so that increasing numbers of U.S. citizens, especially youth, are caught in deadly courses of drug and alcohol use, promiscuous sexual involvement, and violence.

What do we expect when so many young people cannot find meaning or a home? Drug users often say that they are bored. Gang members participate in vicious crimes in order to belong to a community that will care for them. And the situation will get worse. As I write this, the radio is announcing that hard liquor manufacturers have decided to end their self-imposed ban against advertising on television; people of all ages will more readily see one more way to ease the pain of living. The United States will never solve the problem of drugs and alcohol as long as we fail to address the spiritual issues that drive so many to use them — the powers of evil that steer the hopeless attempt of many to repress the nagging *Sehnsucht,* their (unidentified) longing for God.

11. Much of my recognition of postmodernism's effects on young people arises from simple observations and conversations. For an excellent overview of manifestations in popular culture of the postmodern ethos, see Stanley J. Grenz, *A Primer on Postmodernism* (Grand Rapids: Eerdmans, 1996). Some aspects of my description above of postmodernism were gleaned from J. Richard Middleton and Brian J. Walsh, *Truth Is Stranger Than It Used to Be* (Downers Grove, IL: InterVarsity Press, 1995).

4. *"It's Not My Problem"*

Also, the United States will not solve its substance abuse problems as long as the national mood is "I'm-OK–you're-not." An article in a recent issue of *U.S. News and World Report* summarizes what many have observed as a pervasive syndrome. We need not dwell here on the first result of this syndrome, which is that voters exaggerate national problems and distrust the government to solve them. But the second result cited is important for our purposes — that people "understate problems in their own back yard and cannot be roused to address them." These consequences "breed paralysis in civic life" and compel complacency.[12]

The report shows how television, in connection with other forces, has shifted the cultural *Zeitgeist* (the spirit of the times). The media's constant bombardment of violence and casual sex has lowered everyone's expectations for the safety and morality of other communities — though not for their own. This observation rings true for me; I always thought the violence was everywhere else until two boys were murdered by a sexual predator in a park a few blocks from my home.

Finally, the report comments on the universality of this syndrome:

> Scholars are just as susceptible to it as are high-school dropouts. Rich, poor, black, white, young, old — virtually all groups of Americans simultaneously hold sanguine views of themselves and pessimistic appraisals of others. One poll of university professors, for example, found that 94 percent of them thought that they were better at their job than was their average colleague. Reports from around the nation illustrate how insistently the I'm-OK–you're-not phenomenon is woven into the daily lives of Americans — and why it presents obstacles to liberal and conservative reformers. (26)

12. David Whitman, "I'm OK, You're Not," *U.S. News and World Report* 121, no. 24 (16 Dec. 1996): 25. Page references to this article in the following paragraphs are given parenthetically in the text. A similar note is sounded in Gordon D. Marino, "In the Drug Culture," *Christian Century* 114, no. 1 (1-8 January 1997): 5.

The article concludes with a section on the potent barrier to reform erected because U.S. citizens are unable or unwilling to sacrifice (29-30). Of course, we are concerned only tangentially about political reform here, but the obstacles are the same for spiritual/religious/ecclesiological reform.

At every church I visit most members think the congregation is doing fine — but then I talk with the youth or children and discover how little they know about the faith, how negligibly it affects their daily lives. People agree that certainly we need more adults to help with the youth group — or Sunday school or whatever — but they themselves are too busy and don't want to sacrifice.

A *U.S. News* poll cited in the report discovered that 65 percent of voters think that religion is losing its influence on national life. But at the same time 62 percent insisted that its impact is growing in their own lives (27). Something is seriously wrong if we think we are more religious, but at the same time recognize that religion is having very little effect on our culture.

I don't think Christianity is powerless to influence (not control) the culture around us and to enable our children to find a different way from its madness and meaninglessness, violence and valuelessness. The problem is that we have lost the heart of God and the heart of the Church in falling prey to the attempts of the world around us to satisfy or repress *Sehnsucht*.

For further reflection, discussion, transformation, and practice:

1. Which aspects of the culture around me are useful for raising children in the faith? Which should be rejected outright? Which can be transformed?

2. How do I notice *Sehnsucht* in myself? What do I chase after to satisfy it? Have I ever stayed satisfied for long? Or how do I try to push it under? Am I successful?

3. How do some of my friends handle their deep longing in life? Are they satisfied? Could I in some way help them to see that at root what they really long for is relationship with God?

4. How has my understanding of the biblical notion of the principalities and powers widened by reading this chapter? What manifestations of the powers at work are readily noticeable around me in society?

5. How has postmodernism affected my life?

6. How has postmodernism affected my children's lives?

7. Do I recognize the "I'm-OK–you're-not" syndrome in myself? in my congregation? How has it hurt me? my community?

CHAPTER 3

The Heart of God
Revealed in the Scriptures

O word of God incarnate, O wisdom from on high,
O truth unchanged, unchanging, O light of our dark sky:
we praise you for the radiance that from the scripture's page,
a lantern to our footsteps, shines on from age to age.

The church, from you, dear Master, received this gift divine;
and still that light is lifted o'er all the earth to shine.
It is the chart and compass that all life's voyage through,
'mid mists and rocks and quicksands,
still guides, O Christ, to you.

O make your church, dear Savior, a lamp of burnished gold
to bear before the nations your true light as of old.
O teach your trav'ling pilgrims by this their path to trace
till, clouds and darkness ended, we see you face to face.

William Walsham How (1867), alt.
Tune: Munich, *Neuvermehrtes Gesangbuch* (1693), alt.

31

When the needs of the world around us are so great — the *Sehnsucht* of our neighbors so haunting, the principalities and powers so controlling, postmodernism so despairing, and noninvolvement escalating — how will Christians respond? For the sake both of our children's faith and life and also of our ministry to our neighbors, what must we be? In this chapter we will consider the way in which God's Revelation[1] teaches us about the heart of God; in the following one we will discuss how, consequently, God's people are formed to be an alternative society. These chapters could be reversed, for certainly, as the hymn above suggests, the Scriptures cannot be known unless there is a genuine Christian community in which to study, memorize, and obey them. I chose this ordering, however, because I think it is important to emphasize that it is the narrative of faith — the Word, the Revelation of God — from which, around which, out of which the community must be formed. In the words of the hymn above, "this gift divine" of the Scriptures "guides" us to Christ and teaches us "trav'ling pilgrims" to "trace [our] path" by that gift until we know God's heart perfectly in seeing him "face to face."

An extremely destructive development for our children's faith and life — and our own — that afflicts numerous church bodies at this time is the extensive loss of the Scriptures. At the 1992 Presbyterian Church (U.S.A.) General Assembly in Milwaukee, Elizabeth Achtemeier of Union Theological Seminary in Richmond, Virginia, gave this warning:

---

1. In this book I am following French sociologist and lay theologian Jacques Ellul's example in capitalizing the word *Revelation* and preceding it with the word *the* to underscore it as *the* decisive gift of a gracious God and the Revelation of what cannot be discovered by human intellect. Ellul also most brilliantly demonstrates that the real problem for biblical interpretation is not the hermeneutical gap between the culture/language of the first century and that of the twentieth century, but the gap between those who receive the Word as the Revelation of God and those who don't. See Jacques Ellul, "Innocent Notes on 'The Hermeneutic Question,'" in *Sources and Trajectories: Eight Early Articles by Jacques Ellul That Set the Stage*, translation and commentary by Marva J. Dawn (Grand Rapids: Eerdmans, 1997).

There is a virus eating at the PCUSA, a deadly disease that is making us sick, gradually but surely destroying our life together. The disease is characterized by the attempt to turn the Scriptures into a relativistic document that takes two forms, and both of them are found in the majority report on abortion that was adopted by the General Assembly. . . . First, the Scriptures are viewed no longer as the ultimate authority for our faith and practice but only as a unique authority, one differing from other authorities yet not necessarily superior to them. Second, the Scriptures are said to have no objective meaning in themselves but rather contain only that message which the individual interpreter brings to them.[2]

It is my goal in this chapter to present warrants for recovering our belief in Scripture as the highest authority for knowing the heart of God for ourselves and our children. Moreover, I intend to offer guidelines for learning again the fullness of meaning that can be found in the Revelation of God, as it has been passed on by a faithful people for centuries.

To be true to the Hebrew/Christian Scriptures of the Church, first of all, we must reject the individualism of Western civilization. This individualism has caused us to read the Bible singularly and to think about our faith only in personal terms — which is exceedingly devastating for our children's faith, as we shall see below. Contrarily, almost all of the Scriptures are addressed to communities (with the exception of the letters to Timothy, Titus, and Philemon), and interpretation of those texts takes place in the Church as a corporate body.

Jesus called a group of disciples and never sent them out alone. He himself enjoyed deep friendship with women who cared for him with gracious hospitality; he asked his best male friends to watch with him in his most difficult hour. At the beginning God said that it was not good for the man to be alone — and yet many Christians try to live a solo faith. Our children need the entire

---

2. Elizabeth Achtemeier quoted in Richard John Neuhaus, "Presbyterians: Where Have All the People Gone?" *First Things* 28 (December 1992): 66.

community for their growth in the life of faith and, especially, for their learning the heart of God through his Revelation.

Second, the Christian community, to be true to our children and a genuine gift to the postmodern world, must deliberately be an *alternative society* that understands itself according to what God has revealed about his heart — that is, his will for us. We find God's heart in the Word, Christ, who displayed it in his earthly life, and in the Word of the Revelation. The Holy Spirit inspired the Church's process of preserving and passing on that Word and continues to inspire our interpretation of the Word in all its forms.

To faithfully be this alternative community of the Church, I believe we must work seriously and strenuously to understand the social forces of the culture that surrounds us and disavows Christianity. The next several sections of this chapter might be hard going for some readers — I struggle constantly to understand and articulate these things myself — but I think it is important for us to be able to place our Christian belief in the context of our neighbors' rejection of it. For the sake of truly being the Church in postmodern times, I hope that pastors, leaders, and parents will work through these next sections with me and equip our congregations and our children with insights to answer the critiques of Christianity that are offered, to know deeply that our belief in the triune God is justifiable, to celebrate the gift that the Bible is to us and to our world, to cherish the Revelation of God that we have been given to teach us God's heart and form us as his people.

Postmodern Denial of Meta-Narrative

One of the most important aspects of this era's postmodern thinking that we must understand in order to emphasize the Christian alternative especially in our reading of the Scriptures is postmodernism's general rejection of meta-narrative. The term *meta-narrative* refers to an overarching story that gives focus, cohesion, commonality, and meaning to life. When I lectured at a seminary in Oslo a few months ago, we acknowledged that

Norway's meta-narrative includes the sagas of the Vikings, the grievous dominion by both Denmark and Sweden, the courage of church and government leaders and school teachers in resisting Nazism, and, in the present day, the people's respectful relationship to the king, their leadership in world-class skiing, and their careful stewardship of oil reserves for the nation's future. These elements of that nation's story link the people together and give them common understanding of, and pride in, themselves and their heritage.

In contrast, the United States displays much greater postmodern breakdown as various interest and victim groups compete with one another. The larger, overarching worldview of the United States — including its founding by religious groups, the heroism of some pioneers, the splendor of its democratic vision — has in recent years given way to fracturing stories of anger over the brutality of the first explorers and settlers against the native peoples, resentment against government leaders who have mishandled their office, indignation toward religion, and fear of the crimes and violence of our neighbors. Much of that rejection of meta-narrative is accurate and deserved, but in its present form the repudiation leaves people without a story for understanding themselves, their work, and their place in society. We must also recognize the logical fallacy of postmodernity's outright rejection of meta-narratives, since its very insistence that all of them are violent and oppressive is itself an example of an imperious meta-narrative.

Postmodernism especially rejects the meta-narrative of Christianity, claiming that it is harsh and patriarchal. It is alleged that in a pluralistic world no religion can be seen as universal. Meanwhile, retaining the modernist elevation of *choice* as a major value, many persons who claim to be Christians have assembled their own belief system from a mixture of biblical elements with a hodgepodge of ideas from other traditions, together with the rejection of what they find "oppressive" in Christianity, such as the doctrine of the Atonement or narratives exhibiting God's wrath. Consequently, our children are growing up in a society that either rejects Christianity outright or blurs it into a pseudo-Christianity for the sake of a false understanding of tolerance.

The Biblical Meta-Narrative as God's Eternal Gift

Those of us who believe that the Word of God does offer a genuine meta-narrative that is universally available and applicable and that is not violent or oppressive must especially remember that we make these claims, not because we stand outside of the biblical narrative as objective observers, but because God does. Though postmodernists reject the Christian claim of its meta-narrative's comprehensive inclusivity, we believe that the triune God has revealed himself potentially to the whole world through a Word entrusted to a faith community that passes it on, incarnated in the flesh in the person of Jesus Christ who lived among us, and transmitted through the centuries by the guidance and empowerment of the Holy Spirit.

Whereas the modern world rejected this claim because it could not be scientifically proven, now postmodernity has opened people up to recognize other kinds of knowledge and uses of reason. We can address the epistemological barriers to faith (that is, *how* we know what we know about God) by accepting the supra-rational mystery of God and the community-attested Revelation and by recognizing the reasonableness of Christian faith as the best answer to the existential questions of who we are and why we exist, of what is wrong with the world, and what can be done about it.

These are the insights our children need for postmodern times. Because the God who has disclosed his heart to us in the Bible is eternal, because his relationship with human beings encompasses all of time, because those who believe in him already have eternal life and so share in God's freedom beyond time, and because his Word offers the standard by which we can assess what is of God and what is alien to his purposes, the alternative Christian community can retain from the world what is warranted for our thinking and reject what conflicts with God's Revelation to us. We don't need a fundamentalistic retrenchment into premodernity in order to uphold the Christian faith. Instead, I believe Christians can be at the forefront in offering to our children and also to the world around us a new postmodernism, not of fragmentation and chaos, but of community and faith.

It is crucial to teach our children that there are several reasons why the biblical narratives can be seen as universally applicable.[3] The Revelation knits all human beings together because all are equally created by God, because Christ died for all, and because the Spirit has been poured out upon "all flesh" — and the result of that outpouring originally was that each person heard the disciples speaking in his or her own language. The Revelation of the Trinity encompasses all human beings threefold.

Furthermore, the Revelation carries within it counterideological elements — that is, elements that prevent us from becoming fixed on certain ideas, political doctrines, or social systems as earthly solutions to human problems. The Scriptures include, for example, texts that prevent us from siding with the voices of victors, prophecies against Israel herself, oracles demanding justice-building and peacemaking, narratives of suffering and oppression that call human dominion into question, and accounts of the apostles' misunderstandings and the contrasting comprehension of the "little people." Jesus himself is the most obvious counter element, for his submission to suffering demonstrates most graphically that God does not work through the power structures and ideologies of the world. Furthermore, at the cross he exposed and triumphed over all the principalities and powers of politics, economics, and religious institutions.

Against the violence and oppression, the injustice and legalism of the society around us, it requires extra effort to nurture our children in the kind of alternative vision the Bible delineates.

Postmodern Critique of the Christian Meta-Narrative

Much of the postmodern critique of the larger story of Christianity (but not of the biblical meta-narrative itself) is valid. It is imperative that we help our children see that throughout its history supposed "Christianity" has violated the very tenets of the faith and has itself often become one of the powers of evil. Training in

---

3. This is clearly articulated in J. Richard Middleton and Brian J. Walsh, *Truth Is Stranger Than It Used to Be* (Downers Grove, IL: InterVarsity Press, 1995), pp. 87-99.

repentance and humility — founded on a profound sense of biblically exposed human sinfulness — is essential for children growing up in a world that pridefully rejects God as the center and reason for existence.

We join the postmodernists in discarding Christendom's premodern attitudes toward authority — that the pastor or priest is able to pass on the Truth of God absolutely truly, that truth can be totally objectively known. We confess that God is absolute and that he is absolute Truth, and we know that God has revealed himself to us objectively in his Word, but we also acknowledge that our comprehension of God is affected by our social situation and that we thus need the whole creation, including also those who do not believe the Hebrew and Christian Scriptures, to reveal more of what we can know only relatively.

Contemporary Christians (and our world) need the premodern focus on God and recognition of the supernatural that were lost in the modern era of anthropocentrism (that is, life centered on human beings instead of on God, which is theocentrism). Everyone most deeply yearns (usually without recognizing it) for belief in God's Truth; that is part of the *Sehnsucht* originating from humanity's creation in the image of God. However, we dare never forget that we know that Truth only partially and can share it with others not as authorities but as fellow students of the Revelation. This attitude is particularly fruitful as we seek to pass on the faith to our children because they need to see us as co-learners, always eager to grow in knowledge and wisdom, the love of God and neighbor.

We also join the postmodernists in rejecting modernism's myth of progress. God's Revelation clearly exposed that myth long ago and named as *sin* the oppressions that result from unequal distributions of "progress" and power. Why, then, do so many Christians buy into that illusion?

Christian theology gave in too much to modernity. Not only did we buy into society's fantasy of human progress, but we also allowed the rules of science to determine how we studied the Scriptures. We accepted modernity's over-rationalistic rules instead of retaining our sense that there are many kinds of knowledge and wisdom and that Scripture carries within itself guides to the ways to study it — with a foundation of belief in Christ as the Revealed and Revealing One and with methods of openness to the Holy Spirit, the counsel of the community, trust, meditation, memorization, obedience, and submission to the text's formation. We allowed modernity to turn us toward entertainment in our worship and toward ministry to people's "felt needs" instead of offering them what is truly needful. In a society of choice, churches became false democracies — for example, in deciding doctrine by majority vote — rather than communities of gifted people equipped by their leadership for a corporate life formed by the biblical narratives and guided by the Holy Spirit.

Theologians recognize that the tools modernity gave us — such as form, source, historical, and redaction criticisms[4] — are inadequate if they are used only to atomize the text and leave us with nothing that forms us as a people of God. For the sake of all that can be gained from them, we retain these study methods from the modern epoch, along with its sense of the relativity of our own knowledge, but the postmodernists (and, even more, the Bible) show us that we need more — for example, the people-forming results of literary, narrative, and canonical approaches to the Scriptures.[5] I do not wish to be simplistic about the arduous tasks of interpreting and being formed by the Scriptures,[6] but we will be more willing to invest ourselves in those disciplines if we retain, cautioned by postmodernity's critique, our belief that the biblical meta-narrative reveals God's superior will to us under the guidance of the Holy Spirit.

4. These methods of study look, respectively, at literary genres, at the various sources or traditions from which a text came, at historical details that enable us to understand texts in their context, and at the work of biblical editors as they put together into a narrative the traditions available to them.

5. These methods of study look closely at literary devices, such as word choices or repetitions and grammatical forms, at the whole narrative of an account in order to study the broader structure and elements that give the story its emphases, and at the whole canon of the Scriptures, in order to see how a text fits in with what Jews and Christians have passed on as the entire Revelation of God.

6. The best book I've seen for demonstrating the work of interpretation so that God's people can be formed by the Scriptures is Richard B. Hays, *The Moral Vision of the New Testament: A Contemporary Introduction to New Testament Ethics* (San Francisco: HarperSanFrancisco, 1996).

Christianity in Relation to Other Aspects of Postmodernism

Certainly on the basis of God's Word Christians can agree with postmodernity's rejection of the modern world's myth of progress. We concur with its deconstruction of the technological mind-set, of political ideologies, of Enlightenment rationality. We have seen the failures of technology to truly fix our problems, the destructive use of science for evil ends, the inability of economics to bring equitable wealth to all. Being biblically formed, we know the source of these defects in human pride, narcissism, and greed.

What we cannot accept from postmodernity especially for and with our children is its total decentering, its reduction of life merely to a carnival, with myriads of consumerist opportunities and entertaining sideshows. Most of all, we observe the emptiness, the hopelessness, and the despair created by postmodernity's repudiation of God and want our children, growing up in a society characterized by that despair, to know instead the hope that is ours through life enjoyed in union with Christ.

We acknowledge, however, that there is no going back to "the good old days" of premodern absolute conviction, of infallible authorities who passed on God's truth. We readily confess that God's people throughout their history have not passed on the whole truth of God, nor passed it on in ways compatible with the character of God himself. We realize that Christendom distorted its convictions and authority with disastrous results in the violence it perpetrated, the oppressions it fostered, and the suffering it caused countless peoples. In past eras, for example, Christendom misconstrued the biblical formulation of "Holy War," which was actually a pacifist notion in the Scriptures in that Holy War was intended to teach Israel not to fight and not to gain any booty from fighting.[7] The Crusades are an appalling manifestation of human perversion of the biblical meta-narrative.

---

7. See Marva J. Dawn, "What the Bible *Really* Says about War," *The Other Side* 29, no. 2 (March-April 1993): 56-59.

40

The Biblical Meta-Narrative
as Gift to a Postmodern World

Accepting the postmodernist critique of our *abuse* of the biblical meta-narrative, how can we recover the true Word of God as a crucially necessary gift for our time in the raising of our children? First we must examine the meta-narrative itself, and then we must clarify how it forms us all.

The Revelation as Story

The biblical meta-narrative is the story of a faithful God. When we read it in its entirety, we realize that it is different from other religious narratives because it focuses on *God in relationship with a specific people*. There are many other creation accounts in religious literature, for example, but only the Hebrew/Christian Scriptures emphasize that this Creator God is also a Covenant God. As Deuteronomy explains,

> Because the LORD your God is a [compassionate] God, he will neither abandon you nor destroy you; he will not forget the covenant with your ancestors that he swore to them. For ask now about former ages, long before your own, ever since the day that God created human beings on the earth; ask from one end of heaven to the other: has anything so great as this ever happened or has its like ever been heard of? Has any people ever heard the voice of a god speaking out of a fire, as you have heard, and lived? Or has any god ever attempted to go and take a nation for himself from the midst of another nation, by trials, by signs and wonders, by war, by a mighty hand and an outstretched arm, and by terrifying displays of great power, as the LORD your God did for you in Egypt before your very eyes? To you it was shown so that you would acknowledge that the LORD is God; there is no other besides him. From heaven he made you hear his voice to discipline you. On earth he showed you his great fire, while you heard his words coming out of the fire. And because he loved your ancestors, he chose their descendants after them. He brought you out of Egypt with his own presence, by his great power. (Deut. 4:31-37)

41

The knowledge of God began with the LORD's intervention in the history of Israel — and from there they discovered that their covenant "I AM" was the One who had created the world.

In the same way, we introduce our children and other people in the postmodern world to the God who loves them and wants to reconcile them to himself. We tell them the story of a faithful, promising God who demonstrated his devotion by always remembering his covenant with Israel. The dependability of his Word is established most profoundly in the resurrection of Jesus, for in the empty tomb we see the culmination of God's work on our behalf, the fulfillment of all the prophecies concerning the Messiah, the down payment on all God's promises for the future.

The Revelation is indeed a convincing Word of hope for our children and all those who are searching in these postmodern times. It proclaims a God of compassion and gracious mercy, who gives meaning and focus to lives tossed around by postmodern randomness. It announces forgiveness and reconciliation to those torn by guilt and lacking skills to build relationships. It describes the Trinity our children and neighbors need — a loving Creator for those who think they have to create their own identity, a perfect Model for those who have no mentors, and an empowering Spirit for those who think they have to do everything on their own.

How the Revelation Forms Us

The Revelation is not a book of rules to give us step-by-step procedures for life and for raising our offspring. There could never be enough rules to cover all the possibilities, and usually our children's (and our own) response to rules is to resist them. Nor is the Bible a collection of timeless truths from which we draw out basic principles or goals toward which we teach our youngsters to aim. Since the Bible contains many dialectical tensions, opposing sides on various issues can draw out contradictory timeless principles, and often people use biblical goals to justify any means. Rather, to modify a basic schema from Norman T. Wright,[8] the

8. See N. T. Wright, *The New Testament and the People of God* (Minneapolis: Fortress, 1992), pp. 140-42. See others' use of this wonderful idea in

Scriptures form us as we dwell in them, as we inhabit them; then we live out of the character shaped by all of God's Word.

Imagine what would happen if we found an unfinished drama by Shakespeare, that we uncovered the first five acts and the last bit of the seventh.[9] How would we produce the play? We could try to write the missing parts, but we know we haven't got the talents of Shakespeare and could hardly draft a version that we could be sure would suit him — and we could not check out our attempts with the author.

Instead, we would try to find actors who were highly experienced in the theatre, who knew Shakespeare's work inside and out, who understood all his writings and his life and his personality — perhaps performers from the wonderful Shakespeare festival in Ashland, Oregon. Then they would have to immerse themselves in the acts of the new play that had been found. With this basis, they could improvise the missing parts.

Similarly, in the Church we have passed down the unfinished drama of God. The first act of the play is the Creation, which teaches us that all the people of the world are brothers and sisters — and prohibits the violence toward other people against which the postmodernists rightfully protest. The second act of the drama is the Fall, which enables us to understand our own sinfulness and the world's brokenness and failure, and which deconstructs modernity's myths of progress more thoroughly than the postmodernists do. Acts III and V include the stories of Israel and of the early Church, respectively, to offer us examples of both disobedience and trust and to demonstrate the consequences of each. Act IV is the record of the life of Jesus and manifests God's covenant action on behalf of the world as the pinnacle of all God's interventions in Act III and as the foundation for the Spirit's work through the saints of Act V. We

---

Middleton and Walsh, *Truth Is Stranger Than It Used to Be*, pp. 182-84, and Rodney Clapp, *A Peculiar People: The Church as Culture in a Post-Christian Society* (Downers Grove, IL: InterVarsity Press, 1996), pp. 138-39.

9. Wright uses a five-act schema, but I find it helpful to divide his fifth act in order to stress the differences in our lives from those of biblical characters in immediate touch with Jesus and of the end of time as an entirely new kind of drama.

know a little bit of the end of the drama (Act VII) from the book of Revelation, but what we know of the culmination of the world is only a sketch meant to encourage us in the struggles of the present.[10]

Act VI is where we fit in, formed by what we have learned in the preceding parts. Immersed in the commandments, goals, stories, poetry, warnings, promises, and songs of the entire Revelation, we are formed to act with the character of God's people, imitating the virtues and deeds of God himself. We have not the same immediacy as the early Christians of Act V, who knew Jesus and/or the first witnesses, so it is necessary to immerse ourselves deeply in these previous acts to imbibe the virtues, attitudes, behaviors, and practices of faithful followers. But we have a great advantage over the Shakespearean actors, for as we improvise Act VI in keeping with the spirit of the rest of the drama we know that the Author is still alive!

What a great gift this meta-narrative is! It offers our children and the people of the world around us a story into which they can place themselves and find forgiveness for their past, purpose for their present, and hope for their future. It forms us to be a people who truly know ourselves, offers us reconciliation with both God and our neighbors, and fills us with new life created by the Holy Spirit at work in us.

The Truth of God as Gift to Our Children in a Postmodern World

Premodernism asserted that there was an objective truth that could be known by those who had the skill to see it. Modernism objected that truth is relative, that different people see truth differently according to their own situations. Postmodernism insists that there is no truth at all, that whatever truth there might be must be created by each person. Instead of these three options, we offer to our children the meta-narrative of the Church, which compassionately demonstrates that Jesus is the Truth, an objective

---

10. See Marva J. Dawn, *Joy in Our Weakness: A Gift of Hope from the Book of Revelation* (St. Louis: Concordia Publishing House, 1994).

Truth who can be known. We know him only partially, but because we know him we do not have to try to create truth for ourselves.

Jesus, who is the Truth, provides the center and focus for all that our children learn in our fractured postmodern times. He is the Way to the genuine home for which everyone in our postmodern culture searches. He is the Life who gives us hope for eternity — and that hope "does not disappoint us" (Rom. 5:5).

I believe that this is a critical time for raising children with God's Truth — and the confusions of the world around us make that task more difficult, although they also provide a momentous opportunity for the mission of the Church. Every one of our neighbors is deeply yearning (though probably without identifying the longing) for what we know — rather, for the One we know. Will our Christian communities as a whole and individual parents and pastors be formed by, and work to form our children by, the biblical meta-narrative so that we can improvise well — and thereby draw to the triune God the world he loves and longs to save?

For further reflection, discussion, transformation, and practice:

1. Do I usually read the Bible in singular terms? How might my understanding of formative texts change if I read them plurally? In what ways do I dwell in the texts so that they can form me?

2. Is my Christian community an alternative society? In what ways? In what ways not?

3. Have any postmodern people whom I know rejected the Christian meta-narrative as oppressive? How might I respond to them?

4. In what ways is the Christian meta-narrative a gift to the postmodern world? How could I explain to someone else my understanding of the Bible as authoritative in my life?

5. How is the Church's meta-narrative a gift to our children? How can I help them appreciate its value and stir in them a desire to be formed by the biblical narratives?

6. What is my understanding of how the Scriptures form us? Does the above analogy to an unfinished Shakespeare play give me any new insight into the formative role of the Bible? What other images could I use to explain to my children what it means, and how it happens, that the Revelation of God affects how we live?

7. How well are my children learning the Scriptures from our congregation and from their parents? Are they being formed by the biblical narratives? In what ways? In what ways not? How could I directly participate in helping them to be more formed by the Revelation?

CHAPTER 4

The Heart of God Revealed through the Church as Parallel Society

Church of God, elect and glorious,
holy nation, chosen race;
called as God's own special people,
royal priests and heirs of grace:
know the purpose of your calling,
show to all God's mighty deeds;
tell of love which knows no limits,
grace which meets all human needs.

God has called you out of darkness
into this most marvelous light;
bringing truth to live within you,
turning blindness into sight;
let your light so shine around you
that God's name is glorified;
and all find fresh hope and purpose
in Christ Jesus crucified.

Once you were an alien people,
strangers to God's heart of love;
Christ has brought you home in mercy,
citizens of heav'n above;
let his love flow out to others,
let them feel the Savior's care;
that they too may know his welcome
and his countless blessings share.

Church of God, elect and holy,
be the people Christ intends,
strong in faith and swift to answer
each command your master sends:
royal priests, fulfill your calling
through your sacrifice and prayer,
give your lives in joyful service,
sing his praise, his love declare.

James E. Seddon (1982)
tune: Ripley, Lowell Mason (1839)

How should the Christian community respond to the effects of postmodernism on our children? What gifts do we have in the Church for forming our offspring with the life of faith revealed in the Scriptures? How will we equip our children to offer the rewards of their faith life to those who seek healing and hope and a home in these postmodern days?

The Parallel Society

I'm sorry that I learned the following story so long ago that I can't find the source, but this account has heartened my thinking about the Church for several years. The playwright-president of the Czech Republic, Vaclav Havel, was asked why the "Velvet Revolution" there was successfully nonviolent — and, we might add, why it remains effective when so many other satellites of the former

48

U.S.S.R. are reverting to Communism. Havel answered somewhat like this: "We had our parallel society. And in that parallel society we wrote our plays and sang our songs and read our poems until we knew the truth so well that we could go out to the streets of Prague and say, 'We don't believe your lies anymore' — and Communism *had* to fall."

The same is true for the Church. Because we take our direction from the Trinity and the Revelation, because we are citizens first of heaven, God's people are a society parallel to the world surrounding us. When we gather for worship and education, we tell the narratives of the faith, sing our hymns, and say our prayers until we know the truth so well that we and our children can go out to our neighbors and offer alternatives to the lies of the principalities and powers that dominate U.S. society. As royal priests (see the hymn above), we offer to the world around us the gifts of the One who is the Truth, the Way, and the Life.

I like both words, *alternative* and *parallel*, for describing the Church. To be parallel keeps us from being so alternative that we don't relate to our neighbors; to be alternative prevents our parallel line from moving closer and closer to modes of life alien to the kingdom of God. Rather than becoming enculturated and entrapped by the world's values of materialistic consumerism, of narcissistic self-aggrandizement, of solitary superficiality, and of ephemeral satisfaction, members of Christ's Body choose his simple lifestyle of sharing, his willingness to suffer for the sake of others, his communal vulnerability, and his eternal purposes. By continual hearing and study of God's Word we and our children are equipped with new visions of God's heart for our mission and ministry of communicating the Christian story, of enfolding our neighbors in God's love, of deliberately choosing and living out the alternative values of the kingdom of God.

The Christian Community as Gift to the Postmodern World

Let us return to C. S. Lewis's notion of *Sehnsucht,* the insatiable longing that afflicts us all, that nothing in the world can successfully quench or repress. As Christians we know that the other world for which we are made is God's presence in God's kingdom, to be fully experienced only at the end of time. To some extent, meanwhile, that world can be tasted now in the Christian community, which incarnates God's Truth in its rites and life together. Our children need a very deep process of spiritual initiation into that community, however, for much of what they see and hear in the world around them is inimical to the habits of God's kingdom.

For those outside the community, the same sort of deep process of Christian formation is necessary because the post-Christian society of the United States leaves many young adults bereft of the basic Christian understandings that once could be assumed in our culture. Therefore, if we and our offspring want to help postmodern people in these times enter the new creation — that is, the alternative society of the parallel Christian community — we must understand their attempts to satisfy or push under the *Sehnsucht*. (These attempts will be explored more fully in Part Two). Then, by life-forming processes, we can incorporate them into the Body that will truly fulfill their desire by nourishing their relationship with God.[1] The recognition that both our children and those who are not members of the Church require similarly deep foundational training in resistance to the allures of the society around them should increase our deliberate educational work on behalf of both groups.

The most convincing testimony to the existence and grace of God for our children and other postmodern people will be the embodiment of God's love by, and the embracing of his purposes in, the Christian community. Many books in the United States about "Generation X" or the "Buster Generation" (young people in their twenties and thirties) emphasize especially their need for love and compassion, their feelings of rootlessness and homeless-

---

1. Because so many adults in our culture do not have the background and spiritual training to recognize and deal with the roots of their human longing in relation to God, our churches need entirely new methods for welcoming people, such as pairing seekers with mentors who teach them the *habits* of Christian faith. See, for example, Samuel Torvend, ed., *The Catechumenate: A Lutheran Primer* (Minneapolis: Augsburg-Fortress, 1997).

ness.[2] Those whose lives are perilously fraught with postmodern despair — and with devastating painkillers of all sorts to drown it — need a genuine and vital community with an alternative process of life formation in order to survive and thrive. The processes by which churches educate young people for faith and life must take more seriously the profound pain of the culture surrounding the Church.

No doubt it is obvious in this book that I am profoundly disappointed by churches' failures to employ the very processes of Christian formation that our children and our neighbors need. As I travel throughout the country, I encounter a multitude of other people, too, who tell me that they are worried about their home congregation because it seems to have lost its way. What does it mean to BE Church? In the previous chapter we considered the Scriptures as a way to begin to know the heart of God; now we can consider more deeply what kind of alternative/parallel community we must be to raise our children in the faith.

In recent months of reading some of the fast-selling literature about "how to choose a church" and "how to grow a church," I have become increasingly disturbed that lots of unbiblical advice is being sold and bought. Ought we really to buy into the contemporary consumer notion that we *choose* a church and that we must *conform* our congregation to society's standards so that we can keep our children from leaving and attract enough new people to grow our parish? Don't the Scriptures constantly emphasize that *God has chosen us* and that *we are called to BE the Church*?

How do the Scriptures describe the Church? What kind of parishes must we be to develop the genuine parallel communities our children need? What would our congregations look like if they were truly being Church — listening to the Word of Christ and being formed by that Revelation?

In this chapter let me suggest a few questions to guide our

2. See, for example, Kevin Graham Ford, *Jesus for a New Generation: Putting the Gospel in the Language of Xers* (Downers Grove, IL: InterVarsity Press, 1995), for a Christian perspective, and see Douglas Coupland, *Generation X: Tales for an Accelerated Culture* (New York: St. Martin's Press, 1991), for the longing of those without God.

thinking about what it means to be a congregation for the sake of our children. This is not blind optimism, but a biblical vision for the alternative society that the Church must be as God's faithful people. No parish, of course, can perfectly encompass all the dimensions of "Church-being" that these questions urge, but I mention these ten topics here to widen our thinking, to give us directions to pursue, and to raise some issues that are being overlooked.

Are Our Churches Biblically Formed?

1. *Does the pastor preach the whole counsel of God and not just what is politically correct? Do the congregational leaders urge you and your children to wrestle with the whole Bible and not just read the parts you like?* How else will we constantly widen our understanding of God and our perception of his attributes and interventions? How else will we, young and old, realize that God is infinitely beyond us and that our human understanding is always inadequate?

The question of our congregations' whole use of the Scriptures must begin this section (and be based on what we discussed about the Bible in the previous chapter) because the community cannot be rightly parallel unless it balances all of the diverse disclosures of God in the Word. We do not falsely attempt to harmonize seemingly contradictory statements — instead we bow before the mystery of an infinite God — but we dare not leave out aspects and tensions that we find uncomfortable.

We hear lots of talk these days about how much God loves us. When was the last time you heard a sermon about God's holiness or about his wrath? Our liturgies rarely use the psalms of lament, and new hymnals leave out or retranslate the old hymns of judgment. God is increasingly turned into a warm, fuzzy teddy bear and is rarely pictured with omnipotent authority, sovereign dominion, the absolute perfection that cannot tolerate our sinfulness. The end result is that adolescents don't even recognize how blasphemous it is to reduce God to a buddy or to sing in "worship" some of those trite campfire songs, as if they were fitting to honor the God before whom we would fall on our faces if we actually saw him.

The Bible is full of dialectical opposites in what it reveals about God. We and our offspring need to see both the ruling arm of power and the tender arm of carrying in Isaiah 40:10-11, both the interventions on Israel's behalf and the oracles against her in the First Testament prophets, both the ardent kindness of Jesus and his momentous anger against hypocrisy in the Gospels.

It is crucial that our children experience a community that wrestles together to comprehend texts, that acknowledges the incomprehensible ones, that obeys those that make clear God's heart, that treasures all the narratives (recognizing that some have more weight than others) as part of God's Revelation to form his people, that is eager to keep on learning. We can train ourselves and our children to ask, as we hear a text proclaimed in worship or study it together, how this passage forms us to be the Church, the parallel society.

2. Does the pastor preach sermons and do the leaders teach classes that rebuke and challenge you and your children? Do the elders admonish you? How else will we become more formed by the biblical narratives and better disciplined for persevering in the life of faith?

The letters of the New Testament, and especially the seven letters in the book of Revelation, demonstrate Christian rebuke — and we know that in certain instances the churches paid attention to Paul's reproof and repented. I do not see much loving admonishment in churches these days, perhaps because we are not willing to receive it.

To see a Christian humbly receive deserved admonition and take steps to remedy the situation is a very important lesson for our children. To observe that in connection with a loving community's support of the offender is even more compelling.

The lack of godly rebuke in churches is the end result of a spiral of decline. Modern and postmodern biblical criticism has made us unsure of ourselves in relation to texts; declining numbers in churches make us afraid to take the risk of discipline; clergy are overwhelmed by "administrivia" and do not devote much time to meditation on the Word and prayer; the overly legalistic (and not mutual) admonition of fundamentalistic churches repulses us. Nevertheless, I am convinced that contemporary Christianity is so weak in the United States because there is not enough constructive criticism and stirring challenge.

It is true that the old literal*istic* methods of interpreting Scripture are no longer viable, but it seems to me that we have given in too much to modernity and postmodernity if we disavow the clear texts, the basic ethical guidance that is consistent throughout the Bible and therefore normative for those of us who claim the name *Christian*. Certainly, for example, a great proportion of us in the United States — both adults and children — deserve the biblical denunciations of greed.

Of course, such admonition is put in perspective by the Church's rite of confession and absolution. What a great gift it is in the Church's worship for all of us to hear the clear announcement of our forgiveness for all the ill that we have done and all the good that we have left undone!

3. Do the congregation's small groups — including youth groups — hold you and your children accountable, support you in your times of weakness, and pray for you consistently? How else will we really grow in our discipleship, have our character formed by the biblical narratives, increase in our ability to live all aspects of our lives in light of the Word of God?

Sociologist Robert Wuthnow's research has shown that most small groups in the United States have become simply places to share feelings — against which nobody can object. When other members of the group do hold individuals accountable, the ones urged to be responsible often leave for another group that is "more supportive."[3] Young people, especially, don't want to hang around if they don't "feel" bolstered.

Biblical support, however, includes accountability. First Thessalonians 5 incorporates in its summary of attributes of the Christian community the indispensable combination that we both rebuke and encourage each other. Churches become so worried

3. See Robert Wuthnow, *Sharing the Journey* (New York: Free Press, 1994).

about numbers that they fail to form functioning *members*. Our teenagers need not the bland "self-esteem" programs they get in the public schools, but genuinely affirming support that also challenges them to faithfulness and follows up with them so that they develop a Body member's faithful habits and practices.

4. Are there some people in your congregation that you don't like? If not, where else (within such a protective covenant framework) will we learn, as God commands, to love our enemies?

Popular opinion encourages us to find a church where we feel cozy and comfortable, where we won't have frictions because we think the same way and have the same social values as other members of the congregation. The prevalent attitude is that people should simply leave a parish and find a more compatible one when conflicts arise.

The Bible emphasizes, however, that the Church is the very place where people with different values can learn from each other, where human conflicts can be addressed, where enemies can learn to forgive and reconcile and relate afresh. The believers in Acts 15 worked on issues until they could conclude with the consensus, "It seems good to the Holy Spirit and to us." Our local congregations could be micro-examples, tangible models for our children of God's enormous integrating and harmonizing work.

In one of the first parishes I served, an elderly woman critiqued me so harshly that all I wanted to do was leave or lash back. While praying about her, however, I realized that she contributed in many quiet ways to the well-being of the congregation and received little recognition in return. I wrote her a note thanking her for all her gifts, especially to me — and the resultant turn led to a good friendship. What pivotal lessons for ministry I would have missed if God had not brought me into a congregation with people of whom I wasn't particularly fond at first!

What pivotal lessons for life our children miss if they don't observe us actively loving those in whom we don't delight and if we don't help them learn to get along with those they don't like. Global peacemaking begins with every small act of reconciliation, every release from bondages of fear or resentment, every measure of justice (see below in Chapter 12).

5. Are there people in the congregation from other ethnic and ability groups? Are there refugees, migrant workers, minority peoples in our pews? Does the congregation welcome the mentally disadvantaged and provide accessibility for wheelchairs, sign language for the hearing impaired, large-print hymnals for the visually impaired? Are the extreme poor made to feel at home among us? How else will we fulfill and teach our children God's plan for the Church that it break down all racial, social class, and capability barriers — so that truly there will be neither male nor female, slave nor free, Jew nor Greek?

Present emphases in church growth urge congregations to find their "marketing niche" — that is, to appeal to people just like themselves to create a homogeneous church. The result might be a large, flourishing parish, in the world's terms, that doesn't care directly for those on the margins of society.

The gospel calls us instead to welcome everyone as God has welcomed us, breaking down barriers to discover the unity of God's diversity, the revealing of God's grace that comes from people not like ourselves. When we say *Shalom*, James says, we must be ready to provide whatever is needed for our hearer to experience genuine wholeness (James 2:16ff.). But it won't necessarily be attractive. It might take lots of extra work, additional patience, a burden of time, plenty of translating, scads of inconvenience.

Once when I visited my husband's classroom and mentioned my visual handicaps to the students (so they would write neatly on the papers I was going to grade), one of the boys immediately came to me with gentle sympathy. He disclosed that he helped to care for a little brother who was losing his vision. Children learn life-changing lessons of warmhearted responsiveness when they grow together with persons of other ethnic backgrounds, when they behold and participate in compassionate caring for the needs of others.

6. Does the community's life demand a lot from you and your children and call forth your spiritual gifts? How else will the pastor be freed up for the Word and prayer? How else will the *ministry* happen?

56

The church marketers urge us to ask what we can get out of a church. How do its programs meet our needs? The result is that congregations have become, in George Hunsberger's masterful phrases, "vendors of religious services and goods," instead of "a body of people sent on a mission."[4] If we share the former perspective instead of the latter, we train our children to be merely religious consumers.

Though the Bible seldom uses the word that we translate "church," the Scriptures do make clear that we weren't made part of the Body of Christ for what we can get out of it. We are called into mission by the Father who created and elected us, empowered by the presence of Christ in our lives to extend and build up God's kingdom, endowed by the Holy Spirit with gifts, equipped by the teaching and preaching of the Church's leaders to use those gifts.

The most powerful influence on my spiritual development as a child was seeing my parents use their gifts to honor God. My mother's considerable secretarial and teaching skills were used in the Lutheran school; her profound hospitality welcomed all kinds of persons to our home. My father turned down a promising pitching career in major league baseball to continue as a principal, teacher, organist, and choir director. I was profoundly shaped by their commitment to using their lives to upbuild the Christian community, and I've always wished for my friends that their families would have such a worthwhile focus. From the very beginning I was encouraged (and these challenges form my most distinctive early memories) to use my gifts to serve God and the world. That affected, among every other aspect of my life, how I did such things as my paper route and singing for Christmas programs.

7. Does the whole congregation understand that everyone is responsible for helping to raise children in the faith? How else will parents be supported in the difficult task of helping their children

4. See George R. Hunsberger, "Sizing Up the Shape of the Church," in *The Church Between Gospel and Culture: The Emerging Mission in North America*, ed. George R. Hunsberger and Craig Van Gelder (Grand Rapids: Eerdmans, 1996), pp. 333-46.

to want to be part of the alternative society? How else will children see that the whole community cares about their well-being?

Parenting is not a duty to be borne alone. It is indeed the responsibility of the whole Christian community. Several years ago my husband and I served as table hosts for the midweek program of the congregation to which we belonged at that time. One of the teenagers from my Wednesday table would come to see me on Sundays after I finished teaching adult Bible class to talk with me or show me things he had made. I felt it was a great privilege to maintain a good friendship with that teenager, just as now I try to talk, every time I see them, with all the youth of the small congregation to which we presently belong. I believe it is a sacred duty (and also a great delight) for all the members of the congregation to affirm our community's youth, to greet them warmly and welcome their participation in all our activities, to ask about what is important to them and to encourage them, to be a small part of forming them into godly young people. How can we better instruct our Christian communities so that everyone in the entire Body knows that he or she shares in the responsibility for nurturing the children in our midst?

How can our parishes more thoroughly surround their families, to provide community support and additional persons who care for raising children with the values of the Bible? Everyone knows that it is easier to stick to certain rules and regulations in dealing with one's children if other parents choose the same guidelines. It is also far easier for children to choose positive values if those values are attractively incarnated in all the adults of the Church.

8. Does the congregation give young people meaningful jobs to do in the parish? How open are our parishes to the presence and contributions of children? How else will they learn that being part of the Body of Christ involves us all in mission, that a life of faith is often hard work, that there are intrinsic rewards more valuable than money or fame?

In one congregation in upstate New York the younger elementary school children lead the chanting of the introit every Sunday. They recognize that this is their job — and a very important one at that — and they are eager to play their bells and teach the congregation how to sing. This not only instills in them several worship skills, but especially deepens their faith in God and their self-esteem.

Young people who are bored with their youth groups are often the victims of programs that attempt to compete with the kinds of fun that the local high school or athletic club can provide. Let us give youth instead what the world cannot give them — Bible study, meaningful involvement in service projects with definite Christian orientation, participation with their families or other elders in joint efforts to relieve suffering, Christian camps, choirs that do the best of church music (from all eras), instrumental groups that play for worship or at convalescent centers, relationships and conversations with older members to root them deeply in the faith. How much do our churches engage in actual *Christian* formative experiences for young people, or are we letting our children be formed primarily by television and by their peers?

9. Does the congregation encourage and enable your children to memorize the Scriptures, learn essential doctrines, delight in Christian symbols, value the noblest hymns and the best new songs, and cherish the heritage of the faith? How else will they be formed to be part of the ongoing meta-narrative of the people of God? How else will they be nurtured to want to remain part of the Christian community?

We are increasingly told that Sunday Schools should use computers and videos, that confirmation class must be "relevant" sharing of opinions, that Vacation Bible Schools ought not to be so old-fashioned, that Bible study is passé. Such educational policies are having disturbing results in churches throughout the United States: children are not experiencing the faith through the modeling of adults who incarnate the Gospel; they have no ability to "account for the hope that lies within us" (1 Peter 3:15); they are remaining biblical illiterates. Recently in a Bible study composed of serious students at a Christian college I made an offhand remark about the account of Gideon and the fleece (Judges 6) — a story that once was standard fare in Sunday School — and eleven out of the twelve religion majors about to go on to seminary had no idea what I was talking about!

Most of the Scripture that I "know by heart" I learned when I was a child — and those precious memorized passages have carried me through many bouts of severe illness, through seven months of blindness, through cancer and increasing handicaps, through plenty of tough times. The Scriptures encourage us to "hide the Word in our heart," which means in our will. The Holy Spirit works through the renewal of our minds and what is stored there of the heart of God — but so many young people these days are learning to base their faith on their feelings instead, which will not hold them when times get tough.

The prevailing assumption in our culture is that children should be allowed to make their own "intelligent choices" — including choices about religion, about elements of the faith. In contrast, as Stanley Hauerwas reminds us, in the Christian community we will want to raise our children to be worthy of carrying on the traditions of their ancestors.[5] Thus, an important task of the entire community is to celebrate its values and invite children to participate in the delight of choosing to be faithful to them as a gift to the world — and to themselves!

I know from speaking at youth convocations around the country that young people want more than churches are giving them, that they especially want a Christianity worth following and a God worth believing. We need strong churches to pass on the faith strongly. All the best research shows that the young people who come back to churches after rebelling are the ones raised with the most robust traditions.[6]

Poet-philosopher Wendell Berry explained the gift of strong traditions in one's heritage in this way:

> The most complete speech is that of conversation in a settled community of some age, where what is said refers to and evokes things, people, places, and events that are commonly known. In

5. Stanley Hauerwas, *A Community of Character: Toward a Constructive Christian Social Ethic* (Notre Dame: University of Notre Dame Press, 1981), p. 169.

6. See, for example, Benton Johnson, Dean R. Hoge, and Donald A. Luidens, "Mainline Churches: The Real Reason for Decline," *First Things* 31 (March 1993): 13-18, and their book, *Vanishing Boundaries: The Religion of Mainline Protestant Baby Boomers* (Louisville: Westminster/John Knox, 1994).

such a community, to speak and hear is to remember. . . . [That the old is unessential to the young] has been caused by the dispersal of families and communities, and the consequent destruction of local cultures and economies.[7]

The Church's speech, too, is most complete when it is built on all the memories of saints and their deeds, of biblical characters and their stories and settings, of the best poems and songs and symbols of the heritage. How can we maintain the culture of Christianity if we dispense with what is old and give our children the impression that it is unessential?

10. Does the congregation go beyond "evangelism programs" to help each member, young or old, become equipped to share his or her faith, to be hospitable to strangers, to be a friend to those who need the gospel? How else will we fulfill the Great Commission?

We will consider in the following chapter the serious confusion these days between worship and evangelism, but at this point we must recognize that all members of the Body of Christ are witnesses to God's grace in the world. Especially in our post-Christian society, the good news of the gospel must be deliberately shared.

Imagine with me what it would be like if the children in our congregations were so glad about their relationship with God that they would eagerly invite their friends (many of whom have no religious foundations in their homes) to participate with them in the worship and events of the Christian community. We are all witnesses — and children are often the best (because of their frankness and sincerity) if they see from our modeling that it matters.

The Basic Issues

The ten topics raised in this chapter can be summarized in three questions that every congregation must constantly ask itself if we are

7. Mindy Weinreb, "A Question a Day: A Written Conversation with Wendell Berry," in *Wendell Berry,* ed. Paul Merchant, American Authors Series (Lewiston, ID: Confluence Press, 1991), p. 31.

serious about Church-being and about bringing up Christian children to share in Church-being. Does our congregational life keep *God* as the center, the focus, our source for truth and life? Do our parish activities and services form members with the *character* of God's people? Do our church events and worship times create us to be a *community* of faith according to the biblical descriptions?[8]

I will be honest with you: I am worried that so many pastors and leaders in the churches of the United States have fallen prey to the confusions of the "church marketers."[9] Instead of faithfulness, the major goal of many congregations has become success. Instead of deepening the spiritual lives of members and training them for mission, the focus seems to be on parishes growing fatter by attracting consumers to their smorgasbord of ministry services. The results for our children are disastrous, for they are schooled by such congregational life to be narcissistic shoppers of religion instead of faithful followers of Christ.

It seems to me that if we and our offspring are a people formed by the scriptural narratives, an entirely different set of values will guide our thinking. We will want to know what God wants instead of insisting on our choices. We will want to be the persons God designed us to be instead of people like the rest of the world. We will want to be a community that passes on the faith in faithful ways.

For further reflection, discussion, transformation, and practice:

1. Does my congregation live as an alternative, parallel society? In what ways? In what respects not? Have my answers to these questions changed or expanded since they were asked at the end

8. For a wider development of these questions, see chapters 5-7 of Marva J. Dawn, *Reaching Out without Dumbing Down: A Theology of Worship for the Turn-of-the-Century Culture* (Grand Rapids: Eerdmans, 1995), and also the following chapter in this book.

9. See Philip D. Kenneson and James L. Street, *Selling Out the Church: The Dangers of Church Marketing* (Nashville: Abingdon Press, 1997).

of Chapter 3? What new insights did this chapter give me concerning the nature of the alternativeness of the Church?

2. What sort of educational/catechismal processes does my congregation utilize for the training of our youth in the fundamentals of Christian faith? What processes do we use to initiate adults who have no background in Christian truth and practices? What educational processes do we engage in with our children in our family?

3. Does my congregation wrestle with all of the Scriptures (and not just the parts we like)? Does my family study the whole Bible together? Do my children see me as a learner with them of the meaning of the Scriptures for our lives? If not, what can we as a Christian community do to change our reading and living of the Revelation?

4. Am I and are my children lovingly admonished by other members of our Christian community? Do we hold each other accountable for living faithfully according to the values of the kingdom of God? If not, what can we as a family and as a congregation do to encourage greater accountability?

5. Are my children learning in our congregation to get along with those they don't like, to serve those who have needs, to transcend racial and class barriers? If not, what can we as a Christian community and as a family do to encourage God's design for reconciliation in the whole human family?

6. Are my children challenged to use their gifts for the sake of the congregation's mission? Are they given meaningful jobs? If not, what can we as a family and as a Christian community do to call forth their gifts?

7. Do my children eagerly share their faith? Does our congregation train them with skills for passing on the gospel? Am I able to tell others about what Christ has done for me in his death and resurrection? If not, what can we as a Christian community do to equip all the saints for witnessing?

CHAPTER 5

The Heart of God
Revealed in Worship

> *Praise the Lord! You heav'ns, adore him;*
> *praise him, angels in the height;*
> *sun and moon, rejoice before him;*
> *praise him, all you stars and light.*
> *Praise the Lord! For he has spoken;*
> *worlds his mighty voice obeyed;*
> *laws which never shall be broken*
> *for their guidance he has made.*
>
> *Praise the Lord! For he is glorious;*
> *never shall his promise fail;*
> *God has made his saints victorious;*
> *sin and death shall not prevail.*
> *Praise the God of our salvation;*
> *hosts on high, his pow'r proclaim;*
> *heav'n and earth and all creation,*
> *praise and glorify his name.*

The Heart of God Revealed in Worship

Worship, honor, glory, blessing, Lord,
we offer as our gift;
young and old, your praise expressing,
our glad songs to you we lift.
All the saints in heaven adore you;
we would join their glad acclaim;
as your angels serve before you,
so on earth we praise your name.

St. 1, 2 "Foundling Hospital Collection" (1796), alt.; st. 3
Edward Osler (1836), alt.
Tune: Hyfrydol, Rowland Hugh Prichard (1885)

The only thing that the Church does that no one else can do is worship the triune God. Therefore, if we want to raise children to rejoice in being members of the Christian community, what we do in worship is critically important. Both parents and congregations have enormous — but also enormously worthwhile — work to do to train our children in the habits and practice of worship.

Are We Worshiping Yet?

The scene was the closing, Sunday-morning worship service for a large youth convocation. The band on stage, whose wonderful contemporary music is quite singable and theologically sound, was working very hard to get the youth involved, but none of the young people in the rows around me was singing, although all the adults were attempting to participate in spite of not previously knowing the songs. I had asked a pastor who was temporarily serving a congregation in the area before returning to Madagascar to observe with me the behavior of the young people, and he also reported that none of the ones he watched throughout the weekend was joining in the singing.

During the sermon time a seminary professor really revved up the youth, offering among other things a dramatic retelling of a popular writer's famous story — thus ignoring that writer's own

65

plea that readers not use his stories except exactly as he had written them since his choice of details was significant for the meaning as a whole. The professor never got around to saying much related to the Scripture texts that had been read in the worship service, and after all the hype he jumped off the stage and turned a flip, to the raucous shouts and wild applause of the youth.

During the distribution of the Lord's Supper, various youth wandered out into the hall, came back with glasses of water, chatted with their friends, and ignored the music a few of us were bravely trying to sing in the midst of the hubbub.

Similarly, at another youth convocation's highlighted worship service, a small group sang a lovely modern version of the Lord's Prayer — and meanwhile a female teenager in front of me was clipping her fingernails.

What is wrong with these pictures? What has happened to worship involving youth? The church marketers say that contemporary people don't want reverence, so we shouldn't insist on it if we want to appeal to the crowds — but we must ask if those gurus are paying any attention to what the Bible says about worship. More personally, we must ask what *our* behavior in worship says about our understanding of, and relationship with, the triune God.

Obviously many of the teenagers (and some of the leaders) at these two events understood worship as only another form of entertainment, which must be replaced with another activity when it is not amusing enough. If we believe — and I do — that the worship of the Church is a very important formative agent in the community, what should characterize that worship if we want to raise genuinely Christian children, and how can we get young people involved in it?

Recently a pastor criticized my book on worship, *Reaching Out without Dumbing Down*, because he thought it gave too much credit to worship as a formative agent. In that book I never say that worship is the only, or even the primary, molding force — but I do insist that because worship is, usually quite subtly, a strong formative agent, we must be sure that what we do in worship nurtures the kind of people we want our children and ourselves to be as Church.

The spirited participation of the children and young adults is one of the most stunning aspects of Christianity in Madagascar, where I spent three weeks serving the Lutheran mission and teaching various Malagasy seminary, clergy, and medical groups. I have never seen such a large proportion of young people at worship services nor heard such vibrant singing (in at least eight-part harmony). My pastor friend who serves there and I grieved to see youth at the convocation here in the U.S. so jaundiced and jaded with worship. There the churches are packed with a preponderant number of youth. In Tolagnaro, about five hundred people jubilantly sang the hymns (translations of old Norwegian hymns with new Malagasy tunes). They sang mostly from memory (because few had hymnbooks), and they made up all kinds of harmonies — such an extraordinary sound. At the time of the offering, everyone processed to the altar with their gifts; with the girls almost all dressed up in white, it was a stunning sight. Their exuberance helps me not give up hope for the practice of worship by young people.

I realize several things, however: the interest of the Malagasy is higher because there is not much else in their society to do; their love of singing is a cultural trait — one often hears little children singing as they play (without any toys); and Christianity is for many of them a wonderful release from the witch-doctor faith of their ancestors. Perhaps we need more poverty to recapture worship for our children here. All kinds of other things are being tried in the attempt to urge young people to get involved in our congregations' worship. Why don't they?

Some of the Whys

Simplistically, youth don't participate in worship because they don't understand it. More basically, they don't understand because they have not been taught. Even more foundationally, they have not been taught because our churches have been too busy doing other things — and perhaps because their parents and/or the community's leaders don't know what worship is either. Probably these comments are too harsh, but as I travel around the country and work in various denominations I am grieved by the massive confusions I encounter regarding worship and by the worship services I have had to endure that are destructive to the formation of godly character in the youth and adults who attend them.

That young people to a great extent are not being taught about worship is due to a combination of multiple factors — and let me hasten to add that some children are beginning to learn through such innovative new programs as "Logos"[1] and "Children in Worship."[2] Our immigrant forebears in many cases struggled with the tension between practices of the "old country" and being respectably "American"; worship was sometimes held in the old language and therefore disdained by the younger generation. Some Protestant ancestors deliberately rejected anything that smacked of being "Catholic" and turned away from everything worshipful except preaching for education with a few songs thrown in. The "boomer" generation rejected authority and dispensed with anything traditional. The "busters" are the generation of choice — and usually prefer the freedom to go skiing or sleep in to the restraints of the worship hour. The technological milieu demands efficiency, so the meaningful ordering of worship is often truncated and thereby confused for the sake of the hourly limit. Declining numbers in parishes and denominations have caused church leaders to panic and do silly things with worship to make it "appealing" (see the next section). We could list many other kinds of factors, but that probably wouldn't help us much to counteract the failure.

More important is the question of why it should matter. Is worship really all that significant in the formation of Christian children?

Fundamentally, we must recognize that every action of our

1. "Logos" is a midweek school program involving worship skills along with Bible teaching, games and sports, and common meals. For information contact the Logos System Associates, 1405 Frey Road, Pittsburgh, PA 15235.

2. "Children in Worship" is a Sunday morning "children's church" program for children up to six years old that actually engages them in worship practices and in learning about the Church year. For information contact Professor Sonja Stewart, Western Theological Seminary, 86 E. 12th St., Holland, MI 49423 (telephone 616-392-8555). See also *Young Children and Worship* by Sonja M. Stewart and Jerome W. Berryman (Louisville: Westminster/John Knox Press, 1989).

lives molds our character. If a teenager chooses constantly to elevate herself, she reinforces her growth into more of a narcissistic person. If a young adult wants to be an outreaching person, he must make daily choices that are generous. Good worship will bring young people out of themselves and into an encounter with God. An environment of humility, reverence, obedience, and eagerness (some of the most prominent reactions of biblical characters when they encountered God or his messengers) will train children in essential aspects of a faith-full disposition.

Our children are best formed if we make use of all the means in the Christian community to nurture in them a godly character — all the narratives and rules and invitations of the Scriptures, all our images for God, our specific worship practices, our prayerful consideration of means and ends, the tiny choices of daily life, the values of the community, and their interactions with its members. All of these things together contribute to who they will become and how they will live.

These days churches get so little time to nurture children in the faith (unless they have a Christian school). Consequently, every aspect of the time we spend together in the worshiping Christian community is critically important for the impression it makes on young people with respect to the value of the Church and their attitudes about who they are in relation to God and his world. Some of the negative influences of unbiblical pseudo-worship are very subtle — which makes them all the more dangerous. We must work explicitly to counteract those destructive influences.

Wrong Turns in the Face of Modernity and Postmodernity

In response to the downward trend in worship attendance that accompanied the massive changes in U.S. society in the 1960s,[3] many congregations made drastic changes in their worship without adequate thinking about the theological, ecclesiological, and educational implications. Though the following list is far too cursory,

3. See Wade Clark Roof, *A Generation of Seekers: The Spiritual Journeys of the Baby Boom Generation* (San Francisco: HarperCollins Publishers, 1993).

it summarizes some of the moves that should be questioned, especially with regard to their effects on the faith of our children:

- In the face of the relativizing of truth, some pastors and musicians dispense less truth instead of more, becoming therapeutic instead of theological — thus teaching youth "feel goodism," for example, instead of forgiveness.
- With the proliferation of entertainments, some worship leaders sacrifice content for form and confuse worship with evangelism and evangelism with marketing (see the following section), thus making worship superficial for our children.
- As society has become more openly pluralistic and less supportive of Christianity in particular, some congregations blur their unique identity as the people of God instead of accentuating it with loving commitment, thus leaving young people without any reason to be Christian.
- As the culture becomes more and more rootless, some denominations and individual parishes give up their heritage as communities with long histories and global connections, thus depriving young people of the continuity of the Church over space and time.
- In the face of the culture's loss of moral authority, some churches become tolerant to the point of ceasing to be a people formed by the narratives of Scripture, thus giving youth the impression that anything goes and that God has nothing to say about how we live.
- In response to the increasing clamor for choice, some congregations foster consumerism according to "felt needs" instead of embracing what is truly needful, thus turning our children into shoppers instead of students of the faith.
- In the face of declining attendance, many congregations are accepting the marketing strategy that Sunday school should be held at the same time as worship, so that parents aren't distracted and so that the Sunday schedule is made convenient for them. The result is that children learn no skills for worship, parents have no Bible study, and all are trained to make their faith efficient rather than faithful. Since research shows that youth who are not trained in the practice of worship are

far less likely to participate as adults, congregations that choose such a schedule set themselves up for failure in raising children for godly life and faithful worship as adults.

- In the face of a culture that celebrates ease (see Chapter 8), some parishes are taking away most of the action of the congregation and giving it to the "worship team," thus reducing participation to expediency and robbing our offspring of the "work of worship" and its training for the vocation of discipleship.

- In the midst of a homogenizing culture, some churches are downgrading the complex and multiform legacy of the Church's music to one style, thus sacrificing diversity for monotony and depriving our children of the excellence and artistry that the Bible always calls for in our praise of God.

- In many congregations "worship wars" rage as pastors and other leaders debate over such questions as "How can worship be made relevant to people in these postmodern times?" or "What style of music should we use to make our worship appealing to the youth and the 'unchurched'?" These are the wrong questions to ask, for they miss the point of being Church; they do not probe the fundamental issues of what worship is, how God's people conduct it, and what it means for raising our children. Let us consider more carefully in this chapter what sorts of questions would be faithful to our tasks as a Church in worship and in order to raise our children to know and spread the grace of Jesus Christ.

Worship Is Not a Matter of Taste

The worst thing churches can do about worship for the sake of their children is to choose music and worship forms according to *their* taste — when their tastes are not yet biblically formed. That would be like letting first graders decide what they want to learn in school. Doctoral research asking young people what they think is "appropriate" for worship came up with entirely different answers from those given when youth were asked what they wanted.

I often wonder how it came about that churches began to

sacrifice their identity in an attempt to please people. The Boy Scouts or 4-H clubs or sports associations do not change who they are to appeal to people — they might use new forms, but these groups still continue to train young men to be virtuous by means of outdoor skills, to teach sewing and cooking, to practice how to play ball. It is commonly known that these organizations serve purposes that people want to participate in, so when a young person wants to join, he or she is grateful for the opportunity and learns how the program works. Similarly, if we want to learn an ethnic dance, those who have practiced it do not change the steps for us. We practice with them so that we can develop the habits of the art. Why do churches throw away their habits and arts — and more deeply, their identity as the parallel, alternative community — instead of welcoming our children and neighbors into the dance and helping them to learn it?

Congregations that cater to taste usually wind up in a "worship war" that rips apart the Christian community by splitting the Body into those who want "traditional" and those who want "contemporary" styles (terms that are quite poorly defined since there are numerous kinds of each). If this war is "resolved" by having one service of each style, the result usually separates the young from the old, so that the young are deprived of their elders' wisdom, experience, and understanding of the faith life, and the elderly are bereft of the youths' energy and enthusiasm. In many other ways this division into styles of worship destroys the genuine community that young people need for spiritual growth.

For example, to choose this solution aborts our being Church because it accentuates the false impression that worship is a matter of taste, rather than of offering our best to praise a worthy God. It also advances the "vendors/consumers" disposition. Moreover, it deprives the "traditionalists" of new expressions of faith and robs the "contemporaryists" of continuity with the Church throughout time. Furthermore, members of the congregation do not learn to appreciate a wide variety of musical styles for the sake of caring for each other in the Body. In addition, all of these results contribute to the narcissistic self-centeredness of young people — and of churches — that prevents genuine witness, concern for the neighbor, and outreach to the world.

I have observed that, if they are taught, young people enjoy a wide range of music. Having directed children's, junior high, senior high, and college choirs, as well as adult ones, I know that people of all ages love old hymns and chorales, new songs and carols, ancient chants, folk tunes, contrapuntal works by Bach, ethnic music from around the world, Taizé choruses, soul spirituals, jazz — the music of the Church! Furthermore, I have noticed invariably that the youth who love to sing in worship are the children of parents who sing with gladness. In one confirmation class I asked the teenagers how many of them liked liturgy, and it matched exactly — each one who did was the offspring of a parent who participated.

Yesterday little Aaron, who is less than three years old, sat quietly next to his mother, who was holding his baby brother, in worship. They sat near the front so that Aaron could participate in what was going on. He sang several of the pieces of the liturgy, leaned forward to catch everything of the children's lesson, and afterward sang for me the first verse of "Holy, Holy, Holy," one of his favorite hymns. His mother said that he also really likes "Once in Royal David's City" and several other Christmas hymns. Of course, not every young child will be equally capable of quiet attention at the same age, but we should expect, encourage, and teach it as much as possible. What if children spent some time in their homes learning elements for worship instead of watching all the frenetic television programs (see Chapter 10 below) that make it impossible for them to be calmly quiet, reverently respectful, joyfully celebrative, and genuinely interested when they come to the house of God?

Instead of changing its music and worship forms to please the young people, a congregation should teach its youth why the older members value certain songs and hymns, why parts of the liturgy are meaningful, how the various things we do in worship contribute to keeping our focus on God and to nurturing us, individually and corporately, in the life of discipleship.[4] Similarly, we should also encourage the youth to continue to bring to our

4. These points are elaborated throughout this and the next section and greatly expanded in Marva J. Dawn, *Reaching Out without Dumbing Down: A Theology of Worship for the Turn-of-the-Century Culture* (Grand Rapids: Eerdmans, 1995).

worship planning group new music that does the same, so that we can teach these fresh worship tools to the older members.

Above all, we dare not fall prey to the cultural demand for easiness. People in the society around the Church do not want to "work" at worship — they want "fast food" speed and ease and accessibility. This contradicts all the biblical instructions about worship, which call for offering God what he deserves — our best in beauty, holiness, and artistry. All the guidelines in the books of Exodus and Chronicles for constructing the worship place and all the directives in the psalms for how to worship call for the highest in excellence and craftsmanship and humility and nobility. Our children will not learn to honor God with the best of their lives if they don't observe and participate in offering God our very best in worship. They will not learn that discipleship demands cross-bearing if our worship practices allow them to be passive spectators or engage them in effortless monotony (of any style).

The most important question to ask, as worship planners, is how we can best glorify God. The issue is not one of style, but of propriety. Certainly we can use all kinds of music (and using a wide variety fosters greater community), but some songs are not appropriate to worship God. Since we are able to worship only by grace, we will want the elements we use to keep reminding us and our children that God is the Subject who has invited us here, who teaches us about himself, who enlightens us to worship. Our glad response to God as the Object of our worship can then take many forms.

Since sharing God's love in word and deed is the privilege and responsibility of all believers of all ages, we must also ask what kind of people our worship practices will form. How will we and our offspring be equipped to be missional throughout the week in all that we do as God's people living and going to school and working in the world around our churches? What is appropriate to bring us all together, young and old, as a community? What will appropriately nurture us corporately and personally for being Church in ways suggested in the previous chapter?

The vitality and faithfulness of our Christian lives and the effectiveness of our outreach to the world depend on these three foundations: our constantly deepening relationship with God, the nurturing of our personal character, and the developing of genuine community. Does everything in our worship contribute to the growth in young and old of this Church-being?

By the use of these three common criteria — keeping God as the Subject/Object of our worship, nurturing Christian character in believers, and developing genuine Christian community — congregations can assess what we do in worship in order to bring together opposing sides of various arguments and a blend of styles. Can we learn better what it means to be the Church as we talk together about worship practices? Can we make sure that old and young worship together for the sake of wisdom and vitality for all? Most of all, can we be theologically faithful about worship instead of being beguiled by the unbiblical advice of church marketers who urge us to do only what is pleasing to youth rather than what is truly worship?

Confusing Worship and Evangelism

Questions that ask about changing musical style or other elements in order to appeal to the youth or the unchurched betray a serious confusion between worship and evangelism, to the detriment of both. Worship ought not to be forced to bear the brunt of evangelism, which is instead the task of all believers. Don't misunderstand: good worship *will be* evangelistic, but that is not its primary purpose. No passage in the Scriptures says, "Worship the Lord to attract the unbeliever." Rather, we are commanded, invited, urged, wooed to worship the Trinity because God is worthy of our praise.

Indeed, the Scriptures frequently tell us that *we* are witnesses. Evangelism happens in our daily lives, our family discussions, our regular encounters, our simple conversations and carings (or at evangelistic events, which have a focus different from that of worship) — in order that we can bring others, especially our children, *with* us to worship God. Evangelism is the means; worship is the end.

Worship can actually be done only by those who recognize the utter worthiness of the Trinity. The labor of helping young people acknowledge God's worthiness happens in the home and in the Christian community where we work constantly to nurture our offspring to know God's preeminent excellence so that they want to respond with adoration and praise and commitment.

The worship service itself is also part of the entire educational processes of the Christian community by which God's people are equipped to introduce others to his worthiness. Evangelism or sharing is done by all of us, including our young people, who realize that everyone around us needs God's grace. Out of our love for God and our love for those neighbors, we are eager to serve them and pass on the witness of faith.

Think of the difference between evangelism and worship with this simple analogy: imagine how I describe my beloved husband to audiences as an example in my presentations, in contrast to how I speak to him when I get home from the speaking engagement. I could hold up a large picture of Myron, to whom I've been joyfully married for 91 months and 11 days today as I first write this, and tell the audience what a wonderful elementary school teacher he is, how beautiful are the gardens he grows, how gently he cares for me with my physical handicaps — all this to introduce him to the listeners, just as we introduce God to others in evangelism. But when I arrive home I will speak to Myron with words of love, listen to what he tells me about his work, talk through my experiences while I was away, sort out problems with him, and so forth — just as we interact with God in worship. Our conversations will be in the language of intimacy and growth, rather than in the idiom of introduction.

Worship is the language of adoration addressed to God and the language of God's Revelation, which instructs us to honor him appropriately and equips us for life and witness. Good worship is purposefully directed to God; it will, as a result, nurture the character of believers and the community and form us to be the kind of people who will reach out evangelistically and in service to the world around us.

The distinction is not total, for if believers worship with gladness and eagerness, anyone who is not yet a part of the community certainly will be attracted to the One who is the object of their worship. But to focus the worship on evangelistic introduction deprives our children and ourselves of the deeper nurturing they and we need to live as Church and deprives God of the intimate worship due his Name.

Worship to Form the Missional Parallel Society

You might wonder why I have spent so much space on evangelism in a book about raising children to be truly Christian. It is because so many churches throughout the country and throughout the denominations have confused worship and evangelism, and in doing so have prevented the community from equipping its off-spring to have the heart of God and, therefore, to be missional — that is, participating in God's mission — in the world. If we in the Church are truly going to be an alternative community, the parallel society, then our worship must contribute to that. It is essential for our young people that their experiences in worship undergird the Joy that is ours because of the different life we lead as God's people — with different values, distinct goals, unique purposes in life.

I capitalize the word *Joy* because I do not want it to be confused with happiness. Ours is a world that does everything it can to escape suffering, that pursues happiness relentlessly, sometimes at great cost to others. I grieve that many congregations have turned their worship services into "happiness" celebrations and thus foster the selfish consumerism that their members have already learned from the world, instead of nurturing in them the authentic *Christian* discipleship that brings genuine Joy and service to the world.

You might think from the preceding comments that I am opposed to the "contemporary" side in many congregations' "worship wars." Actually I'm opposed to the "traditional" side, too, because both sides are asking the wrong questions and failing to nurture a missional people. The Church always needs both old and new music, continuity as well as reformation, a sense of the heritage of faith going all the way back to Abraham and a consciousness of the need to put that faith in accessible forms and new wineskins. The questions we must ask are those concerning how to be faithful to the biblical descriptions of what worship is, to the content of the faith we pass on, and to the God whom we worship.

If the congregational leadership plans worship according to the biblical narratives and the heritage of the Church (throughout time and space), then they can use all the best materials and forms possible, no matter from what era they derive. For worship I have played both guitar and organ, composed new anthems and songs, and directed young choirs and instrumentalists in a wide variety of musical styles from a diversity of ethnic traditions and eras. For whatever music or drama or other materials and forms we use, however, we must realize how much carefulness is required to sort out the best, the most theologically sound and musically excellent, new materials — a process that is already quite well completed, with some notable exceptions, for worship elements passed on in a tradition and therefore appearing in hymnbooks.

Some church marketing gurus frequently tout the misconception that worship should be "user-friendly." I am certainly not advocating worship that alienates or is inaccessible to our children, but the Scriptures help us see that being confronted by God is not always comfortable or comforting. God is not easily understandable, nor is it cozy to be a disciple. We must be careful, of course, that it is not God's earthly servants who offend, but let us always remember that the Lord of the gospel himself is a stone of stumbling and a rock of offense and that discipleship requires hard work. User-friendly worship seems to me to sacrifice an awe-full lot of God.

What We Need Is the Truth

What we need in worship is the Truth — the whole truth, nothing but the truth, so help us, God! That oath from the witness stand gives us good guidelines for what our children require from us in our worship services.

The Truth that the Church has to offer to everyone in the midst of these postmodern times must be shared in all its wholeness. When our children hear from the world around them that Christianity has been (and sometimes now is) violent and oppressive, we must humbly acknowledge that this criticism is right. Beyond accepting the blame for Christians' failures in history, we must help our offspring understand the whole truth that we remain sinful and fallible. We do that in worship with genuine confession (and the announcement of forgiveness). We also proclaim in worship what the Scriptures thoroughly teach us about our nature being helplessly sinful, hopelessly lost. That fact forces us to see that we cannot know the Truth entirely, that our eyes are blinded by sin, that our understanding of God is only partial. But that does not negate the Truth of the God we confess nor our recognition of Christ who is the Truth, the Life, and the Way.

Against the postmodern rejection of meta-narrative — that is, of the possibility that there is any universal, overarching Truth that is true for all people in all places — I believe that we Christians can humbly and gladly celebrate with our children in worship the nonoppressive, all-inclusive story of a triune God who creates, redeems, and unifies as manifestations of his perfect love for the whole world. The Christian meta-narrative, specific parts of which are declared in our worship each week and the whole of which is proclaimed in our worship over time, is the account of a promising God who always keeps his promises — a Truth clearly seen in the First Testament history of Israel and most clearly seen in the history of Jesus of Nazareth, who died and rose again in fulfillment of God's promises. We believe that this meta-narrative will reach its ultimate fulfillment when Jesus comes again to bring God's promised gracious reign to fruition — and thus the meta-narrative of God's kingdom already initiated and celebrated in worship gives us all that our children most deeply need of hope, purpose, and fulfillment in this present life.

This God of eternal mystery condescends to reveal himself to us — a process to which he invites us by drawing us to worship him. That is why our worship needs to be structured as richly and deeply as possible, so that we never lose sight of the fact that God is the One who enables us to come to worship and the One who receives our praise.

Furthermore, our worship must contain nothing but the truth. Music, songs, Scripture lessons, sermons, liturgical forms, architecture, and other accoutrements of art and gesture and ambience are all means by which God invites, reveals, and forms us. If we use shallow (I did not say *simple*) worship materials, they will not reveal the truth about God. Instead, these superficial materials will both shape shallow theology and form our children and ourselves

79

superficially. Songs with cheap or sentimental lyrics or banal music belie the coherence and integrity and supreme beauty of God. Sermons that draw attention to the preacher's eloquence or merely to the exterior needs of the listeners deprive the congregation, old and young, of the formative power of the scriptural narratives for meeting our genuine needs for repentant insight, constant forgiveness, authentic security, unconditional love, absolute healing, faithful presence, fruitful freedom, compelling motivation and coherent guidance for daily life, and eternal hope.

Worship can never give us the whole truth, but worship must never give us untruth or less than truth. Our children's young minds — and our finite minds — cannot begin to grasp all that there is to learn about God, but every time the community gathers we have the opportunity to add to our total store of truth what this time of corporate worship contributes. Only by God's grace and in the context of prayer and the whole Christian community can worship leaders prepare services that present, and our young people receive, as much truth as possible.

Against postmodernity's rejection of the past and of authority, in the Church we realize that we are greatly helped in our planning by the wisdom gathered throughout the Church's existence, by history's sorting of the good from the less-than-good in hymns and liturgies and interpretations. Now it is our responsibility also to sort through what is new in order to choose what is true — keeping God as the Subject/Object of our worship, nurturing the truthful character of individual believers, and forming the Christian community to be outreaching with the Truth that we know.

Christian worship gives the truth of coherence — that in the songs we sing (whatever style, old or new) the music fits with the words, the words fit with who God is and who we are, the song fits with its place in the worship service, the service fits with the time of year in which it is held. In our chaotic, disparate, fractured postmodern world, young people need such appropriateness, such coherence, such order and flow — in short, the harmony of God.

The Christian community makes its worship and communal life as full of truth, beauty, and goodness as possible in order to usher participants into the presence of God. These foretastes are not meant to satisfy our deep longing (our *Sehnsucht*) or to push it under, but to intensify it so profoundly that we search for its fulfillment only in the other world for which we were made, God's kingdom, of which the community's worship is a preparation and a proleptic experience.

Equipping the Saints for Ministry

If worship stays well focused on the Trinity, our children will become better equipped to be God's witnesses to their diverse worlds. To introduce our families and neighbors to God and to God's gifts for them, we need an ever-growing understanding of his promises, his character, his interventions in the world, his truth that underlies our realities. Out of a character formed by the biblical narratives, by their faithful interpretation, and by resulting sound doctrine will flow love that responds to the love of God. Such a character will manifest forgiveness that recognizes the potency of the Father's grace, actions that follow the model of Jesus, encouragement and compassion empowered by the Paraclete.

Of course, it will be extremely difficult to form strong Christian character if the worship hour is the only time the Church has to nurture it, but worship's subtle influence on character dare not be misdirected. If we sing only narcissistic ditties in our worship, we will develop a faith that depends on feelings and that is inward-curved, instead of outward-turned. Worship as Truth and thereby formative of alternative character is a major issue for me as I think about the nurturing of our children because of so many bad experiences lately in worship services that were flimsy, if not flippant. With so much quality contemporary as well as traditional music to choose from, why does so much of the new music used in many congregations lack theological depth, biblical images, motivation to be about God's purposes of witnessing, justice building, and peacemaking in the world? What kind of people are our worship services forming?

Second Timothy 3:14-17 speaks about Timothy being trained throughout his childhood in the Holy Scriptures — trained to *know* them and be formed by them and not just to "believe" as if

81

that were a leap in the dark, to have habits and not simply to make a single choice. Our offspring — and perhaps we — need that kind of training much more than our parents did, since the society no longer supports it and since so many cultural forces alien to the gospel impinge on our lives and urge our conformity. Instead of giving our youth nothing but Sunday school classes and sermons that merely "share opinions" on various issues, let us offer them deep explication of Scripture to lay the basis for genuine Christian thinking, thorough teaching of the biblical narratives in order to form them to react as God's people, with kingdom values, to the problems and social issues of their everyday lives. Instead of giving them only worship ditties that merely repeat a superficial feeling, let us teach them hymns with strong doctrinal content, songs that elaborate metaphors and images, music that contains progressions of thought, choruses that emphasize habits of faith.

I have carefully chosen hymns to head the chapters in this book to demonstrate that poetry and music are excellent tools to reinforce lessons learned or to stimulate new avenues for thinking. If you have been reading these aloud — or singing them when you know the tune listed or can find it in a hymnbook — you have experienced how the sound heightens the enrichment of a wonderful song of faith.

Education about Worship

This chapter has followed a crucial progression — away from making worship a matter of taste into evangelizing our children so that they want both to worship and then to reach out beyond themselves in mission to the world around them. To do this, our worship will be truthful — focused on God and appropriate to who God is, nurturing godliness, developing genuine community, calling and equipping the parallel society to be missional.

I have discovered that, when young people understand these things about worship, musical style ceases to be a barrier. No matter if "traditional" or "contemporary" elements are used, failures to teach and lead are the impediments. Youth's participation in worship will be deepened by joyful leadership and good modeling.

I am profoundly indebted to my parents for the wonderful training and modeling they provided when I was a child. I learned many phrases and melodies of hymns (in German and English) as a toddler because I went with my mother to the "Ladies Aid" and was swept up into the elderly women's love for singing. The first word I ever learned to read was *Selah* because of reading psalms during worship in the parish. My mother always traced the text with her finger so I could follow it and begin to associate words with letters on the page. Soon I noticed that when the congregation said a certain word that I didn't understand, it was printed off to the side. I began to watch for those words in the margin and could shout "Selah" with the community whenever it appeared. Humorous perhaps — but as a wee one I participated in psalm praise with my joy-full Selahs and felt a part of the community.

By the time I was five, weekly worship had taught me to sing entire liturgies. In the Lutheran school I attended for eight years, I learned hundreds of hymn, psalm, and Scripture verses. Every year my father wrote lots of new music for the school choirs — including new carols, descants for older Christmas carols, and once an eight-part angels' song for the Christmas program. The result of my parents' example and instruction was that I was both deeply rooted in the heritage of the Church and eager to compose and use new, faithful music.

I am convinced that, in the midst of the ambiguous, sometimes chaotic, never settled, ungrounded society that surrounds them, our young people crave roots. If we teach them the beauty and truth, the meaning and purpose of what we do in worship, they become more involved and feel more at home in the Church.

I remember vividly one occasion when I led an "explained liturgy" for about two hundred high school students.[5] The pastor hosting the worship was a gentle, elderly man who served a congre-

---

5. The appendix in *Reaching Out without Dumbing Down* suggests some children's sermon ideas by which elements of worship can be taught to youngsters (and their parents at the same time). Audiotapes of explained liturgy services (#33d and e, #66c, #72b) can be obtained from Dottie Davis, Christians Equipped for Ministry tape coordinator, 15500 N.E. Caples Rd., Brush Prairie, WA 98606 (telephone 360-256-1493 or 360-892-3618).

gation of hearing-impaired persons in a nearby city. One especially valuable refrain in the Church's historic liturgy that I love to teach to young people because it increases our sense of the Christian community and our mutual ministry is the pastor's blessing, "The Lord be with you," and the congregational response, "And also with you." Here ritual gesture is extremely important. Pastors extend their hands to the people as they remind them of the Lord's presence; the people greet their leaders with a prayer for a sense of God's presence as they serve the assembly. Four times the traditional liturgy gives congregants this opportunity to say to the pastor, "We are grateful for you serving as the host at the Lord's Table, for giving us the Word of God — and we are praying for you to be filled with the Spirit's presence as you fulfill these tasks." Do the people look directly at the priest and extend their hands to him when they say these words? Does he look at them and receive their blessing?

I had explained these things to the teenagers — this was in the days when the hymnbook still used the response "And with thy spirit" to the pastor's blessing. When we did these lines at the retreat after my explanation, the pastor extended his hands to bless the youth, and all two hundred extended their hands and sang their response with all their might. He received it by pulling his hands to his heart and grinning from ear to ear. His eyes and the eyes of many of the students were glistening with tears. What a profound picture of mutual ministry in the Body of Christ!

The worship service lasted more than two hours by the time all received the Supper, and yet scores of the teenagers told me that they thought the time went fast, that they *loved* the service, that they never knew the liturgy meant so much, that they could hardly wait to tell their friends back home about the wonderful worship we had at camp. The explanation and participation helped the youth feel that they truly belonged to the Church.

The intention of the preceding example is not to advocate only old liturgical settings. I am promoting good worship materials from every era, but all must be well taught as to their purpose and meaning, their beauty and truth. I hope that professional church workers, parents, and others reading this book will gladly seize the initiative to educate their youth for worship, so that worship can educate them for life.

A Few Examples

Last night at the symphony I encountered one of the teachers who had been at a conference last summer in Portland at which I urged the musicians and pastors to engage in deliberate training for worship. She said that she "just had to tell" me what happened when she taught her second graders the responses described above. Now, she rejoiced, "The Lord be with you; and also with you" is a daily part of the class's life, for the children love to begin each day with the refrains. Recently, these seven- and eight-year-olds were given the opportunity to lead chapel for the entire Lutheran school, and their teacher reported that they were thrilled to have the chance to be the ones who, extending their hands, offered "The Lord be with you" to all the classes.

Another, more thorough example is provided by the small, primarily African-American worshiping community to which we belong, which serves its poor neighborhood in Portland in numerous ways. This congregation uses a wonderful blend of musical styles every week. One Sunday we began with a contemporary praise song (that was genuine praise), then sang "We Are Marching in the Light of God" from South Africa, and ended the devotional songs with a chorus from Taizé. Other worship music included three different traditions — a Lutheran chorale, a Wesleyan pietistic chorus, and a soul-fully sung solo.

This community now is learning to sing the Lutheran liturgy — and when I first played it many of the members told me how much they liked it — but previously we spoke it. Contradicting those who say that teenagers don't like liturgy, the students in this parish recite it with full voice. Young people also participate in reading the Scripture lessons and bow reverently at the altar before and after reading. The key is that the grandfatherly pastor there recognizes the value of coherence in the worship service, explains to the members why the liturgy is so valuable, and prints a complete statement of the week's theme at the beginning of the worship folder. Both he and the director of youth and education use illustrations in their sermons that include the youth, and the teenagers also assist with ushering, acolyting, chancel dramas, keeping attendance, caring for the infants, and serving refreshments. One twelve-year-old in the congregation brought three of her friends with her last Sunday.

Hospitality

The great delight of this congregation is that everyone who comes is warmly welcomed; no one is a stranger. In these days of mega-churches, I keep realizing that there are greater possibilities for genuine hospitality in smaller communities, where the same persons remember you from week to week and care if you are missing from worship. Though I have to work to keep up with the names of new members, the present size of the congregation makes it possible for me to know all the teenagers and children and to talk with them as much as possible — as well as to use examples appropriate for them in my sermons or when I teach music for worship.

The hospitality of the congregation is a major key for helping our youth enjoy participating in worship. This includes such things as warm greetings from all the adults and particular avenues for offering their special gifts. Music must be made available for all the songs used. Even if youth cannot read music, they can tell if the notes are going up or down. We must make sure they have what they need — hymnbooks, service folders, or whatever — to participate. One good option is to pair our youth with senior citizens who love the Lord and love to worship, for them to share worship materials, to teach each other the kind of musical style each one knows best, to be friends in mutual faith, and to increase community across the generations.

A Vision

During his earthly life Jesus prayed for us — that is, those who would believe through the witness of his disciples — that we would be sanctified in the truth and then sent out into the world to bear testimony to it (John 17:17-21). This is a wonderful description of worship for us and for our children: that by God's gracious invitation and Christ's intercession and the Spirit's enabling we are welcomed to learn of the Trinity through the biblical narratives passed on by faithful witnesses. Gathered in the community of saints, we are formed by the truth taught in worship music and Word and ritual so that out of our Christian character will flow the witness of our words and deeds.

Growing up in the postmodern world that surrounds us, our children deeply yearn for stability, morality, security, fidelity, faith, hope, and love. These deep needs can only be met through the One who meets our deepest need for Truth. Let us make sure that the worship services we plan and conduct present to them that Truth in all its clarity and beauty and goodness.

For further reflection, discussion, transformation, and practice:

1. What wrong turns in the face of modernity and postmodernity has our congregation made with regard to worship? What could we do now to counteract them or to reverse those false moves?

2. Does our congregation confuse worship and evangelism? Have we turned worship into a matter of taste? What could we do to plan worship that is authentic, biblically faithful, and formative of genuine community and of missional people?

3. How true are the worship services in our congregation? Do they speak truth, use music that is true, give the Truth of God? What could we do to make them more truthful?

4. What kind of people are our worship services forming? How does the music we sing contribute to the formation of genuinely Christian children? How is my faith nurtured by the elements of worship?

5. What does our congregation do to train young people in the meaning and practice of worship? What educational processes for worship could we develop?

6. How hospitable is the worship of our congregation for its young people? How hospitable are we as members of the community?

7. What examples have I experienced of really blended worship — worship that uses new and old music and forms from throughout space and time, that stresses both continuity with the entire Church and also the reformation and revival of new wineskins, that involves young and old people with their gifts, that invites everyone to participate in a hospitable way?

CHAPTER 6

The Pastoral Heart

A Song to Be Sung to our Pastors and Youth Leaders

We bid you welcome in the name of Jesus,
our exalted Head.
Come as a servant; so he came,
and we receive you in his stead.

Come as a shepherd;
guard and keep your fold from all that fosters sin,
and nourish lambs, and feed the sheep,
the wounded heal, the lost bring in.

Come as a teacher, sent from God,
charged his whole counsel to declare;
lift o'er our ranks the prophet's rod,
while we uphold your hands with prayer.

Come as a messenger of peace,
filled with the Spirit, fired with love;
live to behold our large increase,
and die to meet us all above.

James Montgomery (1825), alt.
Tune: Hus, *Cantionale Germanicum*, Dresden (1628)

By this point, many pastors or youth directors reading this book might feel overwhelmed. I'm not giving you simple, easy answers that will help you fix your youth group in six easy steps. In fact, I seem to be making your job much harder by asking you to make sure that your congregation is a genuine community, that it really is formed by God's Word, that it worships with integrity and truth, beauty and coherence. In short, for the sake of our children and ourselves, I want us to be the Church.

In the long run, truly being Church, a genuine parallel society, will make it easier for professional church workers — because the community will free them to use their gifts and not burden them with unrelated administrivia. I can see you pastors and youth leaders laughing now: "This lady is hopelessly idealistic." No, I am simply echoing the apostles and their visions for the Body of Christ in Romans 12, 1 Corinthians 12, Ephesians 4, and 1 Peter 4. None of our communities can fulfill these biblical visions because we are not perfect and our world is sinful and broken, but the Scriptures give us the direction toward which we aim and the picture of what God wants to create the Church to be by the Spirit's power.

Of course, I have to add that in many ways truly being Church will make *everyone's* job harder because then we will all be burdened with the heart of God; we will grieve for all the pain our children suffer because of their own sin, the iniquity and brokenness of our society, and, sad to say, the failures of Christian communities. But then I must hasten to add also that there is no greater Joy than to share the heart of God and no hope outside of it.

My call in this chapter is for pastors to stop being CEOs or marketers and to recover again, for the sake of the alternative community and especially of the Church's children, what it means to be a *pastor.* Similarly, youth leaders need to be more than activities directors; their role in the alternative community requires them to have pastoral hearts, seeking to "shepherd" young people in the paths of righteousness. Furthermore, the leadership of the congregation must support the professional staff in their emphasis on caring for souls wholistically (since the biblical meaning of the word *soul* is "one's true being") instead of raising the numbers or simply providing programs. I pray also that congregational members will uphold their pastoral leadership in their roles of teaching the Scriptures, developing the community life, and leading worship as these three dimensions have been elaborated in the previous three chapters. This chapter for pastors is shorter because I am assuming that readers will also add what was discussed in the preceding chapters to this one.

Equipping All the Saints for Ministry

The fundamental paradigm our congregations have to recover is that the primary task of the pastoral leadership is to equip the saints for ministry. This works in more than one direction in terms of raising our children to be Christian. Not only is our goal to equip all the adults in the congregation to care about all the children, but also we intend to equip the young people for their ministries.

What I am asking for here requires a major paradigm shift. What percentage of "church members," would you guess, belong to a Christian community, as discussed in Chapter 4, for the ways in which it will equip them to serve God's purposes in the world? Most of the pastors I know try valiantly to issue God's call into ministry, but a large proportion of the members are not able to hear it because they have heard too well the siren call of U.S. consumerism. Who knows how large a percentage of members belong for what they can give — we are commanded not to judge each other's hearts — but I know how easy it is for me to start thinking about what I can get out of a congregation instead of what I can give, and I'm even a full-time "servant" of the Church! I'm repeatedly appalled by the narcissism and lack of genuine servanthood in my own heart, which arise usually because I focus on my own feelings instead of on what I know. It is easy for all of us to concentrate on how the community should care for us, rather than growing ever more willing to spend the time it would take to care for someone else. We are all too busy.

How, then, can pastors and youth leaders/teachers fulfill the picture of the Church in Ephesians 4:7-16? Simply, by truly being pastors and teachers — and let me encourage you, servants of the

91

Church, to remember first of all that you are such because God gave you as a gift to the Christian community. In this world where everyone is judged by his or her accomplishments, it is a major paradigm shift for clergypersons to begin with knowing they are the beloved of God, presented as God's treasure to the Body for its equipping, empowered by grace for life and ministry. When the leaders understand themselves in that way, they will more freely nurture in young people the same self-awareness.

Devotion to the Word and Prayer

This can hardly be said strongly enough: *THE* most important component required for a pastoral heart is daily immersion in the Word and prayer. Think in your own life of the people who have impacted you most for faith — really impacted you, not just impressed you — and undoubtedly they were people of profound spirituality. That seems obvious, but I know far too many youth directors and pastors and other church leaders, including myself, who do not spend adequate time for themselves in prayer and Bible study. They prepare lessons to teach others, lead in corporate prayer, "officiate" at worship, but do not allow themselves adequate time for personal prayer, devotion, and contemplation.[1] For some of us it is a matter of poor choices, for others a matter of ignorance, but for far too many it is a matter of being misled by the marketing gurus who demand that they be administratively adept or technologically proficient or masterfully entertaining instead. In fact, church marketing gurus are urging that seminaries should devote more time in their curricula to "management," even as a great number of first-year seminarians are arriving with limited knowledge of the Scriptures and of the practices of faith.[2]

1. See chapter 9, "The Word Ought to Kill Us," in Marva J. Dawn, *Reaching Out without Dumbing Down: A Theology of Worship for the Turn-of-the-Century Culture* (Grand Rapids: Eerdmans, 1995).

2. For an excellent exposé of some of the problems with, and unbiblical advice of, church marketers, see Philip D. Kenneson and James L. Street, *Selling Out the Church: The Dangers of Church Marketing* (Nashville: Abingdon Press, 1997).

No, a thousand times no! The narrative of Acts 6 teaches us a crucially important lesson for the ordering of the Church. When the apostles found themselves overwhelmed by the administration of the meals, others who were also "full of the Spirit and of wisdom" were chosen for the supportive tasks so that the Twelve could devote themselves to the Word and prayer. The criteria for the selection of these other servants shows that their mission was equally "spiritual," but the process also makes it very clear that the Church needs leaders who are thoroughly engaged in studying and meditating on the Scriptures and constantly immersed in conversation with God to gain God's guidance and learn his purposes. Churches are not failing because their pastors are not savvy enough about business, but because they have so little to say if they are not immersed in the Word. They do not have the heart of God if their pastoral practice and care are not formed by that Word and undergirded with prayer for congregational members, for wisdom, for vision.

Children and teenagers know when their youth leader and pastor love them — and that love for them will result if the leaders devote time to praying for them. Because the culture in which we live is not supportive of the Church's purposes in forming young people to be Christian, great prayer is required for wisdom to deal with the youth, for power to resist negative cultural influences ourselves, and for strength to abstain from taking the easy way out in planning our programs for the Christian community's children.

A Pastoral Heart Leads to Modeling and Caretaking

In light of the social issues we will discuss for the sake of the Church's children in Part Two of this book, we must emphasize here that our Christian communities need pastors and youth workers whose absorption in the biblical narratives causes them to be open models of the kinds of choices we desire our children to make. How will our youth learn to care about the poor if their congregational leaders are as concerned about affluence and consumption as the rest of society? How will they learn to be peacemakers if those in authority in the community do not practice skills of stress reduction and conflict resolution?

93

Pastors, youth directors, and parents need to pay close attention to the issues raised in the second part of this book, for their example in following the way of Christ is crucial. Young people will reject a Christianity that is hypocritical; they won't believe the lifestyle of Jesus is worth following if their elders do not care diligently about imitating it. Of course, we can't be perfect — we all have our flaws. I'm not asking for heroics from the pastoral leadership, but I am asking for heroism. Youth in our society are desperate for examples of people who, in the ordinary situations of daily life, make courageous choices — and in this case, choices consistent with the biblical invitations.

In light of the topics to be raised in Part Two, I am pleading for pastors and youth leaders to be rooted in the Scriptures and in the community of faith so that they are willing to suffer instead of anxious to evade or escape suffering, eager to be generous instead of possessive, diligent in what is right instead of passive, not overly tempted by technological toys to the destruction of community and genuine intimacy, active concerning what they know while knowing the limits of information, ardent in peacemaking and justice building, and sexually chaste. In short, we need leadership with a pastoral heart characterized by the wild paradoxes of bold humility and confident dependence.

It is much easier to be a CEO than an SOC — that is, a servant of care. It makes us feel better to be a chief executive officer who pushes papers around and looks successful because of the big numbers on those papers. It is much harder to deal with people; one cannot feel very successful working with people because so often there is nothing to show for it. The same temptation to take the easier way is widespread for all of us who work in the Church with youth. For example, sometimes speakers at youth convocations come in and "drop their wad" and then leave, as if they have nothing to learn from the other speakers or the youth, as if the whole community didn't matter. The teenagers might idolize them — but they don't grow from their modeling, and the young people are deprived of the intimate care they need for spiritual growth.

Perhaps some of us need to confess our laziness. Is that too harsh?

Perhaps some of us need to confess our ego. Is that admonition too blunt?

I know I need both confessions. It takes an enormous amount of energy to keep working with youth formed by our frenzied yet passive culture. Sometimes those young people will mock us for our devotion and spirituality, for our alternativeness and careful choices. It is often not fun to be faithful rather than famous.

Faithfully formed by the Word and prayer, a pastor's heart will be motivated to care and humbled to serve. Contemplating God's Revelation and listening for God's voice, youth leaders and clergy will acquire God's heart for their children and young adults.

One very small but practical aid to such a heart is the naming of the place where we work. It helps me remember what I do in this place where I am presently writing to call the room my study, instead of my office. And one side of this room is called the quiet time place, where my devotional books are kept, as well as hymnbooks and icons and candles. In that place also I keep a supply of get-well, sympathy, birthday, anniversary, and congratulatory cards and my birthday calendar so that my prayer time includes those who are suffering and those who are celebrating. In that way even the writing of cards is wrapped in prayer. Perhaps congregations could support the development of their youth leaders' and pastors' hearts by urging them to have a study or prayer chamber instead of an office. Certainly it will help if we protect their devotional time and their Sabbath days.[3]

The Pastor's Heart for Youth

Probably most of you reading this book do not need these reminders about having a pastoral heart (but probably some of your area colleagues do). The very fact that you are concerned enough about the moral formation of the children you serve to read these chapters proves that you have God's heart for the youth. What I want

3. These ideas will be expanded and other aspects of clergy health and wholeness will be explored in my forthcoming *The Sense of the Call: Theological Principles for Ministerial "Shalom,"* to be published by Eerdmans.

to do, then, is to support you as the apostle Paul does in frequently writing such encouragements as this: "Finally, brothers and sisters, we ask and urge you in the Lord Jesus that as you learned . . . how you ought to live and to please God *(as in fact, you are doing)*, you should do so more and more" (1 Thess. 4:1, my italics). I know how much a simple reminder to include the youth in my efforts at Church renewal changes what I do.

In fact, the most wonderful thing about writing this book has been how it has affected my own preaching and concern for the youth in the congregations I serve. It has been my habit and desire ever since I served as a director of Christian education in campus ministry many years ago to invite young adults over for dinner and conversation or to attend teenagers' sports events or music recitals, but I don't get too much opportunity to do that with my present traveling schedule. Writing on this subject has helped me look for new ways to care for young people when I am either at home or on the road.

Shortly after beginning the final stages of polishing this manuscript, I was a guest in a Christian Reformed Church in Michigan; it was the Sunday in the church year when we celebrate "the baptism of our Lord," and I tried, in my message on Isaiah 42:1-7, to include several references to the concerns of the youngsters and the teenagers. How would they live out their baptismal life in their schools? What persons around them might be dimly burning wicks that they could fan into flame or protect from the wind? Several people in the congregation thanked me for that focus on the youth; a few parents said their children really sat up and paid attention.

In my home congregation, I find myself making more introductory comments when it is my turn to read the Scripture lessons — introducing the children (and perhaps some adults) to the reasons why texts do certain things. Last week before reading 1 Samuel 3 I told the young people to watch especially for the word *LORD* in all capital letters and explained its Hebrew background and the significance of the name *Eli*.[4]

4. All the letters of the title *LORD* are customarily capitalized in our Bibles to indicate that the Hebrew word translated is the name *YHWH*. The original Hebrew noun was composed of these four consonants, Y H W H, which relate

I had acquired a large box of the Moravian *Daily Texts* to use as hostess gifts when I travel for my work, but I wanted to offer all the families in our small congregation a copy first for their family devotional life, since the book includes for each day of the year a text from each of the Testaments, a hymn verse for each text, and a closing prayer.[5] Suddenly it struck me that this book might be perfect for the young people — and I was thrilled that the teenagers responded to my invitation and came to us for their personal copy. Now I have to remember to do follow-up and see how they are using the book, ask them what they think about when they reflect on particular passages, find out if they sing any of the hymn verses and if the prayers seem to fit their lives.

Besides encouragement for practical inclusion of young people in our preaching and caring, let me also urge here that the pastoral heart be applied to specific teaching of the issues explored in Part Two of this book. When we are devoted to the Word of God, we can't help but notice discrepancies between God's designs for human life and the patterns of the society around us — and these lead to general attitudes and particular attempts to counteract the corrupting and injurious influences. For example, I never intended to get involved in talking with young people about their sexuality, but the agonies of the students around me who had never

---

to the root of the verb "to be." Since the Jews honor God's name by not saying it aloud (for fear they might blaspheme it) and since the original Hebrew manuscripts were written with only consonants and not the vowel points, scholars are not sure how to say the word, though now it is often vocalized as *Yahweh* (formerly as *Jehovah*). That is the name by which the LORD revealed himself to Moses at the burning bush in Exodus 3:14-15. It is a term that distinguishes him from all the neighboring, false deities. He is not just a god, but he alone is the faithful covenant God, the great "I AM."

Eli means, in Hebrew, "my [i] God [El]."

5. I find the Moravian *Daily Texts* to be a wonderful tool for my personal contemplation and prayer. Because each day's devotion includes the words for only one or two verses of the songs, I have also purchased the Moravian hymnals so that I can sing the hymns in their entirety in my meditational time. These books are available from the Department of Publications and Communications, Moravian Church, P.O. Box 1245, Bethlehem, PA 18016-1245, telephone 215-867-0594, FAX 215-866-9223.

heard any better ideas than what the media offer them intruded on my prayer life. Still today I find myself far more anxious before speaking engagements with youth (I was so sick and ugly when I was in high school that I probably haven't ever gotten over those feelings of inferiority with teenagers), but it seems that God pushes me to do them by stirring compassion in my heart.

The pastoral heart takes many forms according to each person's gifts. One pastor in a larger congregation near our home is incredibly good at remembering names; he calls each child and teenager by name when they come forward for the Lord's Supper or when he sees them anywhere. This pastor has superb rapport with all the youth in the congregation and is committed to using their gifts as much as possible in the life of the parish. Each year he goes with a group of young people and a few other adults to Mexico to help build housing for the poor.

Our grandfatherly pastor's primary gift is compassion. I have seen tears in his eyes as he spoke about a neighborhood teenager who was shot in an act of random violence. This pastor actually began the inner-city ministry in a poor neighborhood in Portland by walking the streets and talking to the troubled youth.

One special friend, who is not a professional church worker but who has tremendous biblical/historical skills and a pastoral heart, is extensively involved in teaching the youth in her Christian Reformed congregation. She has developed a four-year program that equips the youth with deep knowledge of the Scriptures, of major doctrines in the Christian Reformed Church, and of the history and literature of the Church. She teaches many of the components herself and helps others to be part of the program.

One very close friend, the solo pastor for a very large congregation in a small Midwestern town, has a great gift for conversation with youth. He had tried to urge the seventh and eighth graders to read *The Lord of the Flies* so they could discuss it together, but the teenagers wouldn't do it. At an evening dinner he casually began a conversation at his table with "Let's pretend" and then laid out a scenario in which the whole confirmation class became locked in the home where they were for a year, they had plenty of food and water and whatever else they might need, and all the adults died. "What would happen?" he asked.

Immediately two of the strongest girls declared, "We'd take over."

"And what next?" the pastor asked.

"We'd probably have to kill Brent." What an admission! No one in the class can stand that boy because he irritates them so much. (And, of course, if we look closely, we will realize that his behavior is his way of coping with the pain of his life, just as the girls' control is theirs.)

"But then, how will you be able to live?"

The pastor skillfully steered the conversation, and soon the teenagers were talking in a healthy way about the rules they would need to live and how they could find the patience and hope they would need to wait until they were rescued. The conversation lasted one hour and twenty minutes.

When he recounted this event, the pastor said, "Oh, it was fun."

How many pastors would enjoy such a conversation? Certainly it is this man's special gift, but it is also a habit, a practice he has developed out of long years of applying his pastoral heart to the needs of youth, to helping them think better about the meaning of their lives and of the life of faith.

I have included the diverse illustrations in this section to invite every pastor and youth leader reading this book to celebrate his or her own gifts and the ways they can be used to reach out to the youth of the Christian community and perhaps the wider community. And may all the congregational members reading this book support their pastoral leaders in using their gifts to express their pastoral hearts for the sake of the Church's children.

Developing the Community's Pastoral Heart for Its Children

The conversation that ended the previous section took place at the home of one of the members of the congregation my friend serves. Every year at that home they hold an elegant sit-down dinner for the confirmation students, who dress up and learn formal table manners in the process. Other adults in the congregation help prepare the food, host a table of youth, and do the cleanup. They say that the young people learn important lessons about respect and decorum — and, though initially shy or embarrassed, inevitably enjoy the event. What a great way to develop the pastoral heart of more people in the congregation for their youth.

Shepherding such events is one means by which the pastor and/or youth leader can equip the saints for their ministry to young people. I am convinced that if the professional workers are devoted to the Word, they will be formed in its visions of the Body and then will habitually use equipping language, will be fired by the Scriptures to fulfill the purposes of God, and will invite others into such ministry.

It is also important, I believe, that pastors and youth directors engage the congregation in conversations about the society that surrounds the Church so that the entire community is equipped to nurture our children in the midst of it. All the factors we will consider in Part Two of this book are powerful forces; it will take the entire community to resist them, to train our offspring to reject them, to offer alternative models of what it means to be the people of God. Clergypersons and other leaders in our churches need to equip all the members of the Body to understand the *Sehnsucht* that drives our world to its excesses, to resist the forces of the principalities and powers, to recognize the destructive effects of postmodernist thinking and welcome its contributions, to comprehend the authority of the Scriptures in our lives, to envision the Church in its unity and diversity and mission, to worship with integrity and faithfulness — as these facets have been sketched in the previous four chapters.

What the congregation does on Sunday mornings is key for "equipping the saints" in order that ministry to the youth takes place, for a parish cannot have worship that fosters easy listening and passive spectatorship if we want to encourage everyone to take the time to care for the Church's children. Worship is the community's chief endeavor in which the saints participate in *leitourgia,* the work of the people. Their "work" to worship God trains them in habits of diligence for God's purposes to be done in the world — but this requires the constant comments of the pastoral leadership for them to understand it. Furthermore, if the sermons always ask how we live out these texts in daily life, if the hymns frequently invite active faithfulness, if the prayers issue calls to service, and if the spirit of the community highlights the Joy of involvement, worship will form the character of caring for our neighbors — and specific references to caring for our community's children will channel that disposition.

Leaders of the congregation, especially the clergy and youth director, can train others to welcome the youth, speak to them, challenge them, be hospitable toward them, and invite them to participate. Other members of the Body can be involved in programs of mentoring, youth advocacy, or marriage counseling. The music director can include youth in instrumental groups or handbell ensembles; children can be encouraged to sing in choirs or given opportunities to perform solos. Young people can teach the older adults new music. Teenagers could serve as congregational welcomers, ushers, money counters, readers, or acolytes. The women's and men's societies could be urged to take young people under their wing. The congregation might establish programs for male friendship with kids raised by single moms. The social service committee can specifically include invitations to youth to participate in their soup kitchen, prison ministry, or Habitat for Humanity building projects. In our congregation the youth raised money to buy small Christmas trees, which they decorated and delivered to shut-ins.

All of this is not simply work for the pastor to do. Some larger congregations often call a director of volunteer ministries; we should make sure his or her job description emphasizes involving the children. Often a senior citizen who is homebound is glad to make phone calls to invite the youth to participate in various activities and groups. The pastor's role is to share his or her heart with the whole congregation, so that everyone takes on the responsibility of caring in each person's own way for the children. Perhaps the clergyperson's role might also include rebuking those who are not shouldering their share of the discipling. Paul writes in his first letter to the Thessalonians (5:12) that they should honor the ones laboring among them especially for their loving *admonishment*; such admonishment will be the result of the pastor's and youth leader's devotion to the Word

101

and prayer, attentiveness to the apostles' teaching, and intercession for congregants.

Recently a PBS documentary on the Amish revealed through the comments of the young people how much they loved being part of that community because they knew that everyone was working so hard to love them. Indeed, we need the input and outreach of the entire fellowship to raise our children, and the pastor can never be finished inviting such involvement and equipping the congregation for it.

For further reflection, discussion, transformation, and practice:

1. As a pastor or youth director, what is my primary role in the congregation I serve? What would I like it to be? What is the biblical vision for my role?

2. How thorough is my immersion in the Word and prayer? What materials and forms could I use to deepen my devotional life?

3. Am I satisfied with my present state of spirituality? What is missing? Does my own spirituality lead to obedience in issues of money and power and sexuality and peacemaking? In what dimensions do I need to grow? Who could help me, hold me accountable, guide me?

4. As a member of the congregation, how could I support my pastor and youth director in their devotional life, their keeping of a Sabbath day for rest, their choosing of priorities for ministry?

5. What are some ways in which I could particularly include the youth of my congregation in my sermons, in my allocation of time spent in ministry? How specifically am I teaching young people to be part of the alternative society? What aspects of the parallel society outlined in Chapter 4 are lacking in our congregation? What could I do about that?

6. What special gifts do I have that could be channeled toward the youth? How would a deepening of my pastoral heart through

the Word and prayer equip me to use my gifts better on behalf of young people?

7. What are some ministries to or on behalf of the youth for which I could equip congregational members? What are some ministries of the congregation for which I could equip the youth? Which other people in the community could I enlist in the equipping of youth for ministries?

CHAPTER 7

The Parental Heart

To you our vows with sweet accord,
head of your church, we pay;
we and our house will serve you, Lord;
your word we will obey.
Grant us and all our children grace
in word and deed your name to praise,
and in each family, your will
and purpose to fulfill.

Frederick William Foster (1826), alt.
Tune: Worship, popular melody
adapted at Hernnhut (c. 1740)

Those of you who are parents and are reading this book because you want to think about how to fulfill that role in a truly Christian way are probably frustrated that it took me so long to get to you. I have placed this chapter here deliberately because I believe it is impossible for parents to raise Christian children alone. The powers of evil are too dominant, the culture around us is too post-Christian, our children have too many options. Parents need the total support of the entire Christian community, of a vital Body of believers who contribute to the passing on of the faith. Because our congregations so often fail to be truly the Church, a really alternative society, parents are not equipped for their crucial role in the shaping of character in their children, nor are their efforts enhanced by the community's enfolding and training.

"What a Terrible Time to Raise a Child!"

These are difficult days for raising children in the faith, especially for the reasons that we will explore in Part Two. Here I want to focus on the particular problem that our offspring are spending time in schools and in activities with peers who have not been parented.

Every year in my husband's classroom there are a few students who are diligent workers, courteous and respectful children, pupils interested in learning. Almost all of them are the students who have come from other countries — Japan, Russia, Vietnam, Korea, the Philippines, Romania. These children must have very deep habits from their families and cultures if they are going to remain well-mannered and studious in the midst of the rowdiness and downright disobedience of their peers. Myron grieves as he watches some of these students lose the habits of their home cultures and become as cynical, "bored," flippant, and lazy as are many children formed by television in the United States. Of course, we are not asking for the stilted and stifling classroom atmosphere in which some of us might have grown up; Myron works very hard to develop instructional plans that could lead to enthusiastic involvement in the learning processes and active participation in class discussions. What is extremely destructive to the children who want to be involved is that so many of their peers couldn't care less about learning and are actively participating instead in behaviors that obstruct everyone else's education.

A few years ago when Myron taught third grade, the kinder-garten teachers at his school called together the first- through third-grade instructors and warned them that the class coming up was disturbingly deficient in the normal customs that children learn "at their mother's knee." A large majority of the pupils did not know the basic habits of civility such as saying "please" and "thank you." Numerous pieces in educational journals and district news-letters bemoan the burden that has been loaded onto teachers because so many "parents" are expecting the schools to fulfill their job and because so many children these days are being raised by teenage mothers or by perpetual adolescents.

The schoolroom is just one place (but one that represents a large number of hours) where the Church's children are exposed to practices and habits contrary to Christian virtues. Several news journals have recently featured articles discussing the new models for youth of rebellion and "in your face" transgression of cultural limits. Madonna has been joined, for example, by Chicago Bulls star Dennis Rodman. How can the influences of such perpetually adolescent youth heroes or of rude schoolmates be counteracted if we want our children to grow up caring about others and serving society rather than alienating it?

Christian parents dare not be blindly optimistic about the possibility in this time and place of raising children who are genuinely Christian, because optimism is, by definition, not in touch with the true state of things. Nor, I must hasten to add, should parents be pessimistic, for to despair is to deny the Lordship of the Trinity over our lives and over the world. Instead, we all must be Christian realists[1] — knowing the truth about sinful humanity and about the particular influences and infiltrations of our society, but also knowing the hope that is ours in Christ. As Paul wrote to the Corinthians, those who are in Christ are part of a new creation (see below), and in that milieu — not the milieu of the technological, consumerist society that surrounds us — we raise our children.

Parents, How Can You?

Even as I proclaim hope, I must add a wake-up call for parents (which probably most of you reading this book don't need, but I include it just in case). I shudder when I see adults taking their children to some of the terribly destructive movies showing in all

---

1. I use the phrase "Christian realists" as Jacques Ellul uses it, not as Reinhold Niebuhr does. See Jacques Ellul, "Political Realism," chap. 3 of *Sources and Trajectories: Eight Early Articles by Jacques Ellul That Set the Stage,* trans. and commentary by Marva J. Dawn (Grand Rapids: Eerdmans, 1997).

the other rooms of the ten-plex movie theater where we are attending something rated G. Parents, how can you expose your children to such banality, violence, greed, and narcissism? How can you let your children see such movies that distort their understanding of their sexuality and of its expression?

Parents, how can you let your children watch so much television when its destructive effects on your children's brains are documented? (We will look at this more closely in Chapter 10.) How can you not care about what your children are learning in school, about who their friends are, about how they spend their leisure time? How can you not care about the disrespect your children breathe in from the culture, about how they spend their money, about who their heroes are?

If you care enough about raising Christian children to be reading this book, you most likely don't need these rebukes, but some of your children's friends' parents might. Since the influences of the culture and youngsters' peers are so strong, perhaps you might have to be an agent of admonition with other Christian parents in order to build up a community of believers who work together to train their children in the habits of faith.

On the other hand, perhaps you do need a slight nudge. Maybe you have let things slip a little because it is so hard to hold the line. Perhaps you suffer from the "I'm-OK–you're-not" syndrome described in Chapter 2. David Whitman reports that "about 40% to 50% of Americans think the nation currently is moving in the wrong direction. But 88% think their own lives and families are moving in the right direction."[2] Are we really proceeding on a course that will lead to godliness, firm belief, the character of faith in our children? Are we dealing with our own *Sehnsucht,* that pressing yearning which nothing but God can ultimately satisfy, in ways that point our children to God?

As we dig below the surface of things in Part Two, readers must always remember to keep exploring themselves and their Christian communities more and more deeply. For example, if we ask about the influence of television on our children, then we have

2. David Whitman, "I'm OK, You're Not," *U.S. News and World Report* 121, no. 24 (16 December 1996): 25.

to question why parents let them watch it so much. Then when we think of how much time and effort it takes to raise children without the television set, we begin to get to the real issue: Are parents willing to spend that much time for the sake of raising Christian children? Even under that question, there are more complex issues, such as what takes up parents' time instead or what is the parents' understanding of why they have children.

Why Does the Christian Community Have Children?

It is crucially important in this book about raising our offspring in faith to examine our fundamental perception of why parents in the Christian community have children. This issue necessitates that we be a parallel, alternative society, for our culture's attitude shifted dramatically away from the biblical perspective with the development of effective birth control methods. Let us take seriously how radical a reversal occurred in people's thinking, not only about genital sexual relationships, but also about the parenting of children when human beings learned how to control whether children were conceived. Before conception became a matter of choice, children were more often received as a gift, and life was devoted to raising them; now parents (or even individuals) decide whether having them is an inconvenience or of benefit to themselves. This paradigmatic shift turns the focus away from how parents invest themselves in their children to a new stress on the advantage children will be to them — by carrying on the family name, accomplishing what the parents couldn't, providing fun at the moment or someone to quench the *Sehnsucht*.

This shift in perspective is enormously significant. It changes the major question from "How shall we raise children?" to "Do I want children?" or even "How can I avoid having children and still enjoy sexual pleasure?" Our society has lost the sense that the nurturing of our offspring is a full-time task for both parents. I especially appreciate the comment of an acquaintance who reported that when friends ask her if her husband is babysitting the kids (when she is at a meeting or something), she responds, "No, he is parenting." The very fact that this remark takes most of us by surprise shows how little we honor the calling of parenting as the major vocation of both mother and father.

Consequently, some people choose not to have children for a variety of terrible reasons — they are too expensive, they hamper one's lifestyle too much, the world is too dangerous so it would be too much trouble to raise them in it. (Of course, there are also some good reasons for choosing not to have children, such as limited health or a particular calling in ministry.) If a couple's reason for having or not having children comes from a fundamentally self-centered concern for their own gain, with what kind of character will they nurture their children?

Members of the Christian community must renounce the selfishness demonstrated by most reasons for our culture's positive or negative choices about producing and caring for children. Instead, the Church's primary question always is, "What kind of people are we or are we becoming?"

The Body of Christ thus offers a quite astonishing alternative to the world in this matter. We admit that having children IS a great burden, but one that *God* gives us; therefore, we gladly respond to the gift for the sake of the kingdom of God. Moreover, whether or not a couple has children may depend upon their role in the community. Some Christians might be childless for the same reason that others are single — in order to dedicate their lives more fully to the spiritual care of others.

In a chapter on "The Moral Value of the Family," Stanley Hauerwas reminds us that the main role of the family in former societies was to reproduce and to rear children for the future. He laments that the prevailing cultural assumptions of present society leave parents bereft of any notion that being a parent is an office of the community and not a willful act. To them belongs the primary (but not sole) responsibility for passing on the values of God's people. Their key role enables them to ask children to behave in certain ways, to live as the Christian community lives, to believe as we believe.[3]

---

3. Stanley Hauerwas, *A Community of Character: Toward a Constructive Christian Social Ethic* (Notre Dame: University of Notre Dame Press, 1981), pp. 159 and 173; see especially chapters 8 and 9, "The Moral Value of the Family" and "The Family: Theological Reflections," pp. 155-74.

As an alternative society, we who are members of the Christian community have behaviors, lifestyles, and beliefs worth passing on to our offspring. We know that what we proclaim is the One who is the Truth, who is worthy of our children's acceptance. Moreover, in spite of the state of our world, by bringing children into the world we declare that there is hope, that God is indeed sovereignly good, and that he is able to use us as agents in his care for all his children.[4]

Begin by Having a Heart for God

If we start with the assumptions that children are a treasure and that they are entrusted to us (both parents and Christian community) in order that we will raise them to be members of the Body of Christ, then we will recognize that the most important part of being a parent is to have a heart — that is, a will — formed by God. The community's and pastor's primary task concerning parents is to help them keep God first in their lives.

The book of Deuteronomy is filled with instructions to Israel for living out their relationship with the LORD, and chapter 6 gives the best guidelines for parenting. A close look at the verses in that chapter will set forth the most important elements for raising children in faith.

> "Now this is the commandment — the statutes and the ordinances — that the LORD your God charged me to teach you to observe in the land that you are about to cross into and occupy, so that you and your children and your children's children may fear the LORD your God all the days of your life, and keep all his decrees and his commandments that I am commanding you, so that your days may be long. Hear therefore, O Israel, and observe them diligently, so that it may go well with you, and so that you may multiply greatly in a land flowing with milk and

---

4. The ideas of this section are set in the context of a wholistic ethics of sexuality in Marva J. Dawn, *Sexual Character: Beyond Technique to Intimacy* (Grand Rapids: Eerdmans, 1993).

honey, as the LORD, the God of your ancestors, has promised you." (Deut. 6:1-3)

For our purposes here we don't need to note too many things in these introductory verses. I include them especially because of their declaration that God's goal for our children and grandchildren is for them to "fear" the LORD all the days of their lives. This does not mean to be afraid or terrorized, but the Hebrew word does connote more than awe and respect. Having biblical fear, we will constantly recognize that we deserve God's wrath — but we always hold that awareness in dialectical tension with the sure knowledge that God's love and compassion have removed our sin and guilt and have set us free to enjoy the gifts of home and family that God provides. Genuine biblical fear gives rise to true worship and the reverence that accompanies it, for we will never take it for granted that God allows us to know him and dwell in his presence.

"Hear, O Israel: The LORD is one God, the LORD alone." (v. 4)

This is the great *Shema,* the Hebrew word for "hear" or "listen carefully." This sentence is a creed for Israel, a summary of their faith in *YHWH* as opposed to everything else that claims to be god. The LORD calls the entire community to pay attention and thus reminds parents that they are not in this nurturing job alone. Furthermore, the people of God remember that the LORD is the only true God, a covenant God who always keeps his promises — and therefore we can trust him as we seek to serve him by raising children in the faith. Keeping ourselves focused on God's reign in our lives is the most essential and most beneficial requirement for parenting.

Those of us who practice infant baptism can use that terminology to describe our source of confidence. At our baptism we received the Holy Spirit, who continues to be at work in us to guide and improve our parenting. Furthermore, at their baptism our children received that same Holy Spirit, whom we can trust for his continued nurturing and sustaining of our offspring. The Spirit of the LORD is upon us all — fulfilling God's promises in us and through us to bring to completion that work which he has begun in us until the day of Christ Jesus (see Phil. 1:6).

> "You shall love the LORD your God with all your heart, and with all your soul, and with all your might." (v. 5)

Loving God is not a feeling (though sometimes feelings follow), but it is an act of the will (heart) and of the whole person (soul) and of one's strength (might). Parents will model for their children what it means to live in faith if they themselves keep God as the center of their attitudes and intentions and decisions (heart), of their use of their gifts and talents and personality (soul), of their every expenditure of energy and time and resources (might).

> "Keep these words that I am commanding you today in your heart." (v. 6)

Parents will be more able and more ready to communicate God's desires and purposes to their children if they themselves are formed by the narratives of the Scriptures, if they intentionally keep God's will as the ground and fulfillment of their own. Parents will be equipped more thoroughly for this "remembering" if they are faithful participants in regular worship, if they engage in Bible study both personally and corporately, if they have daily devotional times of study, meditation, and prayer.

> "Recite them to your children and talk about them when you are at home and when you are away, when you lie down and when you rise." (v. 7)

What a delightful command this verse is — urging parents to talk about the Word of God continually with their children. The New Revised Standard Version's translation "recite" sounds a bit too formal for the intention of this verse. The Hebrew root actually means to whet or sharpen, so the recitation is meant to teach, to repeat so that our children understand and appreciate. The New International Version captures the spirit of the Hebrew phrase better by rendering it "impress them on your children." By talking of God's purposes and instructions both when we are home and when we are away (and, of course, we are always either one or the other, so this pair of phrases means all the time), we will really imprint our children with these formative influences. By talking of biblical guidelines and desires when we lie down and when we rise (another pair that may signal all the time or may mean something more specific, like morning and evening devotions and prayers), we will begin and end and continue our days in light of God's direction. Hebrew literature often groups things in sets of four to stress universality; these four phrases concerning talking about God's instructions are meant to emphasize that parents do it all the time with their children. This doesn't mean in an obnoxious, pushy, non-listening, dogmatic way, but that in daily conversation the things of God remain a constant part. Talking about the LORD can be as simple as saying "Look at this beautiful day God created" instead of "What a nice day" or as thorough as explaining to a preteen God's design for human sexuality.

> "Bind them as a sign on your hand, fix them as an emblem on your forehead." (v. 8)

Metaphorically, Hebrew literature uses the word *hand* to signify our actions, and still today the image of the forehead portrays our thinking. Thus this verse urges parents to keep God in all of their conduct and thoughts. Orthodox Jewish men take this statute literally and wear phylacteries or small leather cases inscribed with Scripture verses on their hands and foreheads during morning prayers. I find it helpful to wear a cross to remind me continually that my life is to be lived in ways that glorify God. Before marriage and a wedding band, I wore a cross ring that prompted me every time I reached out to pay a grocery store clerk or to shake someone's hand to make sure my actions served God's purposes. Symbols might help to keep us focused, but the chief emphasis of this verse is that the values of God's kingdom should be firmly inscribed and established in our minds and wills, our behaviors and deeds.

> "And write them on the doorposts of your house, and on your gates." (v. 9)

Just as verse 7 gave us four times (encompassing all times) in which we speak to our children about God, verses 8 and 9 give us four places (thus every place) that we can put symbols to help ourselves remember God's instructions in all of life. Again, the Jews fulfill this verse literally and put their mezuzahs (little boxes containing a piece of parchment on which the *Shema* from Deuteronomy 6 is written) on their doorposts. Their faithful obedience urges us to question whether our homes contain signs that we are Christians. Would anyone entering our home know the focus of our life together? Do the symbols on our walls, the magazines on our coffee tables, the books on our shelves, our habits and behaviors demonstrate God's presence? Our children are formed by the milieu in which they live, both visibly and experientially. Part Two of this book will explore practices and signs that influence our offspring either for or against God.

> "When the LORD your God has brought you into the land that he swore to your ancestors, to Abraham, to Isaac, and to Jacob, to give you — a land filled with fine, large cities that you did not build, houses filled with all sorts of goods that you did not fill, hewn cisterns that you did not hew, vineyards and olive groves that you did not plant — and when you have eaten your fill, take care that you do not forget the LORD, who brought you out of the land of Egypt, out of the house of slavery." (vv. 10-12)

These verses will be especially important when we consider the effects of our consumerist society on Christian faith in Chapter 9. The people of Israel and we ourselves are here reminded that everything we possess is a gift and that we dare not let our belongings or prosperity cause us to forget the LORD. It is essential, if we want our offspring to grow in faith, that we never let God's gifts take the place of the Giver.

> "The LORD our God you shall fear; him you shall serve, and by his name alone you shall swear. Do not follow other gods, any of the gods of the peoples who are all around you, because the LORD your God, who is present with you, is a jealous God. The

anger of the LORD your God would be kindled against you and he would destroy you from the face of the earth. Do not put the LORD your God to the test, as you tested him at Massah." (vv. 13-16)

Do we take seriously enough the righteous jealousy of God? To recognize that God has a *right* to our obedience — because he created and redeemed us, after all — is properly to fear the LORD. Though many psalms and proverbs repeatedly tell us that "the fear of the LORD is the beginning of wisdom," the language of fear is hardly used in our day. We want to turn God into a nice cozy buddy, with whom anything goes. But God's righteous jealousy is directed toward our benefit. Life simply works better when we don't follow other gods, as we shall see throughout the chapters in Part Two.

The Israelites continually rebelled against God's Lordship in their lives — and paid the price in human terms. They deserved and got oppression, destruction, bondage, exile. God certainly doesn't want such things to happen to his people, but our sin carries within it the potential and impetus for consequences. Our enemies are totally different these days — heart attacks and other stress diseases, family breakdown and dissolution, public exposure and legal recriminations, the principalities and powers of our society — but the logic is the same. We wreak our own havoc when we turn to other gods and away from the covenant LORD who is, and promises to be, present with us.

"You must diligently keep the commandments of the LORD your God, and his decrees, and his statutes that he has commanded you. Do what is right and good in the sight of the LORD, so that it may go well with you, and so that you may go in and occupy the good land that the LORD swore to your ancestors to give you, thrusting out all your enemies from before you, as the LORD has promised." (vv. 17-19)

The truth is that life simply works better when we live in tune with the designs of its Creator. God's commands are not hammers over our heads to get us to shape up. Rather, they are his loving instructions for how to do what is right and good, so that life may go well. As a person with multiple handicaps and physical complications, I find this eminently logical and desirable. If I eat according to my strict diet, exercise daily, sleep an adequate number of hours, wear my leg brace, and take all my oral and injected medications, I feel much better, can be more productive, and enjoy life more. Why mess it up? I always pay if I skip or disobey aspects of my regimen. Similarly, God's instructions are not onerous burdens; they are for our good, "so that it may go well" with us. It is critical that we help our children learn that about God. The LORD never gives commands to spoil our fun; rather, his rules are intended to deepen it.

> "When your children ask you in the time to come, 'What is the meaning of the decrees and the statutes and the ordinances that the LORD our God has commanded you?' . . ." (v. 20)

This verse presupposes several things — that our children will be acquainted with the decrees and statutes and ordinances, that they will know the LORD, that they will want to know the meaning of what he has commanded. These assumptions provide clear guidelines for parenting that are being ignored these days. For example, too many youth that I encounter have never heard from their parents anything about God's commands for their sexuality. Too many young people don't ask their parents about the meaning of the latter's faith because they don't see that it makes much difference in their elders' lives. We need the customs and practices and insights discussed throughout this book to make this verse a reality.

> "Then you shall say to your children, 'We were Pharaoh's slaves in Egypt, but the LORD brought us out of Egypt with a mighty hand. The LORD displayed before our eyes great and awesome signs and wonders against Egypt, against Pharaoh and all his household. He brought us out from there in order to bring us in, to give us the land that he promised on oath to our ancestors. Then the LORD commanded us to observe all these statutes, to fear the LORD our God, for our lasting good, so as to keep us alive, as is now the case.'" (vv. 21-24)

Notice that the faith the people of Israel recounted to their children was a communal one — not so much the testimony common today of one's personal relationship with God, but rather a witness to the way in which God has led and dealt with the community. Many of the phrases in these verses are customary creedal lines by which the Hebrew people reported their faith. In the same way, it is essential that we immerse our children in the *Christian* faith, the belief of a community that goes back to Abraham and Sarah, Mary and John, and that stretches throughout the globe. We don't so much seek to develop in them their own faith as to make them an active part of the faith that already exists in a people.

> " 'If we diligently observe this entire commandment before the LORD our God, as he has commanded us, we will be in the right.' " (v. 25)

The original Hebrew sentence of this verse begins with the end of this English rendering: it will be *righteousness* to us. It will be fitting, good, for our well-being. Oh, how blessed our families will be if we live according to God's design! How blessed are the children who grow up in a home devoted to God's purposes, with mothers and fathers who fulfill their parenting role first of all by loving the LORD their God with all their heart and soul and might and then by passing that love on to their offspring!

Children Really Need Parents

Long ago I heard about an unforgettable piece of research. Those conducting the research watched children in playgrounds with and without fences. They discovered that if there was no fence the children played much closer to the center of the park or schoolyard, even if the most interesting equipment was placed on the edges. If the playground had a fence around it, the children played right up to the outside edges, even if the best equipment was placed at the center. The research supports our deepest intuitions: children need to know the boundaries.

God's Revelation made it very clear long ago that the role of parenting implies discipline. Proverbs 19:18 chides, "Discipline your children while there is hope; do not set your heart on their destruction." Surely it is devastating to children to leave them without boundaries, without trained habits that eventuate in their own self-control, without behavior patterns that build relationships and lead to service.

Certainly there are plenty of good books on disciplining children. I do not intend to give advice here — and would not be capable of it if I wanted to. I only seek to highlight the unique slant on discipline that a community context for raising children provides. For example, when Ephesians 6:4 emphasizes, "Fathers, do not provoke your children to anger, but bring them up in the discipline and instruction of the Lord," our faith community can encourage the men to take the plural here seriously. No one can father alone. He needs the wisdom of the grandfathers in the community, the support of all parents, the teaching of those who explicate the Lord's instruction. Children are less likely to become provoked if they recognize that their mothers and fathers are themselves also disciplined and instructed, that their parents are agents of the Lord's work, that all the parents of the congregation are agreeing together on certain standards.

Another aspect of the Christian community's perspective on discipline gives us hope in our struggles. In light of many passages in the Bible, we can realize that in our many tasks as parents we do the best we can to image God. The picture in Genesis 1 of our roles to image God as male and female puts such instructions as Ephesians 6:4 above into perspective. We are not expected to be God for our children; rather, we do whatever we can in God's stead. This perception sets us free to put ourselves under the same grace that we want to characterize our nurturing of our children.

We don't have to pretend we are perfect or expect ourselves to be, for fathers and mothers are fallible human beings. None of us could ever parent as well as we would like to. But we can humbly admit to our children that we are doing the best we can to serve as representatives of God's fathering and mothering. In our failings, we can model for our children repentance and humility; we train them in communal mutuality by asking them for forgiveness. Furthermore, we specifically teach them always to

118

know that their totally successful Parent is unceasingly there for them. Meanwhile, our methods of parenting are guided and our courage for the task is heightened by the way in which God reveals himself in his care for us.

Finally, the Christian community's perspective on raising children helps us recognize it as God's art, the Lord's craftsmanship in which we participate and which then encourages our offspring to make of their life the best art. We get this insight from such texts as Ephesians 2:8-10, which emphasizes that we are saved by grace and not by works and then concludes, "For we are his workmanship, created in Christ Jesus for good works, which God prepared beforehand, that we should walk in them" (RSV). The calling of parenting is cohesive with our life of faith in the same way that Wendell Berry's crafts are unified in this explanation:

> I am a farmer and a poet — a poet who writes about farming, and a farmer who reads and thinks about poetry. But it is more complicated than that. I have come more and more to believe, with Eric Gill, that the only valid kind of distinction to be made between kinds of making is qualitative. Otherwise, human work is all art — all artifice or making-by-art. I do believe that "a *good* farmer is a craftsman of the highest order, a kind of artist." The finest farmers are masters of form. They must know how to do one thing while remaining mindful of many. They must bring many patterns into harmony. They must understand how diversity may be comprehended within unity. They must know how to deal with the unforeseen. And these are all characteristics of the finest poets. Also, there is a kinship among all arts or disciplines, and a knowledge of one imparts a sympathy for others and can be useful in learning another.[5]

Will our work of raising children be artificial — that is, without heart — or will we in the Christian community engage in the highest art of parenting? Since there is a kinship among all

5. Mindy Weinreb, "A Question a Day: A Written Conversation with Wendell Berry," in *Wendell Berry*, ed. Paul Merchant, American Authors Series (Lewiston, ID: Confluence Press, 1991), p. 32.

arts, our disciplines as followers of Jesus will have the best effect on the craftsmanship with which we nurture the Church's offspring. And our goal will always be to help our children be formed to be genuine artists themselves.

Tools for the Craft

Many different tools can be part of the craft of parents in raising their children — depending on the gifts of the parents and the participation of the whole Christian community. *The* most important instrument is time. Probably you have seen the sociologists' statistics on the extremely small average number of quality minutes (or seconds) spent by our society's parents with their children. The most recent one I read reported that a group of high-level CEOs were asked how much time they spent conversing with their children about matters more personal than arranging car schedules. Most of them guessed anywhere from half an hour to an hour each day, but hidden microphones on their children revealed that they spent, on average, seventeen seconds a day! In the Christian community we want to be decisively different, for we know that formation of alternative character takes a great investment of prime time to counteract all the influences of the dominant culture.

One great gift of time that Jews and Christians carry together to the world is God's design for Sabbath keeping — one day of the week in which we cease working and focus instead on resting, embracing the values of God's kingdom, and feasting.[6] I especially use the word *embracing* because the Sabbath day is not designed simply for loafing around, but to be a celebration and sign to the world of God's covenant with his people (see Exod. 31:12-18).

6. I do not argue about which day should be celebrated as Sabbath (which means in Hebrew "to cease" and not "seventh day"), for there are good reasons both to continue the Jewish Saturday Sabbath and also for celebrating Sabbath on the Lord's Day or Sunday. Some church and medical professionals have to choose still another day of the week. This subject is elaborated much more fully in Marva J. Dawn, *Keeping the Sabbath Wholly: Ceasing, Resting, Embracing, Feasting* (Grand Rapids: Eerdmans, 1989).

During the extra time in this twenty-four-hour period parents should take special care for their own spiritual growth and for that of their children.[7] I cannot emphasize enough the positive changes it brings to our hectic lives when we faithfully reserve an entire Sabbath day set apart to deepen our relationships with God and family and to learn more thoroughly who God is and the kind of character he wants to develop in us and in our children.

One key use of time for raising our children to be part of the parallel society is conversation. One reason for the rapid growth of the Church of Jesus Christ of Latter-day Saints is its emphasis on family home evenings. Many converts to Mormonism are drawn to its insistence on a weekly, intimate family evening composed of Scripture reading, special activities, and discussions.

Can our families institute not only such a special night or even an entire Sabbath day, but a regular habit of daily conversations and devotional moments? It is important to do so when the children are young so that the habit is established before they get involved in so many school activities. In contrast to our society's "ships passing in the night" living arrangements, can our families specifically set aside time for devotions, meals together, intimate conversations, and shared hobbies and chores so that the children can easily question their parents when issues, such as sexuality, come up? My former secretary built wonderful relationships with her three children by "tucking them in" every night, even when they were in high school, so that there was always a special time to talk. The mother of one of my godchildren always took time to pray with her son and daughter before they left for school in the morning.

One element of family conversation that is rapidly getting lost in our culture is the telling and retelling of stories — from the family tree, from the local community, from the community of

---

7. Some wonderful family ideas for celebrating the Sabbath can be found in Karen Burton Mains, *Making Sunday Special* (Waco, TX: Word Books, 1987), and Martha Zimmerman, *Celebrate the Feasts* (Minneapolis: Bethany House Publishers, 1981). See also Zimmerman's *Celebrate the Christian Year* (Minneapolis: Bethany House Publishers, 1993).

faith. One of my heroes for emphasizing conversation in the community is the activist/poet/farmer Wendell Berry. In the following excerpt from his introduction to a book about Berry, Paul Merchant examines the poet's ideas in a way that raises the same issues for the Christian community:

> Part of "the work of local culture" (as expressed in an essay of that title in [Berry's book] *What Are People For?*) is the telling and retelling of stories, for entertainment, for instruction, and for the preservation of history. Berry notes that children were always present on these occasions, called locally "sitting till bedtime." His description makes it clear that the entertainment industry has supplanted the art of story-telling, even where it was strongest and most valued, and Berry's urgent determination to tell the stories of his own community, preserving its local idioms, is quite literally the defense of a culture, as important as the preservation of a minority language in the survival of a national identity. The act of memory preserves a valued way of life, exactly as the maintenance of a deep and healthy topsoil preserves the fertility of the land — Berry makes the analogy explicit in the vivid opening paragraphs of this same essay.[8]

Is the parallel society of the Christian community preserving its history and its idioms by telling and retelling its stories in the presence of its children? Similarly, are we singing the songs of the alternative community for the sake of our children's memory, to preserve the fertility of our offspring's faith?

In 1996 the Music Educators National Conference, representing 65,000 members, "compiled a list of songs which they believe must be taught to our nation's children to preserve an important part of our culture." There were forty-two songs on the list, including such favorites as "Amazing Grace," "Danny Boy," "Frère Jacques," "Give My Regards to Broadway," "Home on the Range," and "Puff, the Magic Dragon." The journal in which I read the report — *Cross Accent,* the publication of the

8. Paul Merchant, "Introduction," in *Wendell Berry,* p. 4.

Association of Lutheran Church Musicians — asked its readers which hymns and songs they thought their children should know and wondered if they should identify their own core list.[9] What songs should we be teaching in our homes (as well as in our churches and Sunday schools) to pass on the faith to our children? I learned probably hundreds of songs and hymns through our family's evening devotions and by singing in the car on our way to visit grandparents hundreds of miles away. I grieve that children these days do not grow up with singing in the home; thereby they are deprived of a great deal (pun intended) of faith formation.

Other tools of the craft of raising children in the faith will be given in connection with specific cultural issues in Part Two. We must pay attention to customs and habits, practices and attitudes that counteract the societal influences that pull our children away from God.

Before concluding this chapter, however, we must recognize that some of the best tools we might use can be abused if they replace God instead of leading to him. If we return to the idea of *Sehnsucht* (introduced in Chapter 2) we must note that sometimes people use good gifts of God's superb creation to muffle their restless yearning. Thus these excellent things meant for our enjoyment substitute for God as the true Stillness for our yearnings, instead of serving as pointers to his sufficiency. Some parents have to be careful lest they even try to suppress their innermost restlessness with their religious piety. They busy themselves with honorable Christian activities in the futile (usually subconscious) attempt to avoid facing and responding to their longing for God himself. Their children will see the hypocrisy of those efforts and will probably wind up rejecting, not the true faith, but the "faith" that became for their parents a shield against God.

9. Tom Leeseberg-Lange, "Crosstalk: What Music Will Lutheran Children Inherit?" *Cross Accent* 5A, no. 9 (January 1997): 4.

Don't Forget: You're Not Alone

Before we move on to the specific issues (the principalities and powers in society) of Part Two, I must emphasize once again that you parents are not alone in the spiritual care of your children. Without the support of the Christian community, you fathers and mothers might feel overwhelmed by the impossibility of your roles in the midst of the society that presently surrounds the Church. Two insights from the apostle Paul are crucially important for our sense of hope in the tasks of parenting.

In 2 Corinthians 5:17 Paul writes, "if anyone is in Christ, *there is* a new creation." For the first time in English the New Revised Standard Version made this rendering its primary translation and got the Greek right. It is not just we who are different if we are in Christ. *Everything* is new. We live in an entirely different milieu because we are in Christ, for we are incorporated into his Body, the Christian parallel community. Thus, let me urge parents to discuss the questions raised in Part Two with other members of their congregation or Bible study group or with fellow Christians at their jobs or in their neighborhoods. Find partnering parents to work on the same issues in their families along with you; find senior citizens who can help you learn the wisdom of God through experience and over time for your own situation. If your own congregation is not truly a community, perhaps you parents reading this book can be leaders in helping to make it so — for your own sake and for the sake of the Church's children, including those in your own family.

Finally, the apostle Paul reminds us frequently that the principalities and powers have been defeated by Christ and that nothing — not any of the powers discussed below — can separate us from God's love (Rom. 8:28-39). It is essential, before we take a realistic view at the powerful societal influences that threaten our children's faith, to remember that these forces have already been conquered. That gives us hope for the battle against them, for indeed they must be fought (Eph. 6:10-20). We do not fight alone. We contend with all the saints on our side and with God himself in our midst. Remembering that fact will give us all the hope we need to persevere.

For further reflection, discussion, transformation, and practice:

1. What are some aspects of contemporary U.S. society that make it difficult to be a Christian parent these days? How does realism about these forces make it more possible to avoid them, resist them, defeat them, or surmount them?

2. Am I satisfied with the amount of time and the quality of care I invest in my children? Why or why not? What changes would I like to make in my life?

3. What verses from Deuteronomy 6 were especially helpful for me to understand my role as a Christian parent? Why? How could I pass on what I learned to other parents in my community?

4. What verses from Deuteronomy 6 especially rebuked me for my failings as a Christian parent? What would I like to do to change? How might these verses help me lovingly to admonish another parent in the community?

5. How can I help my children learn to make art of their lives? In what ways do I see my own life as a work of art?

6. What are some of the most important tools for me to raise my children in faith? What practices do we follow for keeping the Sabbath day holy? How are these helpful for my children's and my own spiritual growth?

7. With whom can I partner for support in the task of Christian parenting? Does my congregation have supports for parents already in place? If not, what can I do to change that?

PART TWO

Having God's Heart for Our Children in a Contrary World

A Song Especially for Our Children to Sing

God of creation, you brought us to birth,
gifted us with all the blessings of earth.
Now as your children with futures to face,
we turn to you, Lord, wholly seeking your grace.

Jesus, you modeled obedience. May we
live in your freedom and serve faithfully,
Choosing your will, even bearing a cross.
Suffering for you will not ever be loss.

Christ, you lived simply; equip us to give
from our abundance so others may live.
Teach us to share what we have gen'rously
with all the needy, whereso'er they may be.

In our world raging with violence and war,
fill us with love as we work to restore
justice, equality, mercy, and peace
that all the hatred between people may cease.

127

Jesus, to both men and women a friend,
chastely you loved them; now help us transcend
wanton confusions our culture displays.
Help us live purely throughout all our days.

Come, Holy Spirit, abide with us still.
Grant us your guidance to live out your will.
Amid life's choices aid us to employ
trust, courage, wisdom, faithfulness, hope, and Joy.

Trinity, gracious, empow'r us to do
what you design for us all our life through.
May what our future brings teach us anew
that we, your children, are belovèd to you.

Text: Marva J. Dawn (1997)*
Tune: Slane ("Be Thou My Vision")

---

*This hymn does not appear in the Moravian hymnal. It was composed specifically to match the themes that will be covered in the second part of this book.

CHAPTER 8

No Pain, No Way

Lord, who left the highest heaven
for a homeless human birth
and, a child within a stable,
came to share the life of earth —
with your grace and mercy bless
all who suffer homelessness.

Lord, who sought by cloak of darkness
refuge under foreign skies
from the swords of Herod's soldiers,
ravaged homes and parents' cries —
may your grace and mercy rest
on the homeless and oppressed.

Lord, who lived secure and settled,
safe within the Father's plan,
and in wisdom, stature, favor
growing up from boy to man —
with your grace and mercy bless
all who strive for holiness.

HAVING GOD'S HEART FOR OUR CHILDREN

Lord, who leaving home and kindred,
followed still as duty led,
sky the roof and earth the pillow
for the Prince of glory's head —
with your grace and mercy bless
sacrifice for righteousness.

Lord, who in your cross and passion
hung beneath a darkened sky,
yet whose thoughts were for your mother,
and a thief condemned to die —
may your grace and mercy rest
on the helpless and distressed.

Lord, who rose to life triumphant
with our whole salvation won,
risen, glorified, ascended,
all the Father's purpose done —
may your grace, all conflict past,
bring your children home at last.

Timothy Dudley-Smith (1965)
Tune: Eden Church, Dale Wood (b. 1934)

Oh, the humor of our life's situations! I began work on this chapter this morning — organizing my concerns and ideas, choosing the best hymn, outlining the progression of thought — and then I quit early. I had rearranged my writing, insulin, eating, and exercise schedule in order to avoid a certain swimmer who has been coming to the pool at the same time that I work out in mid-afternoon. I scurried to get to the athletic club early — and she arrived at the very same time! I wanted to avoid her because she moves so ungracefully and fast that it is difficult for anyone to swim laps in the lane next to her. Her speed and lack of consideration for other swimmers combine to make it quite challenging for the senior citizens and me, who chose this time for exercise because it had been quiet. Already slowed by my crippled leg, the lowered blood pressure

130

my kidney medicine causes, the arthritis in my hands and knees, and the atypical residual pain from my mastectomy four years ago and from injuries to both elbows, I get frustrated that the abnormal wake her awkward style creates spoils the fun of swimming. So my efforts today to make life easier for myself were foiled — a perfect example of the very subject of this chapter.

Fortunately my nemesis quit early today and left me the only one in the pool. As I swam very gently to see how long it took for the turbulence in the water to subside, I had extra opportunity to ponder the sources of pain in our lives, the perpetual efforts in U.S. society to avoid any discomfort, the value of some kinds of pain, and the gospel imperative to fight those torments that are unjust and oppressive. Even as I write this now, I am grateful to my parents, who taught me thoroughly in my childhood the value of discipline and hard work in the face of tribulation. Without those formative lessons, I would have quit enduring the pain of exercise a long time ago — and probably would no longer be alive.

The Idolatry of Ease or Happiness

Certainly one of the glaring characteristics of contemporary U.S. culture is the insistence that life be comfortable, easy, entirely without any kind of suffering. Notice how many of our major social controversies — such as the issues of abortion, euthanasia, or the convenient availability of divorce — are argued on the basis of a false compassion that "eases suffering" in the short run, but causes long-term consequences that are only beginning to be recognized. Social analysts perceive, for example, that these three issues cause far-reaching public consequences, including our culture's more jaded attitudes toward children and illness, our escalating inability to trust the medical profession, and the crime, violence, abuse, and character deformation that result from fatherlessness in the home.[1] When

1. I have been shocked reading about all the negative effects of fatherless-ness and the immensity of the problem. The percentage of children without fathers in the home has more than doubled in the last thirty years to 36 percent, and scholars estimate that the figure will be 50 percent by the year 2000. The negative

parents elevate their own coziness as the primary goal of their existence, the results of that idolatry of comfort on the raising of their children are disastrous.

The first of several destructive effects of the coveting of ease on our society's children is this: when parents are not willing to suffer for the sake of their offspring, the latter are deprived of the sense that they are beloved, that they are worthy of care, that they matter supremely to the family. Children in the public schools now are the first generation to be raised by parents who were themselves raised by television — parents and grandparents find and found it easier to set the children in front of the television set than to expend the enormous energy it takes to *nurture* a child. The result is that every year my husband Myron's classroom contains a large percentage of children desperate for attention, unequipped to focus, unable to care about anything except their own pleasure since that is all they have seen modeled in their homes. Raising children is anything but easy; the irony is that the spiral of difficulty gets compounded if parents begin by taking the easy way out. Every step in the direction of selfishness is paralleled in the children and thus makes it many times harder to turn instead in the direction of genuine care.

Certainly, the idolatry of comfort itself is amplified by our mistakes in dealing with its root. Many people in our society — including, I suppose, all of us at times — think that if we can just get past the present difficulties or trials, then we will find deep satisfaction. Life will go better, we are sure; we'll be happy as soon as . . . Of course, if we look carefully, we recognize this attitude as the old problem of trying to quench or repress our *Sehnsucht* (remember Chapter 2). Seeking after comfort, however, can never result in fulfillment of our deep spiritual yearning, for suffering is inevitable since we live in a broken, corrupt world.

Several other aspects of the idolatry of ease in our culture contribute to problems for us in raising children of faith. In Chapter 5 we saw the destructive effects of making worship too easy,

---

results include lower achievement in school, less empathy and other virtues in the child's character, and higher rates of early sexual activity, suicide, alcohol and drug abuse, and violence against women. See sociologist David Popenoe's *Life Without Father* (New York: The Free Press of Simon and Schuster, 1996).

as our children do not learn that discipleship involves a cross, that following Jesus takes work, and that the disciplines of faithful Christianity are well worth the cost. In many other ways, however, this idolatry of comfort and coziness deepens the problems of our society and makes it more difficult for us to nurture our children with genuinely Christian character.

First, focusing urgently on getting out of pain quickly or taking great care to avoid it causes persons in our society not to understand the sources of their suffering. We often undergo tribulations as the natural consequences of our bad choices, and we ought to pay attention to that source to learn crucially important lessons for our future. Many of our afflictions are undeserved, due to the thoughtlessness and cruelties of others; knowing the origin might help us prevent the damage, rectify it more thoroughly, learn how to avoid it, or make us more sensitive to the pain of others who also suffer at the inflicters' hands. These unmerited struggles are times when it is critically important for the Christian community to enfold those who suffer them.

Some miseries arise from the simple fact of bodily aging and the presence in the world of disease — all because our sin brought death. Since the death ratio is the same for everyone — one per person — these adversities could wake us up to see our lives more clearly in the light of our mortality (and then resurrection). Simply to escape these maladies through pain medications allows us to elude necessary reflection on our priorities and practices and purposes. The fallenness of the world guarantees that we can never escape suffering on earth, but people go to great lengths to try — and thereby fail to acquire the gifts of wisdom and character that sickness and sorrow convey.

It is especially important that we guide our children to know the sources of their pain — and, most particularly, that they be allowed to bear the consequences of their poor choices. When the misfortune is not their fault but is caused by the sins of others, we can do whatever is possible to help them avoid it, surmount it, or endure it, and we can help them discover and then resolve that they never want to cause similar harm to someone else. It is essential that we strongly support them and share with them in that suffering, lest it give rise to bitterness instead of empathy.

I think it is also helpful, when an appropriate situation arises, for young people to contemplate death. My own near-death trauma when I was in high school filled me with a deep sense of the gift of life and of my responsibility to use what years I have well. Many of the temptations of the society around us never appealed to me because I had better things to do with my time. I don't wish near-death experiences on teenagers, but I do earnestly wish that they had a better sense of the preciousness of life so that they wouldn't waste it in devastating habits.

Another destructive effect of the idolatry of happiness in our culture is that persons' failures to understand the sources of their pain lead to wrong methods in their efforts to deal with it. People expend an extraordinary amount of energy trying to avoid struggle or suffering, scrambling for self-preservation — and often the result is more problematic. For example, in churches people often concentrate intensely on smoothing things over rather than getting to the root of issues so that conflicts can be genuinely resolved or transformed. Similarly, children waste time and energy trying to evade homework and thereby fall further and further behind in school, when the same amount of time and tenacity devoted to doing the work would lead to the satisfaction of accomplishing it and learning the lessons intended.

The most dangerous dimension of the idolatry of ease is that so many people in the United States turn to alcohol or drugs to avoid pain — and, of course, that behavior leads to much greater suffering in the end. I don't think it is necessary here to cite statistics of recent rises in alcohol consumption and drug abuse among young people since we read and hear them frequently. What is urgent is that we recognize the spiritual roots of such addictions. As I noted in Chapter 2, our society will never solve the problem of drugs and alcohol as long as we neglect the underlying spiritual yearnings that propel so many to use them — their cravings for comfort and "freedom" and escape from life, which at root are hopeless attempts to satisfy or repress the nagging *Sehnsucht*, their (unidentified) longing for God.

Recently several school teachers were discussing the finding that mandatory drug and alcohol education programs in the public schools have been found to be ineffective. Some children who are determined to experiment will do so anyway, in spite of the programs; others who are equally committed to resisting the temptation will abstain regardless of the instruction. The complication researchers have discovered is that the children in between these two groups, who could be swayed either for or against addictive substances, are reacting to the mandatory programs with experimentation instead of resistance.

In contrast to such unfruitful efforts, the Christian community can offer hope, healing, and a home to those in the bondage of addictive lifestyles. Social analysts recognize that rehabilitation programs centered on Christian faith have the highest success rate at producing genuine deliverance from addiction — which the Scriptures suggested to us long ago in passages that reveal God as the one true Liberator. When the Church embodies and extends God's deliverance through community members' profound love for the neighbor (and for their children), followers of Christ can bring those in the captivity of substance abuse to the only One who can set them free from the ravages of their attempts to silence the profound yearning.

Though I have not seen any documentation to support this contention, it seems to me that faith-based programs would be the most successful in promoting abstinence and prevention as well as rehabilitation since they would get at the spiritual roots of the temptations. I believe that the Christian community could offer great gifts to our society if we teach our children well that life in Christ is much more satisfying than life inebriated. We can give young people many strong reasons, such as the following, for preferring not to engage in destructive addictions: if involved in service projects instead (see the next section) they will have too many other interesting things to do; belonging to the Christian community, they will have a large family of other people caring for them richly; knowing, above all, the love of God, they will find their deepest satisfaction in his grace. The Church's entire process of training its children (and its catechumenal process for adult new believers) is in some ways a form of rehabilitation, for it is a nurturing in an entirely new way of life.

Finally, we must note that our society's massive efforts at

trying to be comfortable lead to many of the other idolatries that we will look at in this part of the book. Gluttonous consumerism (Chapter 9) — especially of media and information (Chapters 10 and 11) — violence (Chapter 12), and sexual immorality (Chapter 13) all result from choosing the easy way out.

The Model of Jesus

As the hymn at the head of this chapter reminds us, Jesus himself suffered in every way imaginable — not only the pain and shame of the cross, but also homelessness, foreign oppression, the need to escape terror and live as a refugee. He lived as one who had no place to lay his head.

Because Jesus lived intimately connected with those who suffered the evils and oppressions of this world, his insistence is all the more poignant and compelling for us that when we, as his disciples, serve the hungry, the thirsty, the stranger, the naked, the sick, and those in prison we are serving him (Matt. 25:31-46). In contrast to our society's attempts to avoid discomfort or suffering, what a great adventure this is into which we invite the Church's children: to participate with us in finding ways to serve Jesus through our brothers and sisters who suffer and to enter willingly into their suffering. My goal is that every child in the Christian community be involved in some form of compassionate care for the needy of our world.

Families can include their children of all ages in their efforts to minister to the less advantaged. Many people in homeless shelters, for example, seem to enjoy greatly being with children — and our own offspring will not take their own homes for granted if they play with other youngsters who have had to move frequently, who have never known a stable home, or whose families have never owned their own residence. Broadway Christian Parish in South Bend, Indiana, serves Sunday dinner every week to the people of the neighborhood, and lots of youngsters come; children of the congregation work with their parents in the teams who prepare the meals and clean up afterward. The children of the Christian community learn powerful lessons of generosity and of humility when they sit at family tables with those who do not possess, as they do, what is needed for daily life.

It inspires me that so many congregations are now involving their youth groups in "Servant Events," activities of genuine care for the marginalized of our world. Young people are helping to tutor in the inner cities, serve food at soup kitchens, distribute blankets and clothing to the homeless, or prepare places for them at shelters. I hope that we can increasingly get our offspring involved in fighting the systemic roots of poverty, too. For example, Bread for the World offers numerous ways for youth to become associated with endeavors to change congressional and presidential policies.[2] Any efforts our congregations can make to enable teenagers to understand better the root causes of joblessness, ghettoization, homelessness, lack of health care, and so forth will contribute to their growth as truly caring persons, eager to combat evil inequities in our society's structures.

Goshen College, a Mennonite school in Goshen, Indiana, requires that all its students spend one term serving in a Two-Thirds world country. I wish more Christian colleges required such exposure, for it is also critically important that we introduce our children to the resiliency, creativity, and generosity of the poor. As the Chinese aphorism says, "Go to the people. Live among them. Learn from them. Serve them. Plan with them. Start with what they know. Build on what they have."[3] Those who participate in such ventures almost unanimously agree that they gain far more than they contribute, that they learn immense lessons about faith and neighborliness, that they realize the impediment U.S. wealth often is to genuine community.

One way to nurture compassionate care in all our offspring, but especially the younger ones, is through their reading. Many

2. For more information, contact Bread for the World at 1100 Wayne Avenue, Suite 1000, Silver Spring, MD 20910; phone 301-608-2400; fax 301-608-2401; e-mail: bread@igc.apc.org; WWW: http://www.bread.org.

3. This aphorism is often quoted by John Perkins, founder of Voice of Calvary Ministries, which emphasizes racial reconciliation and the development of cooperatives, medical resources, and training programs to combat poverty. See Stephen E. Berk, "From Proclamation to Community: The Work of John Perkins," *Transformation* 6, no. 4 (October/December 1989): 4.

excellent children's books raise issues, deepen understanding, foster concern, offer possibilities for service. For example, the Scholastic book club from which my husband and his students order paperbacks has recently featured a large number of superb novels related to the Holocaust. These books are not overly gruesome, but they tell the story well enough so that young readers gain insight into the customs of the Jews and the utter tragedy of their losses, so that children will never want to let such a thing happen again, so that youngsters realize that there are many ways to fight such evil, so that they see the work of heroes who triumphed in spite of their circumstances.[4] Other children's books can help our youngsters recognize the evils of prejudice, the importance of family, the gift of faith.[5]

4. I especially recommend Olga Levy Drucker, *Kindertransport* (New York: Henry Holt and Company, 1992), a memoir of the wanderings of German Jewish children who were sent by their parents to England for safety; Isabella Leitnor, *The Big Lie: A True Story* (New York: Scholastic, 1992), an autobiographical account of a Hungarian Jewish family; Lois Lowry, *Number the Stars* (New York: Dell Publishing, 1989), a story showing the effective protection by the Danes of their Jewish fellow citizens; Michael Morpurgo, *Waiting for Anya* (New York: Puffin Books, 1990), a narrative of the efforts of a French village to smuggle Jewish children over the border into Spain; Marilyn Sachs, *A Pocket Full of Seeds* (New York: Puffin Books, 1973), the story of a French girl whose family takes in refugees and then is taken away by the Nazis when she is absent from home; Steven Schnur, *The Shadow Children* (New York: William Morrow, 1994), a mysterious account of residents of a French village dealing with their memories of World War II; Ida Vos, *Anna Is Still Here*, trans. Terese Edelstein and Inez Smidt (New York: Viking Penguin Books, 1986), a portrait showing a Dutch girl's struggle to uncover herself after having hidden for three years; Jane Yolen, *The Devil's Arithmetic* (New York: Viking Penguin Books, 1988), a fictional story of a contemporary girl who is suddenly transported into a World War II–era Polish village, the whole of which is arrested and taken to prison camp.

5. Two that especially do all three of these things are Isabelle Holland, *The Journey Home* (New York: Scholastic, 1990), a tale of two orphaned girls that explores prejudices against Catholics, Irish immigrants, and the poor; and Sara H. Banks, *Remember My Name* (Niwot, CO: Roberts Rinehart Publishers, 1990), a story that exposes the tragedies of Cherokee deportation and slavery in the United States.

No Pain, No Way

The Call to Holiness

The verse that strikes me most in the hymn above is the third one:

> Lord, who lived secure and settled,
> safe within the Father's plan,
> and in wisdom, stature, favor
> growing up from boy to man —
> with your grace and mercy bless
> all who strive for holiness.

As we contemplate the wanderings, the rumors, and the derisions of Jesus' earthly life, we are nudged to deeper reflection when we discover his security and safety at the center of his Father's will. In the midst of a world besieged by troubles of all sorts, what a wonder it is to discover the sanctuary available to us in seeking holiness. It is a great gift — and a sure one in the face of the impossibility of true ease in this world — that we can promise our children the safety of God's eternal care and the security of the resurrection.

Furthermore, God has promised, and Jesus reiterated this promise, that we *shall* be holy as his Father is holy. By Christ's work of grace, we are counted as saints — and our genuine safety lies in living out that sainthood. But rarely in the Church do I ever hear anyone, young or old, say that his or her main goal in life is holiness! What a startling contrast to our society's goal of being happy.

In the midst of the world's anguish because no one can find permanent happiness or ease, those who suffer sometimes look to the Church — and what shall we give them? Do they see in our lives a better goal? Do our children see that to aim for holiness is much more fulfilling than to be ceaselessly chasing after an elusive happiness?

We cannot respond to the yearning of our children and neighbors with easy answers or the guarantee of ease. God and his people do not promise an end to suffering in this life, but instead the Scriptures and the Church train us in the truths of faith, which enable us to recognize sorrow's source in sinfulness and its meaning in the grace of God. Members of the Christian community can even "boast" in our suffering, for we know that it produces per-

139

severance, then character, and then a hope that will not disappoint us (Rom. 5:3-5). What our children need is not the illusion that they can escape from suffering, but purpose to endure it. Rather than pursuing an exhaustively fleeting comfort, we all need to be immersed in a faithful community that supports us in our adversity, that works to alleviate what can be eased, that embodies the presence of the God who genuinely comforts the afflicted and also afflicts the comfortable, that enables us to cultivate holiness in the midst of, and in spite of, our struggles and sorrows.

Right now, as I revise this chapter, the comments above are much more poignant for me because I recently learned that the thirteen-year-old daughter of a friend of mine has a high-grade Burkitt's lymphoma, one of the fastest growing cancers known, which needs to be treated aggressively with the harshest chemotherapy possible. I wish that I lived close to Kia and her family, so that I could be part of the community to embody the presence of God for them. What I can do instead is write this chapter — and urge all of you who read it to be, and to train your children in being, the community of presence for those who suffer in your neighborhood. I can plead with you and your children to resist our society's idolatry of ease and to choose instead the goals of holiness and fellowship with those who suffer as a response to the sanctifying grace of God.

"Sacrifice for Righteousness"

Jesus was, of course, the perfect Sacrifice so that we might be covered over with a righteousness that is alien to our sinful nature, but perfectly conformed to the kingdom of God. Can we ever grasp these truths: that God has declared us holy, that Christ has made us righteous, and that the Holy Spirit empowers us actually to live out that holiness and righteousness?

The fourth stanza of the hymn above invites us and our children to follow, as Jesus did, where duty leads in order that we, too, might sacrifice for the sake of righteousness in the world. It is an amazing answer to give children who are screaming for candy or toys to suggest that we choose not to indulge ourselves, that we sometimes sacrifice pleasures for the sake of justice for others.

We will consider this more thoroughly in the following chapter on consumerism (and actually in all the rest of the chapters in this section of the book), but it is important to note the idea here. We don't give up certain things to be more holy, but out of our holy calling we gladly renounce some pleasures in order to contribute to the goodness of the world.

All of family life is a sacrificing for the sake of righteousness. We each give up some of our leisure time to do the chores that have to be done to keep the house clean, to feed ourselves nutritiously, to care for each other's physical and emotional, intellectual and spiritual needs. We must help our children to see that their contributions to these processes are as important as anyone else's. Fathers and mothers need their hugs as much as children require strong affection and enfolding. Both parents require the spiritual lessons that come "from the mouths of babes," and our offspring need careful nurturing in the faith.

The fifth verse of the hymn at the head of this chapter especially encourages us to think of others in the midst of our own sufferings. Let these words again remind us of the work of Christ:

> Lord, who in your cross and passion
> hung beneath a darkened sky,
> yet whose thoughts were for your mother,
> and a thief condemned to die —
> may your grace and mercy rest
> on the helpless and distressed.

God now wants to use us as agents of that grace and mercy toward those without recourse and without hope. As our society becomes more and more fragmented by various victim groups clamoring for their rights, the Christian community knows the privilege of giving up our rights for the sake of working toward God's justice and righteousness in the world. It is essential that we model for our children a willingness to turn toward the needs of others instead of focusing on our own pains. (I don't mean by this that we ignore the sources of our own sufferings. We certainly will take whatever medical or spiritual steps we can to alleviate our afflictions.)

Of course, the heavenly Joy of focusing on others is that we wind up feeling better ourselves, too. To complain and dwell on my anguish only increases it. When I lose myself in service to others, I feel less pain and I worry a great deal less. That happens in the pool each day that the fast swimmer is there. As soon as I activate my usual prayer practices and start thinking about persons with great sorrows and sufferings, it is much easier to swim against the tide.

Someday No More Tears

And someday I will be able to swim (or fly or whatever we'll do) as I want to — with no pain and frustration! Someday I won't care about any of these struggles because I will see God face to face and will enjoy his presence forever as he has promised.

It grieves me that churches these days rarely teach much about heaven. Many pastors and congregational leaders seem to me to be embarrassed by the whole idea — as if it were as flaky as "pie in the sky in the bye and bye when you die." The modernist world of scientific rationalism has stolen heaven from Christians.

It is true that heaven was used falsely as a recompense by oppressors in days past. And, indeed, many Christians have been "so heavenly minded that they are no earthly good." However, these serious errors in the application of the biblical basis for awaiting God's heaven are no reason to reject what the Scriptures say — and our children need the sure hope that someday all suffering will cease.

The Bible does not tell us much about heaven; I suppose if it did we would be so eager to get there that we wouldn't be able to fulfill God's purposes here. God's Revelation does make clear that all sorrow and sighing will be gone, that evil will be forever annihilated, that God has promised us eternal life with him — and the entire narrative of the Scriptures absolutely demonstrates that God always keeps his promises.[6]

6. For further study of the book of Revelation and the gift of heaven for our present suffering, see Marva J. Dawn, *Joy in Our Weakness: A Gift of Hope from the Book of Revelation* (St. Louis: Concordia Publishing House, 1994).

Heaven is not an *escape* to help us ignore our suffering now. It is not a *reward* for getting through these present pains. Rather, it is a *gift*, already received, that enables us to know the truth of God's love and presence underlying our present realities. As the final verse of the hymn above states, we can *know* that the Lord will bring his children home at last because Christ rose, ascended, fulfilled the Father's purposes entirely, triumphed over the principalities and powers, and completed our salvation. That we will someday experience God's presence face to face makes us not less involved with this world now, but more so, for salvation invites us to be agents of God's purposes, too. Furthermore, living in the light of eternity gives us a freedom for that service that the world cannot give. We don't have to justify our existence, prove our worth, make a name for ourselves, or accumulate wealth. With our *Sehnsucht* genuinely stilled by our present possession of eternity, we can expend our energies for others instead of chasing after our own happiness. Heaven and its holiness, sacrifice and its righteousness are the perfect antidote to our society's fruitless pursuit of comfort and ease.

What greater gift can we give to our children than knowledge of heaven, assurance of the promise that the Lord will "bring [his] children home at last"? What greater life can we nurture them in than that of the kingdom of God? What greater purpose can we imbue them with than making heaven known to the world by the way we live now?

For further reflection, discussion, transformation, and practice:

1. In what ways do I see that people in our culture do everything they can to avoid suffering? Are they ultimately successful?

2. What suffering have I had to bear because of my own bad choices? What lessons did I learn? How can I help my children learn appropriate lessons when they have to bear the consequences of their choices or behaviors?

3. In what projects of compassionate care are my children engaged?

What services to the needy does my Christian community provide? What possibilities could we explore as a congregation and as a family for deeper involvement?

4. Do any of the youth that I know have trouble resisting drugs or alcohol? Is there any way I could help them? Does our congregation provide the healing, hope, and home that so many in our society need to combat their addictions? What could we do to equip our Christian community more thoroughly to provide these gifts?

5. What changes might it make in my life if I were to claim holiness as my major goal? How can we encourage such a goal in our children without turning it into "works righteousness" or phony piety?

6. What sacrifices do I make for others? What sacrifices might I make or do I wish I could make? How can I help my children learn the Joy of sacrifice?

7. How is it helpful to me to think about heaven as my home? How would it change the way I live if I lived "in the light of eternity"? How could I talk about heaven with my family to avoid some of the false ideas mentioned above and to stress its values for us today?

CHAPTER 9

"Santa Claus Is Coming to Town"

God, whose giving knows no ending,
from your rich and endless store:
nature's wonder, Jesus' wisdom, costly cross,
grave's shattered door —
gifted by you, we turn to you,
off'ring up ourselves in praise;
thankful song shall rise forever,
gracious donor of our days.

Skills and time are ours for pressing
toward the goals of Christ, your Son;
all at peace in health and freedom,
races joined, the church made one.
Now direct our daily labor,
lest we strive for self alone;
born with talents, make us servants
fit to answer at your throne.

Treasure too you have entrusted,
gain through pow'rs your grace conferred,
ours to use for home and kindred,
and to spread the gospel word.
Open wide our hands in sharing,
as we heed Christ's ageless call,
healing, teaching, and reclaiming,
serving you by loving all.

Robert Edwards (1961)
Tune: Beach Spring, *The Sacred Harp* (1844)

"God, whose giving knows no ending," came to earth out of pure grace and was born into poverty and degradation. How is it that our celebration of that Incarnation has come to be, in the United States, the major supplier of retail stores' profits?

Don't worry. I know that most of you reading this book bemoan what has happened to Christmas in its hypercommercialism. I don't intend to lambaste you for what probably causes you some confusion and regrets and a lot of tension and frustration. I propose instead that we use what we detest about Christmas as a symbol of a much deeper sickness in our society, a sickness that fiercely endangers the possibility of our raising children in the faith. In this matter of dealing with the god Mammon the Christian community must deliberately choose to be, and diligently practice being, an alternative society.

That Christmas in the United States is all about the god Mammon and that people of faith must intentionally elect to be different is readily recognized by people of other cultures. Just before Christmas last year, National Public Radio's "All Things Considered" interviewed citizens from other faiths. Some Muslim girls remarked that they could not understand why parents teach their children about Santa Claus "as if he were some kind of god or something." Some Hindu immigrants said that they would provide for their daughters a reduced celebration of Christmas; the mother declared, "They are Indians. They can never be mainstream, so we have to maintain our identity."

146

How can we as Christians form our children to realize that it is good not to be mainstream, that our identity in faith is worth preserving, that the gods of this world will never satisfy our *Sehnsucht,* our infinite yearning for the Infinite? First we must understand the roots of our society's consumerism and the hopelessness of it.

Materialistic Consumerism

Truly it is a tragedy that U.S. society's perpetual pursuit of material possessions brings on a great proportion of the suffering experienced in our culture — even as people chase after those treasures to escape their suffering. The interminable spiral discloses the impossibility of extinguishing *Sehnsucht* with human solaces or stuff.

Consumerism takes many forms, and the idolatry of having more to consume has plagued the world since the beginning of time. The biblical narratives are filled with accounts of human beings seeking inordinately to possess such things as wisdom (Adam and Eve), the birthright (Jacob), sons (Jacob's wives), or money (the rich young ruler who came to Jesus and turned away sorrowfully). Isaiah 55, which Jesus quotes in John 6, records the impossibility of possessions ever quenching our hunger for more of them; in those texts the LORD asks us, too, why we continually waste our money on what is not bread and our labor for what will not satisfy.

In the twentieth century, however, consumerism is aggravated by many media forces (see the following chapter). Worldwide advertising causes people around the globe to want what citizens of the United States supposedly have and causes people in our society to confuse their priorities or to work like crazy or to go into severe credit card debt in order to have those things too. Marketers with enormous amounts of money at their disposal specialize in inflaming our endless lust for possessions with commercials that constantly convince us that we need more (especially to create the ease we have never found). The merchants don't tell us much about their products; instead, they spend all their energies and imaginations appealing to our anxieties and fancies. Thus, the idolatry of possessions plays to the deeper idolatry of our selves — and, in an endlessly consuming society, persons are always remaking themselves with new belongings.

I especially worry about teenagers in our society for these reasons. Since so many young people are growing up in homes that do not provide them with a family story and a web of reality by which to understand themselves, they constantly remake themselves according to the latest fads or heroes of rebellion; they bow to peer pressures and choose a lifestyle of addiction to things. "You are what you own," the world says, so they look to the marketers to know what is important.

These ongoing refabrications of self arise because there is no core of character by which the young people can set their priorities and guide their life's choices. Constant consumption — of things, of this era's narcissistic music, of sex, or whatever — makes the person's character increasingly pinched, more "inward-turned" as Martin Luther would say. Avaricious attention only to one's own happiness leads to stinginess, greediness, and a complete lack of skill for serving others. My husband frequently remarks that teaching elementary school is so hard these days because all the children care about is themselves.

I am also especially concerned about parents and churches because, as J. Christoph Arnold of the Bruderhof writes, in our society "all too often what sways our decisions is not really our children, nor even their futures, but money." Arnold continues,

> What does it really mean to give a child love? Many parents, especially those of us who are away from home for days or even weeks at a time, try to deal with our feelings of guilt by bringing home gifts for our children. But we forget that what our children really want, and need, is time and attentiveness, a listening ear and an encouraging word, which are far more valuable than any material thing we can give them.
>
> We cannot deny that, as a whole, our society is driven not by love but by the spirit of materialism, which the Bible calls Mammon. Mammon is more than money — it is greed, selfishness, and personal ambition; violence, hatred, and ruthless com-

petition. And it is diametrically opposed to the spirit of child-likeness and of God. . . .

If we are determined to go the way of Jesus, we must see Mammon for what it is — an enemy of childlikeness, of children, and of God. Jesus declared war on the spirit of Mammon; his way was and is the way of sharing, of serving and loving others, even if that means bearing a heavy cross.[1]

Are we, as parents and congregations, willing to bear a heavy cross for the sake of nurturing our children in genuine Christian faith? Our churches might not be the most "successful" ones in town if we nurture children for the rigors of discipleship instead of catering to their consumerist tastes. Are we willing to wage war against the principality of Mammon for the sake of genuine spiritual growth in our children and ourselves?

"Simple Gifts"

In our acquisitive and covetous world, God's people must deliberately nurture their children in an entire community of generous and self-sacrificing Christians if they want them to choose the alternative culture of the kingdom of God and to resist society's materialism and greed. I believe that if Christian churches truly manifested the gracious emptying and self-giving of Jesus, that love would draw their children into the community. It would also attract many persons whose still-unfulfilled *Sehnsucht* has driven them to seek deeper and lasting satisfaction beyond possessions. Only by the life-forming process of participation in the community's benevolence and true charity will our children and our neighbors be helped to find their deepest yearnings gratified as God fashions them to be selfless and truly themselves in relationship with him.

Let me emphasize that I am concerned with much more than money — and that my remarks about money are particularly con-

---

1. J. Christoph Arnold, "A Little Child Shall Lead Them," *The Plough* 51 (Spring 1997): 13, 14, 15. See further his book by the same title, available from the Plough Publishing House, Farmington, PA 15437; telephone 1-800-521-8011.

cerned for the deep attitudes that channel our expenditure of it. As we will see especially in the following two chapters, our families must deliberately counteract our society's passivity about care for the world. Also, our money should be directed not only to address immediate needs but also, more deeply, to counteract the systemic roots of poverty and oppression. Calls to our congressional representatives and senators and the president to support economic development throughout the world, protests against excessive military spending and other governmental policies that hurt the poor, activities that organize our neighborhoods to fight prejudice and racism and unfair business practices — these are a few of the ways in which our money can be paired with actions of true love for those in need. However, since our society is so distorted in its expenditures of money, it is critical that we begin with new assessments of our family's stewardship and think carefully about how we are training our children to understand the purpose of money.

I am so grateful that I grew up with not much money. My father was a Lutheran school teacher and principal in an era when churches expected them to live on piety. That was good for my brothers and me, for we were taught early to manage our money carefully — and ten percent always went first for the work of the Church. I learned to sew so that I could save money by making my own clothes; we learned not to need instant gratification. I did all sorts of jobs, beginning in the fourth grade, to have enough money for college — including a newspaper route, ironing dress shirts, teaching beginning piano lessons, and tutoring in French and math. During college I worked as a lifeguard and swimming instructor, waitress, housecleaner, publicity agent, and research assistant.

As I observe children these days, so many of them seem to have no idea of the value of things, no ability to delay gratification, no sense of the meaning of life and work. I remember distinctly when I received a bicycle in the third grade (my father still rides it) — what a wonder it was to have it. I never took that gift for granted.

I don't write these things to romanticize the past, to say that "life was better in the good old days." I do know that most of the children in our churches do not know how to feast because they

150

don't know what it is to fast. Nothing is special because they can have everything. Psychologists know that life is happier if a person is content, and contentment is a greater possibility if one has learned to want only what one needs, rather than to need everything one wants.

To live more simply in this rigorously overcommercialized society requires us to know a better way to deal with our *Sehnsucht*. Let us look again at Christmas as a test case.

Holiday or Holy Day?

What might we do in our families to celebrate Christmas as a holy day?[2] Of course, we remember that its date was first set purposely to coincide with the Roman festival of the returning of the sun, so that it was indeed initially a pagan holiday. In order to celebrate it, however, the first Christians used that riotous festival to mask their holy one; we need the same anti-establishment consciousness to re-create a Christian season. What can we do to help our children not only to learn that we have different understandings about this holy time but also to enjoy being different in our celebration of it?

My parents followed many old and lovely German Lutheran customs to make the days different for us so that we both knew what the celebration was all about and didn't feel deprived not to have all the material possessions other children had. One of my favorite traditions was the Advent wreath. My father had built a board with nails to hold candles for every day of the season. There were tall candles for the Sundays (the first two and last one purple for repentance and the third one in the row pink for Joy), short red ones in each line for all the weekdays, and two large white ones at the end for Christmas Eve and Christmas Day. Every evening we lit candles for however many Sundays we'd already celebrated and the weekday

---

2. Lots of ideas are available from Alternatives, P.O. Box 2857, Sioux City, IA 51106; telephone: 1-800-821-6153; e-mail: AltSimLiv@AOL.com. Every year Alternatives publishes a resource booklet called "Whose Birthday Is It Anyway?" and their catalog offers many other resources for simpler living.

candles in the line for the particular week we were in. Then we had our nightly Advent devotions with hymns sung in four-part harmony. I loved that singing together every night, but the highlight for which we were waiting came on Christmas Eve after we came home from the Lutheran school's worship service. We lit *all* the candles except the one for Christmas Day and sang Christmas carols for the first time that year — youngest to oldest picking their favorite and singing from memory and in harmonies and descants. I *always* picked "Joy to the World," and I *always* told everybody not to pick any slow ones or I'd cry, and my dad *always* picked either "Away in a Manger" or "Silent Night," and Mom and I *always* cried. It was so beautiful and holy — only the candlelight, only the worship, only the childlike sense that the Christ Child was born into our home.

The Christ Child coming — that was what we waited for, not Santa Claus. We didn't even know who Santa was when we were little because we had no television and didn't go shopping. We didn't miss him at all because our preparations were for the Christ Child. A few days before Christmas my brothers and I would find the glass doors to my father's study papered over and the blinds closed so that we couldn't peak into the room from the inside or outside of the house. Then we knew that the tree awaited us; my parents had secretly decorated it the night before to remind us that the Christ Child came to our house.

After the singing of the carols with the Advent wreath on Christmas Eve, my folks would open the doors to reveal the lighted Christmas tree. What a surprising, luminous, beautiful sight it always was to teach us that Jesus is the Light of the world, that Christmas celebrates his coming to our world — and to our house. There were some presents under that tree, but they were not the main focus. We had already participated in worship with all the school children and soon we would go to the sanctuary for the midnight service. Our heads full of beautiful music, we opened presents one at a time, so each person could enjoy the others' gifts, too; there never was a ripping into everything too quickly and a big disappointment afterwards. If the Christ Child's coming to our house is the main event of the evening, we are never disappointed!

My purpose in all this description is to encourage parents to help their children have a different goal for Christmas, a slower pace, an alternative to offer to their friends. If worship is the focus and full participation in it the means, then presents can take their proper place as signs of affection and symbols of God's immense generosity.

When I was in college, I tried to persuade all my friends not to teach their future children about Santa Claus, but to talk about the Christ Child coming to their house instead. For a few, at least, that might have made a difference; one of those friends one year gave me a homemade card that said on the outside, "I *know* you will have a very merry Christmas," and added on the inside, "For the *Christ Child* comes to *your* house."

My brothers and I did have an advantage, I know. Since my father was the choir director, our home was always oriented toward the Christmas worship. All through Advent Dad would be sitting at the piano and arranging songs for all eight grades in the school program and for the adult choir at the midnight service. I have directed many of those arrangements with choirs since then, and I realize with what skill and devotion he worked on them. Meanwhile, Mother helped write the speaking parts for the school children and was immensely hospitable in welcoming to our home those who had no family with whom to celebrate Christmas. Thus, the model that we always watched in our home was that of two parents using their gifts to make the season and Christmas worship meaningful to hundreds of others. My happiest memories of my childhood are of almost three hundred school children singing descants while about a thousand others sang the familiar Christmas carols; when I got to high school I could join the adult choir as they sang for the special Advent services every week and then for worship at midnight on Christmas Eve and again on Christmas Day. What bliss! And I was never disappointed as long as I kept my focus on the worship; if presents started to become more important, there was *always* a letdown.

Now my husband and I try to keep presents out of Christmas entirely by opening them instead on Epiphany (January 6th) in honor of the gifts of the Magi. Families whose children couldn't wait that long could open gifts on the Festival of Saint Nicholas (December 6th), as long as the parents help their children to see that the original saint devoted his life to serving the poor with his gifts. Emphasizing the goodness and social concern of the original Saint Nicholas invites our offspring to imitate him in the ways he exemplified the gifting of God.

A Theology of Grace and Genuine "Gifts"

You might ask, "But what is wrong with Santa Claus?" The way he is described in our society gets Christian theology backwards. Santa Claus, as the United States customarily idolizes him, teaches children that if they are good, then they will be rewarded. Presents, in that case, turn out not to be gifts. The Christ Child comes instead to tell us that even though (or because) we cannot be good, God gives us the greatest gift of all anyway. Furthermore, since Santa is connected with endless advertisements, he fosters children's gluttony, and then "gifts" are lost in the overkill.

Probably few of the families reading this will be as devoted to Christmas music as my childhood home was, but parents can practice other disciplines related to their own situation and talents/gifts. Perhaps a family can make Christmas cookies together to take to the local homeless shelter, or they can help serve a meal there on Christmas Day. One Christmas Day when I was in college I didn't know what to do with myself while my parents napped, so I walked to the local hospital and visited those who had no one with them for the holy day. Listening to their childhood stories was a great gift to me. Now Myron and I enjoy inviting those who have no relatives in the area to share Christmas dinner with us. Could households invite some poor children to be part of the family's sledding outing, go caroling for shut-ins, shovel snow together for elderly members of the congregation or neighborhood, practice ethnic customs that some people in the community miss? Our youngsters can probably come up with all sorts of creative ideas for letting our celebration of the holy day be a gift to others.

Perhaps family members can limit their presents to each other and take gifts to the poor instead. We have encouraged our siblings and parents to contribute to global food and medicine projects instead of giving us gifts. We enjoy presenting our friends and family with Heifer Project's buffaloes, llamas, bees, sheep, goats, pigs, and chicks to provide an economic foundation for other people around the world.³ We use MAP Christmas cards to advertise their distribution of medicines to global clinics.⁴

Several years ago, one friend of mine responded to his four children's whining and complaining about their Christmas gifts by telling them to pick their favorite toy — and then they took them all to a shelter. At first the children were angry that they had to give up their prized possessions, but when they saw the faces of the youngsters who received them they were overwhelmed with repentance for their ingratitude.

The crucial point in all this is that we help our children know that what we believe influences the way we celebrate Christmas — namely, that salvation is not only an enormously wonderful and totally essential gift, but also the entire reason for the season — its decorations, its customs, its practices. Our children need to observe us, and to participate themselves in, applying our theology to daily life. Jesus said that we cannot serve both God and Mammon; that choice needs to be made more apparent especially at times like Christmas.

Choosing a Different Way

Two key biblical ideas help us teach our children resistance to our society's materialistic consumerism. These concepts are not old-fashioned or quaint, but are vital and stunning. Imagine with me the adventure of enabling our children to choose to be different from the gluttony that surrounds them.

All 100 Percent Is God's

The first biblical notion is that of stewardship. This idea gives children dignity because it emphasizes that God, to whom all things

3. For more information, contact Heifer Project International, P.O. Box 808, Little Rock, AR 72203-0808.
4. For more information contact MAP International, P.O. Box 215000, Brunswick, GA 31521-5000.

belong, has entrusted them with material things, personal talents, and all the years of their life for the good of everyone and the praise of God. Recognizing that our possessions really belong to God encourages us all to be careful of our things, to use them well, to offer them freely for the needs of others. It also trains us not to be performers, because our skills are not our own, but are God-given gifts. That gives us a freedom and a passion to use our abilities without needing to be falsely humble about them. The stewardship of our lifetime provides us with both urgency and peace — urgency to use our time well for the sake of God's purposes in the world and peace because we are not responsible for the outcomes of our efforts at faithfulness. My parents' talks with me about stewardship when I was young, but even more their modeling of faithful use of their possessions, talents, and time, have deeply molded my life since childhood.

If children know that their bedrooms and their toys are gifts to be stewarded, they will be more willing to share them with the homeless children and the neighbors we invite into our residence. We can build in them a sense of gratitude for what they have if we train them through household conversations and decide together how to apportion the family's finances. We can point out to them the lies of the media (see the following chapter) that try to convince us that we need more stuff and that the products being advertised will satisfy our deepest longings, and we can work with them to dismantle the peer pressures to conform to the latest, temporary fads.

I don't think I'm being too idealistic, for I have seen many Christian families (those of my godchildren and of some of my husband's cousins are the ones I know best) where such stewardship is modeled, practiced, and explained, and thus becomes the habit of the children. In *Beyond Chaos,* Chris William Erdman tells a powerful story of a family he knows in which the teenage son Brad had a hard time with his parents' decision to spend Thanksgiving Day serving dinner at a local homeless shelter. Erdman reports that after dinner Brad flopped in front of the television and watched football for the rest of the day, chatting occasionally with a teenage shelter resident named Michael. That night Brad apologized to his parents for his bad attitude and asked them if

Michael and his mother really didn't have a place to live. After learning more about them, he responded, "Maybe we could do something for them . . . I mean, if they don't have anywhere else to go, maybe they could come over for Christmas." Erdman concludes, "There are signs that Jesus is still loose in the world."[5]

A Symbol of Grace

The other scriptural notion that really assists our children in gaining a new attitude about consumerism is that of tithing. I will not argue here for an insistence on giving God 10 percent of one's income (primarily because I think most of us are capable of giving away a lot more). I am instead concerned that children learn that all 100 percent belongs to God (and therefore we are stewards of it) — and tithing is a good symbol for teaching that. Tithing is not a law for us New Testament people; it is a grace.

My first recollections of having money are directly connected to my parents' stipulation that 10 percent went for God's work. I want to note first that this was not a burden; it was a privilege to be a part of what the congregation was doing. It is essential that parents themselves recognize the privilege, the actual possibility of contributing to a greater good. Second, tithing was a gracious reminder that God cared about what I did with the rest of my money. From the age of three I wanted to serve God by being a teacher of some sort, so I was careful to save most of the rest of God's money entrusted to me so that I could go to college. Third, tithing was a great reminder that God provides for our needs. Though my entire life's income has been tithed at least — as has the income of Christians Equipped for Ministry (CEM) under which I freelance — we have never run short. Always there has been enough to live and to do what I believe I'm called to do.

For a while CEM sponsored a crisis house — a place where women coming out of drugs or abuse or other problems could live temporarily. At first we hired a house director, and all the time she worked with CEM there was enough income from my honorar-

5. Chris William Erdman, *Beyond Chaos: Living the Christian Family in a World Like Ours* (Grand Rapids: Eerdmans, 1996), p. 129.

iums and from gifts to CEM to pay her salary as well as mine. After she left to return to school, there was never enough for that extra salary. Since that time, CEM has used our extra funds to send me to teach in places that cannot afford to pay me such as Madagascar, Mexico, and Poland. Also, for all but one of my books we have given the royalties to an agency that helps the poor or to some ministry doing what the book is about. The royalties of this book, for example, are providing scholarships for parents who cannot afford it to place their children in the Lutheran Inner-City Ministries Child Development Program in a struggling neighborhood in Portland. CEM has now existed for eighteen years, and, even apart from those royalties from books, we have always had more than adequate finances to pursue ministry.

Tithing is a wonderful way for families to experience this provision of God. I urge you to think how far beyond the tithe your family could go in giving to your local congregation, to associations that feed the poor and shelter the homeless, to advocacy agencies like Bread for the World, to coalitions working for peace and justice. When the children suggest and participate in deciding each month who should be the recipients of the family's gifts, they will gain and maintain a vision for mission, for, as Jesus said, "Where your treasure is, there your heart will be also" (Matt. 6:21; Luke 12:34). Furthermore, since the word *heart* in that passage means "will," let it remind us all that the needs of the world require more than our money. We must deliberately engage in actions that put our lives and work and fellowship where our money is in the service of the world.

Even our savings can be working for the poor through the efforts of some Christian organizations; Jubilee Housing in Washington, D.C., lets you choose below a certain point how much interest you want to receive (so you can choose not to get any) and then your savings are used to fund rehabilitation of run-down buildings to provide low-income housing.[6] Dwelling House Savings and Loan in Pittsburgh gives your deposits standard interest while using them to make low-interest loans to the poor in an inner-city

6. Contact Jubilee Housing, 1750 Columbia Road NW, Washington, DC 20009-2814.

neighborhood; the Christian owners of this bank also provide banking services for prisoners.[7]

Because the pile of pleas for money gets so large all the time, Myron and I focus on one major category (besides our congregational tithes) for giving each month.[8] Then we also allot a small

---

7. Contact Dwelling House Savings and Loan Association, 801 Herron Avenue, Pittsburgh, PA 15219-4696; telephone 412-683-5116.

8. These are the monthly categories that we have found helpful and a few addresses to give you some suggestions for accountable agencies:

- *Evangelism* — Bible and Bible translation societies; the agencies of your church denomination for global mission; campus organizations; specific missionaries your family knows and writes to.
- *Church planting* — we support some friends who are establishing Christian churches in France; new congregations in your denomination.
- *Homes* — the best agency I know for building new homes is Habitat for Humanity, 121 Habitat Street, Americus, GA 31709-3498. Jubilee Housing (the agency to which you can lend money at no interest) rehabilitates rundown housing for the poor; their address is listed in note 6 above.
- *Racial reconciliation* — groups like Voice of Calvary, P.O. Box 10562, Jackson, MS 39289-9980.
- *Christian camps* — these are valuable places for our children and, increasingly, for family events; check out the camps and retreat centers affiliated with your denomination.
- *Agencies that influence the U.S. government for biblical principles* — for example, Bread for the World, 1100 Wayne Avenue, Suite 1000, Silver Spring, MD 20910, or Friends Committee on National Legislation, 245 Second Street NE, Washington, DC 20002-5795.
- *Building funds* — for churches, camps, Christian institutions.
- *Areas of crisis in the world* — one of my friends has gone as a doctor to Kenya, Somalia, Sudan, Rwanda, and Bosnia with medical personnel sent by Samaritan's Purse, Rt. 4 Bamboo Road, P.O. Box 3000, Boone, NC 28607; telephone 704-262-1980.
- *Agencies working for peace* — like the Carter Center, P.O. Box 105515, Atlanta, GA 30348-9711, or denominational groups like Lutheran Peace Fellowship, 1710 Eleventh Avenue, Seattle, WA 98122.
- *Higher education* — Christian colleges, Bible institutes, seminaries; groups that provide scholarships for poor students.
- *Medicines* — besides MAP (listed in footnote 3 above), consider denominational health agencies or regional ones like Maasai Health Systems (which supports a hospital and doctors in Tanzania), 12019 E. Maxwell, Spokane, WA 99206.
- *Food* — besides Heifer Project International (listed in note 3 above), con-

amount for miscellaneous gifts, for sudden emergencies that arise among our community's members, or for extra pleas that raise our concern. The advantage of this system is that it keeps us from getting overwhelmed by all the needs and at the same time reminds us of the whole gamut of types of needs to care about. I urge families to have just as careful a plan for giving as for their personal budgetary items, since there are plenty of hoaxes in the mail appeals and since the immense needs of our world call for deliberate stewardship and generous "tithing." Since we do not have the responsibility of children to care for, Myron and I have more to give away than most families, but always I realize that we could all give so much more. Tithing is an important symbol to remind us that God himself calls the accounts of our stewardship.

We Need the Whole Community to Resist

In order to raise children who can withstand the allures of U.S. materialistic consumerism, we need the support of the whole community. If Christian parents band together, they will be more able to help their children resist the peer pressures demanding that they buy certain name-brand (that is, unreasonably expensive) clothes or enable them to rebel against the bombardment of media advertising that fosters greed.

Furthermore, the whole society needs the support of the Christian community to withstand the extremely destructive effects of rampant market capitalism. After writing in the *New Oxford Review* about the issues of its excessive, overbearing control (I would call it the functioning of the principalities and powers), Robert Bellah concludes as follows:

---

sider your denominational relief agency; World Vision International, P.O. Box 70005, Tacoma, WA 98481-0005; or Food for the Hungry, 7729 East Greenway Road, Scottsdale, AZ 85260.

Other important agencies to consider supporting might be your local shelters, Salvation Army, and foodbanks; your local symphony or arts centers; libraries; groups that work to save U.S. farmland; and college students from your congregation.

It is easy to see these reactions against the domination of our lives by the market economy as purely individual decisions based on personal reasons. We know, however, that without institutional support, without role models and exemplary stories, few people are able to withstand the pressures of consumerism and competition. It is here that all the institutions that embody moral standards are important, and the church is chief among them.[9]

He believes that the solution for our society's problem of the market economy becoming a totalitarianism that destroys genuine democracy "is right before our eyes. It is in the renewal of community, and of those institutions that make community possible and vital."[10]

Not only is the Christian community valuable for support in dealing with our own children, but also our family's orientation toward community gives us the best reason for refusing certain purchases. When our children whine for extra treats, when they scream for instant gratification, we can remind them that it is our godly *choice* not to indulge ourselves, that we sometimes sacrifice pleasures for the sake of justice for others.

A *"Gift Economy"*

Instead of the increasingly dominating market economy, Christians can offer to the society around them a model of a "gift economy," a phrase used by Jean Bethke Elshtain to denote the believer's ability to give the free gift of himself or herself to others. In our society, contrarily, people make even their relationships contractual so as not to get cheated. The generosity in the life of Christ and his people can give those outside the Church models to resist consumerism.

I would encourage both parents and congregations to consider seriously what kinds of special activities we could engage

9. Robert N. Bellah, "The Triumph of Capitalism — or the Rise of Market Totalitarianism?" *New Oxford Review* 58, no. 2 (March 1991): 13.
10. Bellah, "The Triumph of Capitalism," p. 14.

in to build in our children the mind-set of a gift economy — that we make careful decisions as Christians so that our behaviors and attitudes follow the generous way of Jesus in offering ourselves and our possessions for the sake of the world's well-being. Perhaps we can live more simply by saving up particular treats to make the Sabbath special[11] — to teach our children that we cannot truly enjoy feasting if we never fast and that pleasures are more delightful and meaningful if we forego them at times in order to be able to share more thoroughly with others. It is possible to prevent our children from engaging in childish whining that we should buy them something in stores if they have already learned childlike faith, a contentment and agreement that we choose carefully how to spend our money so that we have more to give away to those in need. They develop an orientation toward a gift economy if they participate with us in a Habitat for Humanity building project or a tutoring service for the poor or if they go with us in any other endeavors of sharing our wealth with those less fortunate. We can invite our children to help make good choices in the grocery shopping or to assist us when we deliver food to a shelter.

These ideas are especially important for training our children in a biblical understanding of sharing and generosity. Our gluttonous society will never understand that pleasure is heightened when it is reserved for special occasions, or when it is extended to others, or when it is anticipated or celebrated in community. A gift economy must be explicitly proclaimed and incarnated in our own daily habits if we want our children both to discover that God is the giver of all good gifts and, consequently, to delight in God's desire that we share them with the world.

---

11. See Marva J. Dawn, *Keeping the Sabbath Wholly: Ceasing, Resting, Embracing, Feasting* (Grand Rapids: Eerdmans, 1989), especially Part IV: Feasting.

For further reflection, discussion, transformation, and practice:

1. In what ways do I see that the materialistic consumerism of U.S. society has invaded our household? In what ways have we resisted it? How is it destructive of community and generosity in general society? In our congregational life?

2. Do our family's Christmas customs promote spirituality or consumerism? What traditions are especially helpful for making the day a holy one? Which ones might we want to change?

3. How does it affect my spending habits if I remember that all 100 percent belongs to God? How might it affect our family discussions about spending?

4. How much of our budget do we give to our Christian congregation and to other agencies doing the mission of the gospel? How much do we give for the needs of the world? Am I satisfied with these percentages? Are my children? How might we as a family make faithful decisions about our giving?

5. What agencies do we support? Have we checked into their reliability, their own faithfulness in spending the money they receive for the cause they publicize? How could we as a family discover good agencies that serve the purposes we care about?

6. Does my Christian community support me in trying to make wise and generous financial decisions? How could my family help our congregation to be a model to the world around us of resistance to the god Mammon?

7. Does my lifestyle reflect a gift economy? Do we talk about it and live it as a family? How can I encourage my children to be more generous with their possessions and with themselves?

CHAPTER 10

"Amusing Ourselves to Death"

God of grace and God of glory,
on your people pour your power;
crown your ancient Church's story;
bring its bud to glorious flower.
Grant us wisdom, grant us courage
for the facing of this hour,
for the facing of this hour.

Lo! The hosts of evil round us
scorn the Christ, assail his ways!
From the fears that long have bound us,
free our hearts to faith and praise.
Grant us wisdom, grant us courage
for the living of these days,
for the living of these days.

Cure your children's warring madness,
bend our pride to your control;
shame our wanton, selfish gladness,
rich in things and poor in soul.
Grant us wisdom, grant us courage,
lest we miss your kingdom's goal,
lest we miss your kingdom's goal.

Save us from weak resignation
to the evils we deplore;
let the gift of your salvation
be our glory evermore.
Grant us wisdom, grant us courage
serving you whom we adore,
serving you whom we adore.

Harry Emerson Fosdick (1930), alt.
Tune: Rhondda, John Hughes (1907)

How can we help but be overwhelmed? The information superhighway is entering our homes; five hundred different television channels are an imminent possibility; the Church's children are exposed to all kinds of new opportunities for media involvement.

We will discuss here not how Christians can influence the television and movie industries — though there is a great need for that to be done in positive ways — but how we and our churches must understand the stakes of our technological times and what Christians must do in the present media revolution to raise children of faith.

Please understand me carefully. I am not criticizing media or technology *per se.* The problem is that both media and technology share in the attributes of the principalities and powers as elaborated in Chapter 2 and easily overstep their proper spheres. They foster what Fosdick's hymn above decries — the scorning of Christ, the assailing of his ways, the warring madness, the wanton and selfish gladness, the accumulation of things that leads to poverty of soul, and the resignation to evils we deplore. As the media are consumed in our present society, they wreak all kinds of destructive effects that are not readily noticed, but that are physiologically, psychologically, or sociologically documented.

In the brief space of this chapter I cannot thoroughly elaborate the ideas I want to introduce, but will sketch for your further consideration six dangers of media consumption. (Other hazards concerning information overload, violence, and sexual immorality will be discussed in the next three chapters.) With greater awareness of the problems, Christian families and congregations can strategize how to take advantage of media benefits without falling prey to their great perils.

Six Dangers of Media Consumption

1. The most obvious problem with the proliferation of media options, most clearly demonstrated by television consumption, is that involvement with them wastes so much time. In *Winning Your Kids Back from the Media* Quentin J. Schultze reports that television watching accounts for 40 percent of adult women's free time and 50 percent of men's. Nielsen Media Research informs us that children and teens consume three hours of television daily, and adults more than four hours. Since the average family television set in the United States is on seven hours each day just for broadcast and cable television, think how much time is spent altogether with the media, including videotapes, video and computer games, and the Internet.

Peter D. Hart Research Associates have discovered that 63 percent of U.S. residents watch television while eating dinner, including 76 percent of young people between the ages of eight and twenty-four. What a tragic loss of congenial time for conversation! Reading has decreased by half since the 1960s.[1] Other leisure activities, especially family interactions, have declined comparably. Think what these statistics mean for involvement in the growth activities of the Church, such as worship and Bible study and projects of compassion. Twenty years ago, the average U.S. citizen could read the entire Bible fifteen times in the amount of time spent watching television in one year! What must it be now?

2. Watching television or scanning web pages stifles the imagination. I notice this especially while traveling — children who are saturated with media in their homes cannot manage to entertain

---

1. Quentin J. Schultze, *Winning Your Kids Back from the Media* (Downers Grove, IL: InterVarsity Press, 1994), pp. 42-43.

themselves when forced to be away from their televisions. I have often had to endure on airplanes youngsters who whine and fuss if they can't have their "Game Boy" and the constant noise of their battery-operated, ping-pong ball–sized basketball shooting games. Their interest in these gadgets flags quickly, however, and then the whining begins again. They often don't know how to play without electronic toys, aren't interested in nature or the wonderful sights outside the airplane window, cannot make up stories (without violence), won't read books, and give up easily if learning requires creativity.

Closely related to the lack of imagination is the loss of attention span. My husband and I noticed this once when playing with our nephew, who was almost five at the time. He is an extremely bright and gifted child, very creative and gentle. While we were playing, however, the television was on — and right in the midst of things, even his own sentences, Erik would suddenly be distracted by some flashing image on TV. It was almost as if he momentarily went into a trance as his face went blank for a minute and he lost his train of thought. Then he would turn away and return to his play. Both Myron and I noticed it separately, and we commented on it later that night because we know that this child has more attention from his parents than most youngsters, reads more books, plays outside frequently, and has learned to do all kinds of things. Think how much television numbs those who do not participate in so many other types of activities. Myron struggles constantly to retain the attention of his students and recognizes that he cannot compete with the rapid, hyped pace of the media. How will we help children learn if we cannot *engage* them in anything that requires effort, continued attention, and imagination?

3. A much more critical point is that educator of educators Jane Healy has demonstrated thoroughly through her research that children who watch a lot of television develop <u>smaller</u> <u>brains</u>. Without verbal output, constant input fails to bridge the hemispheres of the brain, and lack of involvement with the environment decreases the proliferation of dendrites. Only in conversation and by manipulating things — toys, a musical instrument, one's legs in running — does the brain build new pathways and the information

167

received actually get learned. Thus, Healy emphasizes, the media's bombardment not only causes our children to be unable to think; it also prevents them from actually having the brain space in which to think and learn. She pleads as follows:

> If we wish to remain a literate culture, someone is going to have to take the responsibility for teaching children at all socio-economic levels how to talk, listen, and think . . . before the neural foundations for verbal expression, sustained attention, and analytic thought end up as piles of shavings under the workbench of plasticity.
>
> . . . Students from all walks of life now come with brains poorly adapted for the mental habits that teachers have traditionally assumed. In the past, deep wells of language and mental persistence had already been filled for most children by experiences at home . . . Now teachers must fill the gaps before attempting to draw "skills" from brains that lack the underlying cognitive and linguistic base.
>
> We care deeply about the "smartness" of our children, but our culture lacks patience with the slow, time-consuming handwork by which intellects are woven. The quiet spaces of childhood have been disrupted by media assault and instant sensory gratification. Children have been yoked to hectic adult schedules, and assailed by societal anxieties.[2]

You might wonder why this discovery of less brain space caused by a lot of television viewing hasn't been extensively broadcast and why our society isn't "up in arms" to remedy this problem. Certainly none of us wants our children to be less gifted. One reason for our inability to do something about the crisis is that the situation's immensity is masked by the tendency of schools and agencies to "dumb down" tests. Healy proves this by displaying the obvious disparity between a fourth-grade reading test from 1964 and one from 1982. She also reproduces a section of an "Advanced" Reading Achievement Test for ninth grade from

2. Jane Healy, *Endangered Minds: Why Our Children Don't Think* (New York: Simon and Schuster, 1990), pp. 277-78.

1988 — and the "advanced" ninth-grade test is disturbingly simpler than the 1964 fourth-grade test![3]

Of course, teachers know that they are dumbing things down, but society places enormous burdens on them. Parents complain about the teachers if their children are not "doing well" at school, though the teachers could not possibly offset all the bad influences of children's homes. Many youngsters have no background vocabulary or working skills to reach expectations, so teachers are forced to give them passing grades anyway by reducing the requirements. My husband constantly bemoans the fact that his students cannot do the kinds of projects and perform at the reading and testing levels that classes could reach several years ago. Myriads of forces in contemporary U.S. society lead to deficiencies in people's abilities to think, talk, and listen — dysfunctional homes, media assaults, lack of creative play time, and many more factors. The media wouldn't be so bad if none of those other factors existed, if parents followed up with discussions and related activities to help their children process, actively experience, and truly benefit from what is seen or heard.

4. Neil Postman's *Amusing Ourselves to Death* accentuates also that children are <u>less</u> <u>motivated</u> <u>to</u> <u>think</u> because television lulls them into passivity — and this is true even of the supposedly "good" programs. Those who created "Sesame Street" invented it to help children love school, but children learned instead to love school only if it is like "Sesame Street" — with non-sequential learning, no repercussions, and fast-paced entertainment. As Postman reports,

> "Sesame Street" undermines what the traditional idea of schooling represents. Whereas a classroom is a place of social interaction, the space in front of a television set is a private preserve. Whereas in a classroom, one may ask a teacher questions, one

3. Healy, *Endangered Minds,* pp. 27-36. See a similar analysis of lower test results, reasons, and needs for changes in Christopher Lasch, "Schooling and the New Illiteracy," in his book *The Culture of Narcissism: American Life in an Age of Diminishing Expectations* (New York: W. W. Norton and Company, 1978), pp. 125-53.

can ask nothing of a television screen. Whereas school is centered on the development of language, television demands attention to images. Whereas attending school is a legal requirement, watching television is an act of choice. Whereas in school, one fails to attend to the teacher at the risk of punishment, no penalties exist for failing to attend to the television screen. Whereas to behave oneself in school means to observe rules of public decorum, television watching requires no such observances, has no concept of public decorum. Whereas in a classroom, fun is never more than a means to an end, on television it is the end in itself.[4]

My husband struggles daily to help his fifth-grade students become both interested in learning and considerate of others, but they would rather play as the television has taught them, and they have no concept of their disruptions of others nor of the repercussions of failing to learn (see #6 below).

5. In connection with what we discussed about obsessive materialistic consumption in Chapter 9, no one can doubt that television and all the developing computer shopping possibilities promote and foster greed. Much of children's programming is driven by the toy manufacturers whose products are flagrantly pushed. I am disappointed that even the public radio station I listen to is increasingly including advertisements under the guise of news reports or comments about particular programming sponsors. I am so grateful that I haven't yet seen any books containing ads!

The American Academy of Pediatrics reports in its booklet on "Television and the Family" that average children in the United States see more than 20,000 advertisements during the 1,300 to 1,400 hours of television that they watch annually, and more than 60 percent of those commercials are for heavily sugared cereal, candy, and toys. Since only about 4 percent of the advertisements concern the healthy food groups of meat, milk products, bread, or juice, children get a very distorted picture of

4. Neil Postman, *Amusing Ourselves to Death* (New York: Viking Penguin, 1985), p. 143.

what they ought to eat. Recent studies have shown a direct correlation between the amount of television viewing and children's risk of obesity.[5]

6. The greed fostered by media is just one aspect of the larger problem of <u>muddling</u> <u>our</u> <u>perception</u> <u>of</u> <u>reality</u>. Advertisements play to our emotions (particularly fears and desires) and cause us to act on feelings instead of logic and cognitive skills. Neil Postman elucidates that we really don't know from an advertisement how well an automobile functions because the commercial attracts us, not with facts about the car, but with a cozy scene of a family going on an intimate outing. (We will see some further results of these muddled perceptions in Chapters 11 to 13.)

Jacques Ellul also frequently pointed out that daily news on the media features everything horrible, is shown in such short segments, and changes so rapidly from day to day that it fosters a catastrophic, fragmentary, and inadequate view of the world. A doctor friend of mine who has worked in Somalia, Rwanda, and Bosnia in medical missions keeps reminding me that news reports in the United States do not reveal those situations accurately at all.

I don't have space here to discuss other potential subjects, such as the media's invasion of family privacy, but I have highlighted six infectious dangers, all of which merit further conversation and study. (And further dangers of information overload, violence, and loss of intimacy will be highlighted in the next three chapters.) I pray that this brief sketch is enough to make us deeply concerned — and that we will not take lightly the need for a response of limitations and critique! I believe this is a key time for congregations and Christian parents to be at the forefront in setting limits

5. For a copy of this booklet or for more information, contact the American Academy of Pediatrics, 141 Northwest Point Boulevard, P.O. Box 927, Elk Grove Village, IL 60007. Views about commercials and programs (both positive and negative) should be expressed clearly to your local television station. If commercials are misleading, send the specific product name, the channel and time you saw the commercial, and a brief description of your concern to the Children's Advertising Review Unit, Council of Better Business Bureaus Inc., 845 Third Avenue, New York, NY 10022.

to media consumption, in deepening family bonds and faith roots for children so that they have moral values by which to weigh the media they observe, and in offering to the world both prophetic wisdom and workable solutions to the problems that the media inherently engender.

We Can *and* Must *Set Limits on the Media*

We cannot say it often enough that as Christian communities and Christian families we *can* and *must set limits.* Quentin Schultze suggests establishing a three-to-one ratio of family interaction/relational activities and media consumption. Unless we do so, he warns, we will reverse the worldwide, ageless custom of parents teaching their children the wisdom of their faith and heritage, as children instead tutor parents in media-savvy and themselves float aimlessly — without a sense of who they are or what life is really for.

Especially for congregations I want to urge limiting the use of media in Sunday school, for children in our post-Christian culture are now vastly deprived of exposure to many adult models of faith. They need to see the incarnation of God's Word in live people rather than in one more amusing video. An interesting article in *The Plough,* the magazine of the Bruderhof Christian communities in the United States, described what happened when these intentional settlements, which had always lived without TV, began using videos for educational purposes and once in a while for entertainment. Here is their report:

> But the more videos we watched, the more difficult it became to discern which ones were appropriate, worthwhile, or edifying. Dubious footage which might have shocked us months before gradually failed to bother us anymore, and our teenagers and even some adult members began to hanker after each latest box office draw as it hit the rental stores.
>
> The medium itself was problematic, too: it seemed to induce passivity, and the unreal world of images, excitement, and color exercised a greater and greater power of attraction. Watching a

video became "the big thing," whether in the classroom, as a special treat at home, or merely as an easy way to occupy one's time. Relationships between teachers and students, parents, children, and siblings, faded before the screen.

Last fall we decided in our brotherhoods to pack away all our VCRs and videocassettes and live without videos. The results were astounding. Creativity blossomed again among the children at school and at home. Singing, playing, and reading together, arts and crafts work, hiking, and socializing replaced the mass isolation of individuals glued to the screen.

None of us, including our children, has regretted our decision or misses the videos we might have been seeing. And our time, minds, and energies have been liberated for worthwhile pursuits.

Plough asked several Bruderhofers for their reactions to our decision to stop watching videos.

Mavis (5th grade): "It was a good idea to stop watching videos, because it lets us think more about Jesus." . . .

Simeon (10th grade): "I'd rather be birdwatching than watching movies. Not watching videos also gives me more time to practice piano."[6]

I grieve at all the family time and creative potential, the thinking about Christ and the deepening of relationship bonds that are being lost because so much time is devoted to media consumption.

A friend of mine reported that her son asked her to set limits on media involvement when his friends visit because "otherwise they never talk to me." He said that his friends don't know how to quit (as he does because of the creative conversations and interactions of his family), and then they never really *visit* much. In contrast, the mother of one of my husband's fifth graders has placed both a television set and a telephone in her daughter's room — and then wonders why her daughter is not doing well in school.

For the sake of your children's education (and, I might add, for the sake of their ability genuinely to worship) it is crucial to limit their media involvement — for all the reasons suggested by the excerpt above about "Sesame Street" from Postman's *Amusing*

6. "The Bruderhof and Hollywood," *The Plough* 38 (Spring 1994): 25.

Ourselves to Death. Frankly, I don't understand how children —
or adults either, for that matter — can stand to waste any time on
television when so much of it is so destructive to their moral
formation. (I realize that there are some good programs on, but
the number of quality programs is frightfully small compared with
the amount of time spent by the average family in television viewing.) When I was in elementary and high school, I hardly ever
watched the television we acquired when I was ten because there
were household chores to do, family games to invent or attempt,
guests with whom to converse, myriads of books to read, clothes
to sew and other 4-H ventures to complete, sports of every season
to play with all the neighbors at the school playground, musical
instruments to practice, my paper route and later tutoring and
piano teaching jobs to do, science fair projects to create, debate
team information to gather, drama lines to memorize, high school
clubs and church choir practice to attend, worship and Bible class
and youth group activities to enjoy. My husband spent time gar-
dening and drawing and building when he was growing up. Now
it seems many children more often listen to instruments on their
Walkmans than play them, more often watch sports than engage
in them, more often observe activities than discover their pleasures
directly. It seems a sadly vicarious life — with not much proliferation of brain dendrites, not much outlet for responsibility and
creativity, not much of the deep delights of learning many skills.

Of course, parents will have to sacrifice more time initially
to introduce their children to these various enterprises, but ultimately it sets them free from having to hear their children's constant whining about having nothing to do. Indeed, if the children
see their parents' enjoyment of different activities, they will be
eager to learn; I wanted to learn to play the piano so badly at the
age of five that my father merely had to show me where middle
C was and hand me a book. Besides, learning a new skill together
can be a wonderful opportunity for deep conversation between
parent and child about other subjects. I won't romanticize that too
much, for certainly frictions can develop — I remember some nasty
scenes (entirely my fault) with my mother over 4-H projects —
but most of my happiest childhood memories are of moments when
Mom or Dad taught me household skills or sports or music. My

father even let me collaborate with him and write texts for a few of his choral compositions. What a great privilege it is when children are invited into their parents' work and treated as junior partners with gifts to offer.

It really is a choice, and here we are back to the basic issue: Do parents realize that one of their primary callings in life is to invest time in the training of their children for life? The television set cannot accomplish that, but projects and games and chores together as a family can. Moreover, think what security and esteem children savor when they recognize (even subconsciously) that their parents choose to engage in leisure time activities together with them. I think particularly of one family with whom I stayed on a speaking trip. The father, Jim, spent great amounts of time playing ball with and wrestling, tickling, and holding his four boys. Both he and his wife Kathy are deeply involved in the life of their congregation — and the children love to sing the liturgy in the car on their way home from worship! Their oldest son, a pre-teen when I met him, is one of the most spiritually vibrant youths I have ever encountered. It makes me smile to write about this family because in their home my heart rejoiced at the deeply Christian parenting I was observing.

In my attempts to urge parents to substitute family play and creative activities for television watching, I know that many readers might cast off what I write as hopelessly idealistic. As an observer of thousands of young people, however, I must confess that I constantly wonder why so many parents keep serving their children garbage for their spiritual dinner. If we would not feed their bodies with toxic materials, why on earth do we feed their souls with so much violence, sexual immorality, and greed? I cannot imagine letting a small child watch television without my supervision and, as often as possible, my companionship. I cannot imagine letting older children indulge in passive media consumption without any clear and enforced limits, such as Schultze's suggested three-to-one ratio of active family time to passive dissipation.

Personally, I refuse to have a television set in my home and would not make any other choice if we had young children. In order not to speak about this subject uninformed, I continue to sample what is on these days by observing television's offerings in

175

the homes and hotels where I stay during speaking engagements. Almost always I turn the TV off in disgust if I have the choice or turn away in sadness that over time families have become so immune to its escalating immorality or inanity.

About fifteen years ago I shared my house with a family of four and another single woman. We did not have television sets in the house. The parents spent their evenings reading, and the two children were both immensely creative — Hope became a superb pianist and Jess is an extraordinary artist. They both became very active in school activities — Hope was elected princess of her class; Jess was involved in sports. They certainly weren't "maladjusted" because they had no TV. All the families I know who have chosen to go without a television set — and there are quite a few — have said that they have never regretted that decision.

Guidance for the Use of Media

Besides setting limits on the amount of time children spend with media consumption, I want to urge parents to work deliberately as their children grow to strengthen family ties, to develop the children's faith foundations, and thereby to give them constructive guidance as a basis for their own intelligent evaluation of media. We certainly cannot separate our children entirely from media influence, even if we make certain choices about limits. Therefore, we *can* and *must root children in the Christian worldview, its morals and values,* so that they never explore media without consciously assessing it. Since they will be exposed to various computer and media possibilities in school and by their peers, we cannot isolate them from it. Instead, we can equip them with skills for choosing wisely, with deepened conscience for rejecting what is ungodly, and with Christian insights into the meaning of life and the purposes for which they were created and given time.

When parents watch television with their children, they should stop and discuss anything that is offensive immediately, so that youth understand how directly opposed to the things of God much of our culture is and how vigilant we must be to avoid polluting our minds. For example, one evening in a small city in Iowa the evening Lent service for which I was speaking was much earlier than I'd expected, so that I was back in my hotel room by 8 p.m. I was astounded that seven out of eight stations featured programs during that prime-time hour that were glib about sexuality or downright immoral or else were extremely violent. (The one exception was the public television station, which was hosting an opera that probably would not have appealed much to children unless they had been schooled to appreciate it.) I can't imagine that Christian parents would let their children watch any of those other programs. Thorough discussions would have to have already taken place with the youngsters so that they, too, would be repulsed by shows with such values inimical to those of God. We can't reject immoral sit-coms or movies in a way that makes our children immediately want to sneak out to see them. Youth groups can have movie parties and discuss them under the leadership of someone with a committed Christian worldview who deeply loves young people and can talk with them without rigidity and legalism, but with discipline and integrity.

In our own families, we have to create what Susan Douglas calls a "media skeptic." She gives these suggestions:

Don't think your choices are either no TV or a zombified kid. Studies show that the simple act of intervening — of talking to your child about what's on television and why it's on there — is one of the most important factors in helping children understand and distance themselves from some of the box's more repugnant imagery.

I recommend the quick surgical strike, between throwing the laundry in and picking up the Legos. Watch a few commercials with them and point out that commercials lie about the toys they show, making them look much better than they are in real life. Count how many male and female characters there are in a particular show or commercial and talk about what we see boys doing and what we see girls doing. . . . Real life dads change diapers, push strollers, and feed kids, but you never see boys doing this with dolls on commercials. Ask where the Asian and African-American kids are. Point out how most of the parents in shows geared to kids are much more stupid than real-life parents. (By the way, children report that TV shows encourage them to talk back to their folks.) . . .

See, I think complete media-proofing is impossible, because the shallow, consumerist, anti-intellectual values of the mass media permeate our culture. And we parents shouldn't beat ourselves up for failing to quarantine our kids. But we can inoculate them — which means exposing them to the virus and showing them how to build up a few antibodies. So don't feel so guilty about letting them watch TV. Instead, have fun teaching them how to talk back to it rather than to you.[7]

Douglas's advice isn't specifically Christian, of course, but her examples fit in with our desire to build community, reject stereotypes, increase respect for elders, and renounce consumerism and greed. I especially appreciate her suggestion to "have fun" while we equip our children with discerning evaluative skills. It is not an onerous duty or a terrible burden to help our children reject the ungodly values of the world around them. It is instead a great privilege to empower them for choosing the values of the kingdom of God.

Exposing the Principalities and Powers

Let us also realize that the world around us is desperate for what we know as Christians. One of the best gifts we can offer to our neighbors is a precise awareness of the dangers of technology and the media that are hidden by the advertising hype, as well as the genuine opportunities that new media systems entail. Our faith communities can work together to develop workable limits for families and authentic solutions to the generational clashes that arise when parents care enough to limit their children's media consumption. Many nonbelievers genuinely want to join Christians in preventing the emotional, social, intellectual, and spiritual dam-

7. Susan Douglas, "Remote Control: How to Raise a Media Skeptic," *Utne Reader* 79 (January-February 1997): 79.

age their children are exposed to in the proliferation of hazardous media materials.

I am NOT saying that technology and the media are always bad. I use a computer for my theological writing and correspondence, but I impose strict limits on myself because I could spend enormous amounts of time on all the things this machine is capable of doing. I enjoy morally upright entertainments (when those can be found) and find movies helpful for understanding society. I AM saying that the media and technology are inherently dangerous. For reasons given in this chapter and the next three, I decided early in my college years not to own a television set (and fell in love with my husband because he didn't own one either on the same grounds) and have never regretted that choice. I didn't want to train my mind and soul in passivity, time-wasting, greed, violence, sexual immorality, and the numbing of imagination or creativity.

I'm not urging you necessarily to make the same choices. Instead, I am urging you to think prayerfully about this chapter and to discuss these issues with other members of your Christian community. (And three more dimensions of my urgent case against television and media consumption are yet to come.) For the sake of our children, our faith, our service to the world, and our Church, we must be mindful of the perils of our technological milieu and active in giving our world the alternatives and the limits to media our Christian communities can create and set.

For further reflection, discussion, transformation, and practice:

1. How much time do members of my family spend watching television or playing on computers? Is this a reasonable amount or should we look at setting limits? How does time spent in media consumption compare with the amount of time spent in family interactions?

2. Do I agree that persistent television watching stifles the imagination, reduces development of brain space, and muddles our perception of reality? On what basis do I agree or disagree?

3. How much has television watching affected the imagination or perception of reality of members of my family? How could we counteract that in our family life? How does media consumption affect our family's ability to worship, to be silent, to be attentive, to learn?

4. Have I seen evidence in my children's school classmates of the "smaller brains" from television watching that Jane Healy presumes? What differences, positive and negative, do I note between what children are capable of learning now and what we learned when I was in school?

5. How does working with computers or watching videos affect what children learn in school? What are they gaining? What are they missing?

6. What tools do I use for evaluating what I view and experience in my own consumption of media? What tools have I given my children for their assessment?

7. How does the biblical concept of the principalities and powers help me to think about both the blessings and the dangers of technology and the media?

CHAPTER 11

L.I.A.R.

Let your heart be broken for a world in need —
feed the mouths that hunger, soothe the wounds that bleed;
give the cup of water and the loaf of bread —
be the hands of Jesus, serving in his stead.

Here on earth applying principles of love —
visible expression God still rules above,
living illustration of the living word
to the minds of all who've never seen and heard.

Blessed to be a blessing, privileged to care,
challenged by the need apparent ev'rywhere,
where the world is wanting fill the vacant place,
be the means through which the Lord reveals his grace.

Add to your believing deeds that prove it true —
knowing Christ as Savior, make him Master too;
follow in his footsteps, go where he has trod,
in the world's great trouble risk yourself for God.

HAVING GOD'S HEART FOR OUR CHILDREN

Let your heart be tender and your vision clear —
rouse yourself to action, serve God far and near.
Let your heart be broken by another's pain,
share your rich resources — give and give again.

Bryan Jeffery Leech (1975)
tune: Wye Valley, James Mountain (1876)

Three of the effects of too much media consumption are so critically dangerous that I have devoted an entire chapter to each of them. The first of these effects is that frequent use of the media and of the rapidly proliferating technological toys and tools leads to inactivity or merely experiential consumption using such things as the World Wide Web. For example, television offers its viewers tons of data about which they cannot do a thing; consequently, it trains them to receive and discard it without acting on it. This response produces what Neil Postman calls a "Low Information-Action Ratio." Think what such training does to sermons, Christian education, and schools! Have you wondered why your children or your parishioners do not seem to be able to respond to information with appropriate action?

When I spoke about the challenge of this increased passivity in our society at a Global Mission event, one perceptive listener pointed to the truth of the acronym of Low Information-Action Ratio: L.I.A.R. Television makes us liars because we do not do what we could with the truths we learn. We watch news reports of the suffering of the poor in our world, but we do not change our consumption habits in order to counteract the inequities by giving more away to feed the hungry and by building economic possibilities for others. We learn about wars and crime, but we contribute to violence ourselves because we don't take enough time to listen to young people. It makes liars of us in Christ's Church if we rehearse words about the grace of God and do not function as a community that incarnates it.

The severity of the low information-action ratio is escalating rapidly as more and more people get hooked into the Internet. Already scores of people have told me that they fritter away too many hours and too much energy scanning and exploring. When I ask them what they do with the data they accumulate, very few — with the exception of some scholars gathering specific materials for research — give any response other than "I know I waste so much time, but it is so interesting." I'm certainly not opposed to finding out interesting things; I just wish the stockpiling of such data led us into deeper wisdom and more active responsiveness. And I worry about how we will train children to act on their Christian beliefs if they view the narratives of the faith as simply more information that does not really affect their lives.

An editor's introduction to a set of articles in the *Utne Reader* that featured persons looking in new ways at the problems of the media commented as follows:

> It has become commonplace these days to grumble about the Brobdingnagian[1] power of the mass media. After all, no matter how media savvy we pretend to be, none of us is completely immune to the flood of soul-numbing infotainment[2] raining down on us each day from radio, TV, cyberspace, and — yes — even an occasional magazine. But there's not real consensus about how to free society from this overwhelming deluge. Each [person in the following articles] in his or her own way is fighting the battle to reclaim our culture, a battle that is destined to intensify in the years ahead.[3]

1. Brobdingnag was a land inhabited by giants about sixty feet tall in Jonathan Swift's political and social satire, *Gulliver's Travels* (1726). Certainly the problems of media influence seem impossible to fight — without the Champion on our side.

2. We have to realize as a first step that much of the "news" poured out upon us as information is muddled reality, entertainment in disguise. Certainly the talk shows are a blatant example, and yet so many people base their lives on what they "learn" from them.

3. The Editors, "How to Media-Proof Your Life," *Utne Reader* 79 (January-February 1997): 73. The three articles that follow in this issue introduce Kalle Lasn, whose "subvertisements," such as one about "Buy Nothing Day," are intended to jolt people out of their media consumer trance; George Gerbner, who has established the Cultural Environment Movement to counteract the globalization and homogenizing formulas of media and the loss of creativity and integrity in cultures; and Susan Douglas, whose ideas about raising media skeptics were presented in the previous chapter.

As Christians we want to be leaders for the Church's sake and for the sake of the society around us in fighting that battle and reclaiming the culture of the Christian community. Of course, we are not rehabilitating "Christendom," for we must never forget that we are not in charge, but we do want to rejuvenate the genuine alternative community that offers gifts to the world around us out of what we know as God's people. We want to reclaim our heritage of faith and wisdom, the ability to *act* as citizens of the household and kingdom of God.

Information Consumerism

I deliberately wrote *wisdom* in the previous paragraph because it takes the insight of faith to recognize that the unceasing accumulation of information in our present society is often one of the disenchanting goals by which people attempt to satisfy their *Sehnsucht,* their deep yearning for something more. Just as the amassing of material possessions will not ultimately assuage the longing, neither will our society's heaping up of data. In fact, probably you yourself and/or most of the people you know are overwhelmed by it.

Nothing is wrong with information, of course; we need all kinds of it to survive. To be sure, our Christian communities pass on specific details about God, but those facts are anchored in an enduring faith that puts into action what it knows.

U.S. society, however, is glutted with fruitless or contextless (though undoubtedly interesting) data. As Neil Postman thoroughly demonstrates, television, which developed out of the telegraph and photograph, generates an enormous amount of information that does not relate to our lives at all or that is taken entirely out of its original setting.[4] As a result, we are trained to receive those details without really learning from them or acting on them; we develop a L.I.A.R. disposition.

Our children can hardly escape being plunged into this morass

4. See Neil Postman, *Amusing Ourselves to Death: Public Discourse in the Age of Show Business* (New York: Viking Penguin, 1985).

of chasing after information primarily for the sake of entertainment. Perhaps you have been swept into the flood yourself or have been pressured by peers to invest more of your time in becoming technologically adept. I have been hounded by people because I don't yet have e-mail, and because I don't surf the Internet. I am not opposed to these tools, for they can be a great help in one's work and are often used to strengthen communication and deepen intimacy among family members and friends, but I know my own addictive personality and realize that I have to put limits on my involvement with technological toys because my curiosity gets the better of me in ways that pull me away from the work God calls me to do. If I find that these tools will help my ministries more than hinder them, I will gladly use the resources — but meanwhile I am careful to set limits according to my calling and weaknesses.

Because technological tools and toys function as principalities and powers, we have to realize that they easily overstep their bounds and take control of us. The result is that many people do not know how to put limits on their use of them, do not distinguish between mastery of the tools and domination by them. Furthermore, the (often superficial) intimacy of electronic chatter often replaces true friendship with all its open vulnerability and suffering, as well as genuine face-to-face companionship with one's own family.

Finally, we have to recognize that for many of us our continuous pursuit of information is an unfulfillable quest to quench our *Sehnsucht*. Our children, our neighbors, and we ourselves will discover in the end that we can never accumulate enough to satisfy the longing that burns within us — and hopefully sooner, rather than later, we will ask what it is all for.

A vital Christian community has great gifts to offer in response to society's informational and technological overload by connecting us all to the One who alone can satisfy our deepest yearning because we were made for relationship with him. In its formational training, the Church immerses all of us who search in the Truth that infuses everything with meaning and hope, in a Way that brings wisdom out of knowledge, and in a Life that acts on the information of faith.

The most important gift we can give to our children in such

185

an age is the ability to ask why and reasons to say no. As parents and Christian communities, let us nurture in our offspring a profound awareness of the meaning of life that teaches them to be selective about everything, including the information they investigate and how they spend their time. Let us give them reasons for living that enable them to say no to destructive or delimiting technology, to the media's demeaning trivialization, to addictive behaviors, to knowledge without wisdom, to powers that would control them, to any immersion that would tear them away from the Joy of serving God.

A snippet of paper I found torn off from its source in my overcrowded study contains a report from the editor of *The American Scholar,* Joseph Epstein. In his "Aristides" column he mentioned a person who listed in his letterhead along with his address three phone numbers for home, office, and car, two fax numbers, and an e-mail address. Epstein comments, "This guy's altogether too easy to get in touch with," and continues,

> With the information revolution closing in, I ask myself whether it isn't possible to live deeper down, at some more genuine, less superficial level of life than that promised by an endless flow of still more and then yet again even more information. It has taken me a good while to understand this, but it turns out that the only information I am seriously interested in is that about the human heart, and this I cannot find any easy way to access, not even with the best of modems, fiber-optic cable, or digital technology. Pity, though, to have to miss out on another revolution.

Epstein's comments are an open invitation to the parallel society of the Church to be a people who live deeper down, at a genuine level of commitment to God and to each other and to the world. Once again I urge you to think prayerfully about this chapter and to discuss the issues of media/technological overload with other members of your Christian community. What alternative options can we offer our children? How will our faith and the Church's service to the world be affected if we do not recognize the dangers? If we are mindful of the perils of our technological milieu, in what ways will we be active in contributing to our world the alternatives of the limits our Christian communities can set and of the ways we counteract the L.I.A.R. syndrome?

Experiential Consumerism

One romanticized reaction to information overload in the society around us becomes yet another goal that does not satisfy one's *Sehnsucht*. In the age-old dichotomy between "head" and "heart," some people in our culture try to offset the mind trips and appease their spiritual hunger with the inadequate goal, the idolatry, of experiences — often making use of gadgets, the newest technological toys.

Though this is a broad generalization with scads of exceptions, the aspiration to possess more things, the materialistic consumerism of Chapter 9, seems especially to characterize what is called the "boomer" generation (people now in their forties and fifties). Younger persons in their twenties and thirties, those lamentably called the "busters" or "Generation X" or "the blank generation," seem instead to have as their goal the accumulation of experiences or adventures — whether by the virtual reality of the World Wide Web or by actual participation. Members of this generation were often abandoned by their parents because of the latter's drive to accumulate material wealth (or for reasons delineated in Chapters 12 and 13 below), and thus they were raised by television instead. Consequently, many of these young people seek only the next entertainment, the fun of the moment. Frequently I encounter this experiential consumerism on airplanes, where the young people seated next to me seem to be interested solely in their next ski venture or in the rock or esoteric concert for which they will fly halfway across the country.[5]

Experiential consumerism seems to be the primary disposition of the children in my husband's classroom. Most of them want only to play games on the school's computers, to goof around

---

5. For an excellent description of and plea for this generation, see Kevin Graham Ford, *Jesus for a New Generation: Putting the Gospel in the Language of Xers* (Downers Grove, IL: InterVarsity Press, 1995).

instead of reading, to chatter rather than do their math assignments, to watch videos rather than discuss history or literature. Learning is too difficult, they think, and not nearly as exciting as their virtual or real adventures. Similarly, my airplane seatmates, in their responses to my attempts at deeper conversation, often reveal an inability to engage in any sort of spiritual contemplation or reflection about existential questions. Those who do yearn for something more are often at a total loss as to where to find it.

How will our Christian communities equip such people and our children with the ability to discover the deeper life of the people of God? Certainly we dare not make our worship merely entertaining; that would do us all a severe disservice by fostering a consumerist stance toward faith and depriving us of what we truly need.

Rather, our congregations can be models of renouncing the shallow, distracting frivolities of the world around us for the sake of truthful reflection and spiritual study, for the discipline of growth in godly wisdom, for the never-disappointing experience of life in vital union with God. We will thereby offer our children genuine meaning; we will provide an end to the fruitless quest for new excitement to those tired of their idolatry's hopelessness. Instead of frantic craving for instant gratification, we will carefully cultivate in our children — by all the life-transforming educational processes of the entire community — what Eugene Peterson described well in his book title *A Long Obedience in the Same Direction: Discipleship in an Instant Society.*[6]

The Word and the World

The hymn at the head of this chapter displays what it is that calls the Christian community to be different from a world that makes idols out of informational or experiential consumption. Both the Word of God and the needs of the world that surround us call the Church to be an alternative society.

6. See Eugene H. Peterson's excellent study of the psalms of ascent, *A Long Obedience in the Same Direction: Discipleship in an Instant Society* (Downers Grove, IL: InterVarsity Press, 1980).

Rather than having a low information-action ratio, we model for our children and invite them into an active application "here on earth" of the "principles of love" so that we all become a "visible expression" of God's rule and a "living illustration of the living word to the minds of all who've never seen and heard." We know ourselves as "blessed to be a blessing, privileged to care." We let ourselves be "challenged by the need apparent ev'rywhere." The result is that we endeavor constantly to "be the means through which the Lord reveals his grace."

Karl Barth said that Christians should be people with the Bible in one hand and the newspaper in the other — that is, the situation of the world creates the ways in which we apply the biblical instructions and, conversely, the biblical perspective teaches us how to read the world. The scriptural mandates constantly call us all not to let the global news become mere information. They challenge us to work and pray. But we and our children need the steadfast support and enduring encouragement and potent prodding of the entire Christian community to keep us from falling into the slothful, L.I.A.R. patterns of the society around us.

The Antidote of Work

Certainly in the United States the adage is too often true that "we worship our work, work at our play, and play at our worship." We have already discussed in Chapter 5 the crucial importance of worship being genuine worship for the sake of the formation of our children. This chapter will concentrate on a biblical theology of both work and play to equip our children with skills and pleasures to counteract the L.I.A.R. syndrome in U.S. society.

Children suffer from the results of two opposite perspectives on work in our culture. If parents worship their work, they probably don't invest the quantity and quality of time in their offspring that the latter need. Fathers and mothers might be following the L.I.A.R. syndrome in their parental care if they know about the kind of attention their children need, but do not act on what they know because of the idolatry of their work.

If, on the other hand, parents hate their work or perform it carelessly, doing only enough to get by or laboring only for the sake of the money earned, then they do not model for their children the value of work well done. Their offspring are deprived of any reason to invest themselves in schoolwork; they see no importance in learning. Worst of all, their children do not learn that work is a way to glorify God.

A biblical perspective neither elevates work nor degrades it. The Scriptures teach us that work was first given to human beings as a form of stewardship, as a gift. They were invited into the creativity of God to care for the garden of Eden. Work was a delight, full of pleasure and goodness.

All this was spoiled, of course, because human beings were not content. Work became a burden in the Fall, for the result of sin was that now labor shared in the pain and sorrow of broken life. Our propensity to make ourselves gods ravages the delight of work, for labor interrupts our pursuit of our own happiness. Our occupations become mere drudgery; honest toil becomes loathsome or seems beneath us. Employment shares in all the damage of our out-of-order world — marred relationships, natural disasters, things frequently just going wrong, having to bear the results of other people's sloppy labor or bad attitudes, inconveniences and delays and disappointments, too much to do in too little time.

However, the work of human beings also shares in the redemption of Christ, for now it has an entirely new purpose. Ever since Abraham, the people of God have been called to channel their work for the sake of the neighbor, to recognize that they are blessed to be a blessing to others. As the hymn at the head of this chapter declares, now we want to "add to [our] believing [the] deeds that prove it true — knowing Christ as Savior [let us] make him Master too." Ours is the privilege to "follow in his footsteps, go where he has trod," and "in the world's great trouble [to] risk [ourselves] for God." Work becomes an adventure; risk is not a terror but an opportunity.

In the Christian understanding of work, my husband Myron is not simply a public school teacher battling his students' indifference. He is a vehicle for the grace of God, even though he is not able to tell the pupils that. He brings truth, beauty, and goodness

190

into their lives; his own modeling of the stewardship of his life might give them insight into the meaning of their own. Similarly, I don't simply write books and speak at conferences; it is my privilege to be God's agent in those endeavors, to do whatever I can to deepen the spiritual life of readers and listeners.

Artists don't only paint, dance, compose, perform. They use their gifts to express the wonder of God's creation, to make us aware of the brokenness of our world, to stir up compassion, to bring God's Joy to observers, to lift the audience's souls to the other world for which we were begotten. I rejoiced that when the great classical guitarist, Christopher Parkening, appeared in concert with the Oregon Symphony, he included in the program notes about himself the specific comment that his teaching, recording, and performing were due to his Christian commitment.

Farmers don't simply grow crops or raise animals; they labor to feed the world as agents of God's provision. Office workers or store clerks don't only serve customers; they wait on Christ himself. Managers and CEOs do not merely shuffle papers and organize people; they enable their employees to use their God-given gifts.

What a difference it makes if we understand our employment as a means by which to glorify God and love our neighbors — just as it makes an enormous difference if parents understand their role as stewardship of their children for the sake of helping them to love and serve God. And when we understand our labor in such a way, our children learn from that modeling that whatever work they do, they perform it as a sacrifice of praise.

Such a theology of work counteracts the L.I.A.R. syndrome. We don't gather information for its own sake; it, too, becomes a vehicle for God's purposes. The data might specifically be employed so that our work on our neighbors' behalf is more effective. Knowledge might be gathered so that we can more wisely recognize what course to pursue. Details might be important for how they form our character, how they guide our responses, how they help us envision the situation into which we are interjecting our work.

The Antidote of Genuine Play

By emphasizing the value of work as an antidote to the L.I.A.R. syndrome, I certainly don't mean that we never have any fun. In fact, I grieve that one of the great casualties of our present technological milieu is that children in so many cases do not really get to play. Violence in the streets makes parents afraid to let them go to the neighborhood park for a good romp. Sports are so professionalized and technicized that kids less often engage in spontaneous ball games. A friend of mine reported that recently with a group of youngsters he held up a bat the way we did in our childhoods for two leaders to take turns placing their hands up the bat to see which one could choose teammates first — and none of the children present had ever chosen up sides for a game before.

I long for our Christian communities to provide safe places for our children to play, games in which adults and youngsters participate together, with plenty of mutual laughter and fun. One of my happiest Sabbath memories was an occasion when I was with a family whose youngest child chose the activity of the day — and we played with marbles-down-chutes all afternoon.

Genuine play is a great counteractive to the L.I.A.R. syndrome. I am not interested in it primarily in a utilitarian way, but it does offer many benefits besides true enjoyment, as this report shows:

> Play may be instructive, but for animals — as for people — it's of course fun. Early evidence suggests that play taps into the brain chemicals involved in pleasure. . . . Researchers suspect that play also increases brain levels of pleasure-inducing endorphins and norepinephrine, which heightens attention.
>
> Though research into the meaning of play is still nascent, many scientists have come to believe it is critical not only to a young animal's development but to a human child's as well. Children gain physical skills through exuberant motion, just like any young animal. They also gain emotional and mental mastery through play, particularly through imaginative games, according to Jerome and Dorothy Singer, child psychologists at Yale Uni-

192

versity and authors of *The House of Make-Believe* (Harvard University Press). When a child plays pretend, says Jerome Singer, "he is taking a complicated world and cutting it down to size. [When] you are the doctor and the teddy bear is the patient, you have reduced a frightening situation to one you can control." Kids who initiate imaginative play, the Singers have found, show leadership skills in school. They cooperate more with other children than kids who don't make believe, and they are less likely to antagonize and intimidate others.[7]

Since it is not my field of expertise I haven't found any specific research on the matter, but I would like to know the correlation between the amount of active and creative play children engage in and their ability both as youngsters and as adults to resist the L.I.A.R. syndrome and to act on the information they receive. The connection would certainly be strong, for the habits of action and movement, of looking for creative ways to do things, and of responding to the environment would be firmly established. In the Christian community, furthermore, these habits would be nurtured into the virtues of actions on behalf of others, creativity for the sake of fulfilling God's purposes, and responses of compassion and care.

The Antidote of Story

Another gift of the Christian community that counteracts the L.I.A.R. syndrome is our story. The biblical narrative of the people of God is an activist story, one that forms us to be vigorous in sharing our food with the hungry, clothing the naked, sheltering the homeless, and not turning away from anyone in need (see Isaiah 58). Daily family devotions in which we read scriptural accounts and instructions and then elucidate for our children the spirited life of Church-being will reinforce for them the importance of vital response to Word and world. Immersion in this story

7. Shannon Brownlee, "The Case for Frivolity," *U.S. News and World Report* 122, no. 4 (3 February 1997): 49.

produces the character of the people of God; dwelling in it leads to reaching out to others.

Other stories, chosen with care, are also valuable for the raising of godly children. In contrast to informational bits from the Internet, good stories help children find their bearings, adjust their attitudes, gain perspective, and discover some heroes. Psychologists and anthropologists agree on the importance of ethnic and universal myths for the development of peoples' sense of themselves.

My most favorite children's fantasies (also good for adults) will always be the Narnia Chronicles by C. S. Lewis. These seven tales are not only superb stories wonderfully crafted, but they also involve stunning symbolism that helps us understand some of the deep truths of God. My husband has read some of them, especially *The Lion, the Witch and the Wardrobe,*[8] to his public school classes, and the children have always enjoyed them. Lewis himself commented in some of his essays that he hoped to write stories that would stir up people's longings for God and also that *good* stories (not necessarily Christian ones, but those that are good art) are essential for helping children develop their sense of life.

Various groups periodically publish lists of the best children's stories; most likely your local librarian could point you to such resources in their newest updated form. Also, the Scholastic Book Club offers school children really wonderful books; I read many of them for my Sabbath enjoyment when my husband brings samples home to choose the best ones for his class.

Patricia MacLachlan has become another favorite children's author. Her book *Sarah, Plain and Tall* is evocative of the struggles of pioneers, tender in its sympathy, gentle in its romance, very finely fashioned with superior use of images and language, a good story to give children hope and comfort, healing and a sense of home.[9] Its

8. C. S. Lewis's *The Lion, the Witch and the Wardrobe* was first published in 1950. The whole set of seven books — including *The Magician's Nephew, The Horse and His Boy, Prince Caspian, The Voyage of the Dawn Treader, The Silver Chair,* and *The Last Battle,* written by Lewis from 1950 to 1956 — was reissued by HarperCollins in 1994.

9. Patricia MacLachlan, *Sarah, Plain and Tall* (New York: Harper and Row, 1985).

sequel *Skylark* is equally good. MacLachlan is a master writer; many of her lines remain in the reader's memory and issue in later insight, and her exquisitely sculpted characters nurture the reader's own. This book will imaginatively teach a child about loyalty, rootedness, the importance of community in times of suffering, and love — in ways that present television programming doesn't.[10]

An older book recently reissued by Scholastic exemplifies the best of children's literature. In the midst of a delightful tale about an immigrant boy, *The Great Wheel* gives historical details of the construction of the enormous first Ferris wheel at the Chicago World's Exposition of 1893. In the meantime, the novel also rejects class distinctions, stereotypes, and prejudices, and teaches children about zeal and faithfulness.[11]

I mention these particular books to illustrate the kind of materials that parents can use with their children to develop their taste for good literature — and thereby their taste for virtues. When their youngsters are little, parents can read to them stories of the highest quality so that by the time their offspring read on their own they will be drawn to good books. A false parenting notion that has been extremely popular since the sixties is that parents should let their children choose whatever they want in religion, literature, the arts, and so forth. The problem with this is that young people left on their own have no basis by which to make good choices.

All the major civilizations of the world have always cultivated in their young the habits and tastes of the community. Young people might rebel, but they usually return in some measure to the fundamental elements learned in childhood that stand the tests of time and truth. They might live out those values in ways that seem contradictory, and they will undoubtedly expand their tastes, but they will be faithful to the real beliefs they experienced. What is essential for parents and Christian communities is that we clearly delineate the guidelines and values by which we discern and discriminate — and that we live unhypocritically in line with the principles we espouse.

10. Patricia MacLachlan, *Skylark* (New York: HarperCollins, 1994).
11. Robert Lawson, *The Great Wheel* (New York: Walker Publishing Co., 1957, 1985).

The Antidote of Prayer

The most important antidote to the L.I.A.R. syndrome is prayer. That might seem strange to people who view prayer as simply talking to God. But I think at least five dimensions of prayer equip us to counteract the dulling passivity that the media induce and to oppose the mindless entertainment in which so many escape active participation in the purposes of God. There certainly is much more to prayer than we are considering here, but let these points at least initiate further reflection.

First of all, prayer is the means by which we share God's burdens for the world. Both at the beginning and at the end of the hymn at the head of this chapter is the phrase, "Let your heart be broken." Primarily we want our hearts to be broken by the things that break God's heart. Jesus teaches us, as do all the great persons of prayer in the Bible, that prayer is focused on God, not on us. To ask for God's will to be done and his kingdom to come is a means of placing ourselves into God's hands for insights into that will and an envisioning of that kingdom. When we teach our children to pray, we instruct them in "having the mind of Christ"; this is the true meaning of praise — to acknowledge God's character and interventions in the world, to honor his burdens and concerns. We cannot truly develop this mind of Christ without wanting to act on it.

Second, however, prayer helps us comprehend what God wants us to be. If we are active for God's purposes out of a character contrary to those purposes, then our children and the world around us will see and reject our hypocrisy. Prayer must come before our action, because our actions too easily take their character from the milieu in which we live. When we ourselves pray and teach our children to pray, we practice dwelling in God's presence, so that we can become more like him. Consequently prayer is often combat against our worst selves.

Third, prayer is waiting to hear what God would have us do and how to do it. It was praying for the children in my husband's classroom and in our churches that gave rise to this book. In one of the best books on prayer I've ever read (though it is not well known), Jacques Ellul asserts that

196

prayer bestows upon action its greatest authenticity. It rescues action from activism, and it rescues the individual from bewilderment and despair in his action. It prevents his being engulfed in panic when his action fails, and from being drawn into activism, when he is incited to more and more activity in pursuit of success, to the point of losing himself. Prayer, because it is the warrant, the expression of my finitude, always teaches me that I must *be more* than my action. . . . Thanks to prayer, I can see that truth about myself and my action, in hope and not despair.

In this combat, the Christian who prays acts more effectively and more decisively on society than the person who is politically involved, with all the sincerity of his faith put into the involvement. It is not a matter of seeing them in opposition to one another, but of inverting our instinctive, cultural hierarchy of values. The action is not the test of prayer, nor is it the proof of its importance or the measure of its genuineness. It is prayer which is the qualifying factor, the significance, the foundation of the truth of the action.[12]

Ellul calls prayer "the sole necessary and sufficient action and practice, in a society which has lost its way" (175). When we teach our children to pray, we are inviting them into waiting — for God's way and timing, clearer insight, firmer wisdom, giving up our own control in order that God's purposes can really be done.

Furthermore, in terms of preparation for action, our prayers are especially important because they are our major weapon against the principalities and powers of the world around us. Prayer for our world and our life reveals the truth about the various forms of consumerism discussed in previous chapters of this book, about the idolatry of ease, and about the violence to be discussed in the next chapter. Prayer invites us into the love, trust, and obedience that enable us to resist these temptations. In a chapter titled "The Only Weapon Against Falsehood," Ellul insists that

12. Jacques Ellul, *Prayer and Modern Man,* trans. C. Edward Hopkin (New York: Seabury Press, 1970), p. 172. Page references to this book in the following paragraphs are given parenthetically in the text.

the disorders and calamities of the world are but the outer face of the attack directed at turning us away from the Lord. It includes the acclaiming of other lords, and the temptation to despair. The powers of the world especially are at work. There will be devious statements of revelation, and the conflict of the princes of this world grows intense. Prayer is the only weapon for this warfare. (150)

Ephesians 6:10-20 shows how important prayer is for this battle when it stresses that we should *always* persevere in prayer, praying at *all* times, for *all* the saints, with *all* kinds of prayer. When we teach our children to pray with openness to God's wisdom and understanding, truth and freedom, we are giving them the critical weapon they need to withstand the powers of the world around them that would draw them away from faith and service.

Finally, prayer *is* action, for if we have asked for God's will to be done in our lives, our every action is prayer. I like to call it putting legs on our prayers, for to pray truly is not simply to say words or even to sit in silence, but to be available to God for the effecting of his will through us. As the final verse of this chapter's hymn encourages,

> Let your heart be tender and your vision clear —
> rouse yourself to action, serve God far and near.
> Let your heart be broken by another's pain,
> share your rich resources — give and give again.

Of course, if we are part of a vital Christian community, we won't have to struggle so much to rouse ourselves, for all of us in the congregation will be supporting each other's *high* information-action ratio, by which we serve a "H.I.A.R." cause, the purposes of the Kingdom of God.

We can teach our children that prayer means action by simple involvements such as asking as a family what we might do for someone in the congregation whose name is on the worship prayer list. If Mrs. Neighbor is ill, what might it mean for God's will to be done through us for her healing? Perhaps we can send a card or flowers, take over a meal, clean her house, drive her to the doctor, listen to her worries, or babysit her children to give her a break. Truly to pray for her in worship is to participate in helpful actions afterward.

As a community, let us ask our children to help us keep tender hearts and clear vision; let us rouse each other in our personal and corporate families to actions that serve God. In our prayers together, let us seek God's own heart for each other and for the pains in the world around us. Finally, let us thoroughly enfold our children in the awareness of how rich our resources are, so that together we can give and give again and give to eternity.

For further reflection, discussion, transformation, and practice:

1. How do I observe the L.I.A.R. syndrome in the world around me? Is my own handling of information appropriate? in the right amount? with appropriate responses and a high correlation of action?

2. Do I crave experiences and adventures in idolatrous ways? Do my children? What could we as a family do to help each other keep these things in perspective with our Christian commitments?

3. How does the dialectic of Word and world help us avoid the L.I.A.R. syndrome? How could my family become more aware of that constant dialectic in daily life?

4. What are my attitudes about work? What perspectives on work do I convey to my children? What is the relationship of my occupation to my vocation as a Christian?

5. Do I know how truly to play? Do my children get enough of robust and creative play? How could we as a family and as a congregational family play more?

6. Did my parents read to me when I was little? Do I read to my children now? What did I and what do my children gain from that? Do we tell stories of our family history, of the family of faith? Do my children know the stories in which they are a part?

7. Do I really know how to pray? Have I taught my children how to pray? What aspects of prayer do we need to learn together? How could we learn more about prayer? How could we set aside more time to practice it together?

CHAPTER 12

First Class Violence

God, teach us peacemaking, justice and love.
Blessed by Christ's teaching, we're lifted above
all thought of vengeance or envy or hate.
Help us, your children, shalom to create.

God, teach us peacemaking in church and home,
in school and hall beneath Capitol dome,
in shop and industry, city and farm —
show us the pathways that cause no one harm.

God, teach us peacemaking in ev'ry role.
In each relationship make peace our goal.
Yet give us insight that keeps us aware
justice and mercy in balance to share.

God, teach us peacemaking unto the end —
parent or child, or as stranger or friend —
fill all our heart with the pow'r of shalom,
living together, the whole world our home.

Jane Parker Huber (1980)
Tune: Slane, Traditional Irish melody

One day a few years ago I was standing on crutches waiting at the airline gate for early boarding. Next to me was a young mother holding her baby with one arm; on her other shoulder was a diaper bag, and that hand was gripping a small, energetic boy. When the airline agent announced early boarding, suddenly a business-suited man pushed past us to the head of the line, thrust me off balance (fortunately into the wall or I'd have fallen), knocked the pack off the mother's shoulder, and almost dislodged her grasp on the youngsters. Wanting to make him aware of the threat he'd been to her children, I turned to the mother and said loudly enough for him to hear, "Can you believe how rude some people are?" He turned around and hissed at me, "F i r s t   c l a s s boarding" — as if money gives him the right to bully small children and handicapped people.

All Kinds of Violence

How can we teach our children the peace of God's kingdom when we live in such a violent world? Violence takes so many forms — the brutality of the rich who oppress the poor, the warring gangs or hoodlums with weapons who keep whole neighborhoods in terror, nations who rape and pillage other peoples, parents against their children or spouses against each other, the biggest kids in the school against the little ones or the teachers . . . and the violence of each of us. What forms does your ferocity take?

I first became aware of the deep-seated violence in myself during a conversation with two other women, when one of them, a skeptical, more educated woman, derided the other, an honest, trusting, faithful homemaker, for believing in the Virgin Birth. I was so fiercely angry at the first woman's arrogance and her devastation of another's humble faith that I attacked her verbally, using every obscure hermeneutical word I could think of in the vain attempt to show her she was not so smart. Perhaps I won the battle of wits, but I certainly lost the war for community. Ever since that day I keep discovering angers that make me violent — because of selfishness, fear, wounded ego, jealousy, inconvenience, covetousness. Sometimes the anger itself might be righteous, but my violent expression of it certainly is not.

The first step in helping our children prevent, resist, and overcome violence is to recognize it in ourselves and to repent. Sometimes we may bark at them to refrain from something, not so much for the sake of their faithful kingdom life, but because of the nuisance it is to ourselves. Sometimes the destructiveness is more subtle, such as when we fail to encourage our children in ways we could and they need.

Children learn compelling lessons of character when their parents humbly acknowledge mistakes. I remember vividly one time when my mother said, "I am so sorry I yelled at you." That moment built a powerful bond between us, and recalling it often nudges me to be more gentle myself.

My parents made it clear when my brothers and I were young that their punishment was given not from rage, but from love. Usually it was meted out a few hours after our misbehavior — I suppose both to calm them and to let us think about things for a while — and always to see their great disappointment in us hurt more than any spanking or grounding. I also realize how appropriate the penalties they exacted were — and how clear were the boundaries. These aspects of chastisement are very important these days when so many in our society do not seem to be able to make the careful distinctions that prevent discipline, which children thoroughly need, from becoming violent. The result is often that their offspring are either abused or overindulged. Those children, in turn, perpetrate violence through their own mistreatment of others or through their gluttonous selfishness.

Muddled Perceptions of Reality

As we think about reasons for the violence in our culture, the effects of television viewing and some rock-song lyrics come immediately to mind. The problem is so great that I'm discussing the issues of violence in a separate chapter instead of including them as part of my discussion of the negative effects of media in Chapter 9.

Various watchgroups have made it clear that the amount, vividness, and blatancy of television, movie, and rock music vi-

203

olence are escalating at an incredible rate — and that much of the aggressiveness and crime on our streets is directly related. One rural, isolated town had virtually no crime until television was introduced, and then the numbers of youth involved in offenses began an explosive ascent. Our own basic habits of speech and reaction are affected if we constantly hear and see on television nasty comebacks, discourteous remarks, political name-calling, and violent reprisals. If our usual input is a program like "Roseanne" or "Bart Simpson," how will we learn to talk with each other? A great percentage of media productions teach children that the way to deal with petty irritations is to slug the offender; their perception is that violence is the only response to annoyance.

The National Coalition on Television Violence regularly chronicles the numbers of violent acts in television programs and movies; that organization also reports on research demonstrating the correlation between this input and people's actions.[1] Mennonite Media Productions has produced two very useful videos, *Beyond the News: TV Violence and Your Child* and *Beyond the News: TV Violence and You,* to alert us to the great dangers.[2]

One of the frightening consequences of media-violence consumption is that young people — actually, all of us — wind up with severely muddled perceptions (#6 on the list in Chapter 9). The most horrendous account I've read was about a young boy who killed his best friend with a loaded gun and then couldn't understand why his buddy did not get up again like the cartoon characters do after they are shot. Less extreme, but with vastly more extensive ramifications, is the dulling of our sensitivities by the constant barrage of news clips, so that we don't really comprehend the cruel immensity of world hunger, the ferocious brutality of war, the bloody viciousness of street crime, the callous inhumanity that causes homelessness.

In our families and in the Church, we have to be deliberate to offset this muddling and blunting of our perceptions. When I

1. To subscribe to their newsletter, contact National Coalition on Television Violence, 144 East End Avenue, New York, NY 10128.
2. These are available from Mennonite Media Ministries, 1251 Virginia Avenue, Harrisonburg, VA 22801; phone 1-800-999-3534.

was in college, my usual inattentive ignorance of the plight of people in rundown inner-city tenements was shattered one cold weekend when some of my college friends and I participated in a church-run "urban plunge" program in downtown Chicago. Listening to conversations of the neighborhood's residents, sleeping in a frigid, rat-infested room with splintered windows, and wondering if there would be enough food to cover my insulin (which became a luxury instead of a burden) woke me to the truth of poverty.

Such awareness projects are especially warranted when our children are teenagers and no doubt tempted to engage in the typical complaining about, or whining for, material things. Long before that, however, we must awaken them to the numbing effects of television news on our perception of the harsh realities of our world and also help them see the inappropriateness of media violence. We can alert them to the incongruity of fashionably dressed and perfectly coifed newscasters reporting all the murder and mayhem and then adding with a smile, "See you tomorrow." We can heighten for our children the jarring discrepancy between the catastrophic news and the upbeat advertisements that interrupt it.

Neil Postman and Jacques Ellul and other analysts of the effects of media and propaganda have taught me what a poor means television news is for us and our children to learn about the world. Its fleeting, brutal, mostly negative accounts foster a fatalistic, fragmentary, forlorn view of the world; at the same time they overwhelm us so much that we get hardened and paralyzed. We think there is no hope, no possibility for changing things, and thus our perceptions of the truths of God become muddled. We no longer deeply believe that God still reigns sovereignly and that we are called as his servants to labor in and for the world in work that is not in vain.

It is far better to read in-depth news journals, to survey accounts from both sides of the political spectrum, to balance news of crises with accounts of ameliorating efforts. Most of all, for the sake of our children's global view and our own, we must keep in dialectic tension the brokenness of our sinful and corrupted world with the constant realization that Jesus Christ is indeed Lord of the cosmos and that there is much that we can do to bring his compassion to the world.

The Idolatry of Autonomy and Its Violent Consequences

Another reason for the escalation of violence in our society is our narcissistic need to be in control. (It is also one of the reasons why so many people chase after information, for they hope that acquiring more and more information will help them to be more in command of their lives — and perhaps the lives of others.) The modern liberal and enlightened state buttresses the idolatry of autonomy — that is, that each person functions independently and pursues his or her own private prosperity without much consideration for the common good. The repudiation of all external authority that characterized the student rebellions of the 1960s added an unprecedented element to this notion of independence. Such freewheeling autonomy often trounces on other people; for example, the students in my husband's classroom who want to "do their own thing" all the time make it extremely difficult for those few who want to learn to pay attention to what Myron is trying to teach.

In great contrast to previous generations, the boomer population spurned the wisdom of their parents and teachers, of the past, and of traditions (in the most positive sense of that word) without any understanding of what that rejection might mean. Now many of those same people are searching for moral authority and for better answers than they found by themselves, for in their parenting these rebellious boomers have relinquished their mentoring vocation and abandoned their children to their own devices and to the destructive formation of the media — and now they don't know what to do with the results.

The consequences of this lack of discipline are immediately apparent in my husband's fifth-grade classroom. So many children are raising themselves, and their parents say that they don't know what to do with them either. These kids keep trying to figure out who they are. They haven't had the kind of family interactions that form for them a "web of reality" by which to comprehend their experiences. Many of the students have no roots — or too many with multiple parents — and their lives are too disrupted to have any meaning or to have a core of character out of which they act. The result is that they are always "bored" and react with anger and disgust to Myron's attempts to help them get to work.

Tonight he came home from school so discouraged about the future of most of the girls in his class. As he was advising one of them to choose something to read, she responded that everything was boring and then added that she wished she was older, like her fifteen-year-old sister who doesn't have to go to school if she doesn't want to. Other students yelled, "Why not?" and she gloated, "Because she's pregnant." The pregnant teenager seems to be blithely unaware of the enormous responsibility of raising a child and expects her mother to do the job — the same mother who has done such a poor job with her own! "Think," Myron moaned, "about what will become of that baby."

None of the teachers at his school can figure out a way to get these constantly entertained children interested in learning since they refuse to engage in anything that takes hard work — but what will become of them when they are older? Will most of the girls in Myron's class be pregnant, too, in five years? They don't know any other story.

MTV perfectly illustrates the amorphous incoherence of these children's lives, for it has no story line or plot nor any development of character, but only strings of unrelated feelings and images endlessly spun out to entertain. Think what violence such incessant amusement does to these children — and what irresponsible neglect their babies will suffer in turn.

Yet many adults in our society do not realize that the very thing they and their children need — trustworthy authorities to mentor them, to nurture their moral character development, to construct with them a web of reality — is what they have with blind prejudice disdained. Unaware of what has been rejected, their children join their parents in chasing after a (false) freedom (from work, school, responsibility) that does violence to others and that actually enslaves them in their narcissistic selves.

The Lust for Power Megatonned

Of course, our world has always been violent. Jesus himself said that the signs of the times (the broken times of our world before he comes back to end evil forever) include wars and rumors of war, nations rising against nations, family members in conflict with each other. All of us lust after power, for what little autonomy we really have for finding and being in control of our own life is usually not enough to satisfy us. Society has known for a long time that power corrupts and that absolute power corrupts absolutely, but in our time the drive for power is expressed with several new twists and more technological intensity.

One new twist is that now power is frequently obtained by accentuating one's role as the "victim." In terrible perversions of the law, perpetrators of violence can escape punishment by claiming that they are the victims of their environment. Sometimes — and certainly this is a strong temptation in churches — power is accumulated in the guise of servanthood.

The ready availability of lethal weapons multiplies monstrously the evil bent of our human nature. For individuals resolved to harm others, for gangs struggling to maintain their turf, and for nations with long histories of ethnic hatred, the usually unrestricted accessibility of munitions gives assent to brutality.

It seems to me that an important arena for teaching our children the secrets of the kingdom of God is in our work to oppose the proliferation of weapons in our world. As parents and Christian communities laboring to effect a ban on land mines, for example, or to end the massive arms sales by the United States,[3] we can help our offspring recognize that to do so is to fulfill Christ's command to love our (global) neighbors in a way that gets to the systemic roots of their suffering.

Meanwhile, however, we also point out the power plays our children make with their siblings, our own temptations to power, the coercions and manipulations practiced by all of us, so that we

3. For more information about the importance and extent of these concerns and about what we as Christians can do about them, contact the Lutheran Peace Fellowship, 1710 Eleventh Avenue, Seattle, WA 98122.

confess, repent of, and transform, by God's grace, our own violent expressions of might or muscle. In our Christian communities, too, we must confront the subtle patterns of domination that prevent us from submitting to one another out of reverence for Christ.

Everyone Can Be a Peacemaker

Not only must we understand the roots of violence in our culture if we want to train our children to resist, prevent, and overcome it, but also we ourselves must realize and help them to know that we truly can cultivate peace in this world of gross injustice, neighborhood brutality, warring nations, and religious conflicts. The issues of violence are so gargantuan that most of us feel helpless to do anything about them. Yet the Scriptures make it clear that we as individuals and as Christian communities can be effective peacemakers. What can we do to bring God's peace to our world?

In the process of preparing for my comprehensive exams, I discovered an outstanding article, "The Christian Understanding of Peace,"[4] by Gerhard Liedke, a Lutheran theologian writing in East Germany before the fall of the Berlin Wall. He emphasizes that for followers of Christ peace is a *process* rather than a state of being and that it must be grounded in the peace of God. The First Testament's accent on *Shalom* is the foundation for the apostle Paul's pronouncement in his letter to the Romans that the kingdom of God abides in justice, peace, and Joy in the Holy Spirit. Thus, when we pray, "thy kingdom come," we envision the kingdom of God as our ultimate aspiration in the practice of peacebuilding.

To build biblical peace, according to Liedke, we must reduce

4. Gerhard Liedke, "Das Christliche Verständnis von Frieden," in *Christen im Streit um den Frieden: Beiträge zu einer neuen Friedensethik* [*Christians in the Debate about Peace: Contributions toward a New Peace Ethic*], ed. Wolfgang Brinkel, Burkhardt Scheffler, and Martin Wächter (Freiburg: Dreisam-Verlag, 1982), pp. 29-35. To my knowledge, this superb piece has not yet been translated into English; I have summarized it more thoroughly in chapter 28 of Marva J. Dawn, *The Hilarity of Community: Romans 12 and How to Be the Church* (Grand Rapids: Eerdmans, 1992).

violence, need, bondage, and anxiety. Jesus conquered these principalities and powers at the cross and empty tomb, and someday
God will ultimately bring about their complete elimination. Meanwhile, if we mean it when we pray "thy will be done" in and
through our lives, we thereby offer ourselves to be God's agents
in the work of diminishing these four dimensions of suffering.

Liedke emphasizes that such work can be undertaken con-
cretely at all levels — with individuals, in larger groups, globally.
Modifying his list slightly, we can elaborate a chart to ponder how
every single one of us can contribute effectively to the process of
peace.

| | Reduction of | | | |
	Violence	Need	Bondage	Anxiety
with individuals				
in small groups				
in large groups				
in the local church				
in the local community				
in the state				
in the nation				
in the global Church				
in the world				

As long as we don't minimize one dimension at the expense
of another, we actually contribute to progress toward peace by
reducing any one of these components at any level. How hopeful
and empowering it is to see that each of us, as members of the
Christian community, can amplify peace in significant ways!

The chart above suggests all kinds of possibilities, provides
great motivation, and thereby inspires hope. The Christian community can be a significant force in building peace in the world!
Because we know the truth of God's gracious gift of peace, EVERY
CHRISTIAN can reduce violence, need, bondage, and anxiety.

We can teach our children that when they respond to a hateful
remark at school with a gentle answer they are minimizing *violence*

between individuals and thereby contributing to global peace. When they answer their teacher courteously instead of rudely they build peace — and learn habits that will continue to multiply good by snowballing kindness. Some schools train students to be "peer counselors," who serve as agents of reconciliation with small groups; similarly, parents can negotiate conflict resolution on the job or in congregational arguments. Some people are certainly called to be mediators to decrease violence on a worldwide scale, but let us not allow such large contributions to eclipse the fact that every individual effort to reduce any sort of violence on any level contributes to the calming of the world as a whole.

One example of this is the work of my friend Susan, who frequently goes to areas of conflict to serve as a doctor. She has ministered in Sudan, Somalia, Rwanda, and Sarajevo, and in each place she has recognized that more important than her medical work is the spirit in which she performs it, because she is constantly helping to reduce the hostility of the persons she treats. Her involvement helps us to see that these dimensions which must be minimized at all levels are inextricably related to each other, for violence is often the result of inadequate food or medicine. In many of the ethnic struggles of our world, brutality arises because each side in the struggle has a legitimate need for a home.

In Chapter 9 we discussed ways for us as families and as Christian communities to assist in reducing *need* by our monetary contributions to agencies that provide homes or material goods. We can engage our children in actively minimizing need when we work together with them in soup kitchens, take groceries to food banks, stay overnight to help at a homeless shelter, or pound nails with Habitat for Humanity. To get at the systemic sources of these needs we must vote for legislation to combat poverty, question the use of government funds for disproportionate military spending, or "live more simply so that others may simply live." Our children can write letters with us to government officials as part of Bread for the World's annual "Offering of Letters" dealing with structural issues of poverty.

By means of our family and congregational discussions, we can nurture in our children an awareness of the many kinds of *bondage* under which people suffer in our society or around the

211

world and look together for ways to deliver people from those captivities. The legal system in the United States unfairly imprisons many who are poor and unequally incarcerates minorities. We can write to prisoners or work for Prison Fellowship.[5] News journals can help us become aware of the political prisoners of various totalitarian states. We also want our children to recognize, however, that our friends and neighbors and enemies need to be delivered from the bondages of fear or loneliness, the slavery of ideological delusions and narcissistic self-absorption, the jails of self-hatred and rootlessness, the prisons of despair and meaninglessness.

Our children can also participate in freeing others from the many kinds of *anxieties* that plague various levels of our society. Helping one of their schoolmates in a subject that is too hard or offering to tutor someone who has trouble reading can be a way to build peace in the world — especially because lack of education contributes greatly to poverty and violence in our society. Some congregations offer study programs, homework supervision, or tutoring projects in which followers of Jesus of all ages can assist. Activities such as shoveling snow or putting up storm windows for disabled or senior citizens free those people from anxieties. We can send cards to people under stress to remind them of our concern; we can go out of our way to speak a kind word to someone in a difficult leadership position. As individuals and as congregations, we must pray for governmental leaders and world rulers. These are some of the ways in which our families and Christian communities can serve to ameliorate anxiety and thereby build world peace.

It is important for cultivating peace that we continually help our children — and the society around us — to see the interrelations of violence, need, bondage, and anxiety. The downfall of the U.S.S.R. demonstrated that nations cannot massively invest in military weaponry and also maintain necessary infrastructures of transportation and food production systems. The United States must be forced to realize that our society horrendously abets the

5. For more information, contact Prison Fellowship, P.O. Box 17500, Washington, DC 20041-0500; telephone 1-800-497-0122.

world's violence with our production and selling of weapons and, meanwhile, that we contribute abhorrently to the deaths by starvation and malnutrition and related illnesses of 40,000 persons every day by our own gluttony and by our government's cuts in food aid and economic development assistance.

As the hymn at the head of this chapter proclaims, God is the one who teaches us peacemaking — through the model of Christ and the entire biblical concept of *Shalom*. We need to be "lifted above all thought of vengeance or envy or hate" if we are going to be agents creating God's *Shalom*. I especially appreciate this hymn because it emphasizes that we work at peacemaking in all the avenues of our lives — "in church and home, in school and hall beneath Capitol dome, in shop and industry, city and farm" — by what we do as well as by what we do not do, living in order to "cause no one harm." We pray as we sing this song that God would "fill all our heart [that is, our whole being] with the pow'r of shalom, [so that everyone everywhere can be] living together, the whole world our home." As we learned in the previous chapter, to pray these prayers genuinely involves us in bringing about their fulfillment — so that we are thereby submissive to God's work through us so that these peacemaking purposes of God can be accomplished in all that we are and say and do.

Each day as God's agents we and our children can seize many opportunities to contribute to reducing violence, need, bondage, and anxiety on various levels of our world. Even though it might seem that our efforts are only little squares on the chart above, we can trust that these labors are not in vain in the Lord. Ultimately, we know that God himself will be successful in bringing the world to *Shalom*, to wholeness — and therefore we possess enduring hope as we participate in God's work by pursuing our own unique parts of the whole, whatever forms our service might take. May this chapter stimulate all of us to be more generous in finding ways to minimize those factors that keep our world from the peace God intends.

Furthermore, as our families become more involved in "things that make for peace," our children learn that every Christian in the community can find places on the chart to be involved in the process. Consequently, all of us can encourage others around us to become more active in the ministry of peacebuilding. Then, because all Christians throughout the world are contributing to reducing violence, need, bondage, and anxiety at many levels, our local communities can more richly envision the significance and power of the whole. God is at work through each of us — and all of us together — to build peace! Because God has called us to *Shalom,* our children and all the other members of the Christian community can expend every possible effort to bring wholeness to all persons in the world.

The Christian Community as a Place of Safety

Our efforts must begin with making the Christian community a genuine place of safety. A few weeks ago in a workshop, in response to my comment that all of us in our churches should be talking to the young people in our midst to help them feel loved, one participant said, "But we train our children not to talk to strangers."

What a dilemma, for, as we shall see in the next chapter, the very lack of social intimacy causes much of the sexual immorality of our culture as well as some of the violence. Mothers in former generations trained their children to be courteous to strangers; now the violence of the world forces parents to imbue their children with wariness and the skill to flee. Can the Christian community be a safe place where children can freely talk to adults, find mentors, relate openly, play securely?

The flurry of cases of sexual molestation in churches makes many parents afraid. But the solution is not to back off from genuine community; it is instead to love more with all the kinds of love to be explored in the next chapter. It is to talk together to prevent violence, to rebuke and admonish, to take decisive action when community safety is breached.

To make the Christian community a place where children can flourish, basking in the love of all the members, takes time and effort on the part of all of us. I was thrilled last Wednesday when little Ebony finally talked to me after almost two years of greeting her. That same evening one of the teenagers talked to Myron and me at length about her involvement in a school play. By our care

214

for one another in the community we can build our children's security and thereby prevent violence.

As Christians, too, let us find ways to lead in taking back neighborhoods that are being destroyed by violence. Some church groups help rehabilitate run-down tenements, build neighborhood parks, or sponsor area play programs. We can serve as sports coaches, Scout troop leaders, 4-H advisers, study group hosts, and so forth to offer kids positive alternatives to gang warfare.

The authentic Christian community knows the story of God's loving care, of God's action in Christ to defeat violence forever. This Word enables us and our children truly to find ourselves and then to build peace by giving ourselves first to God and then to others. Instead of clamoring for power, we dwell in, and are continually trained by, a community that practices vulnerability, consensus, and authentic servanthood after the model of Jesus. Instead of a greedy grasping for more autonomy to satisfy our *Sehnsucht,* we turn from idolizing independence to find in the community of God's people the intensive mentoring care all of us need, the genuine home we all most desperately want, and the possibilities we all seek for building peace in the world.

For further reflection, discussion, transformation, and practice:

1. In what ways does my violence get vented? Are there any actions or words of anger for which I ought to apologize to my children or spouse? How could we as a family engage in healing conversation about the various kinds of violence we express toward each other?

2. How do the media increase our violence? What could we do as a family to lessen this destructive effect of media on our attitudes and lives?

3. How do the media dull us to the violence of our world? How are our perceptions muddled by the overkill of television? What can we do to offset the L.I.A.R. syndrome with regard to working against the violence in our neighborhoods? in the world?

4. How does my personal push for autonomy produce violence? How does my need for power? How could I learn the vulnerability, willingness to suffer, and compassion of Jesus instead?

5. What are we doing to strive after peace and wholeness for our neighbors? What is my family doing to help build peace in the world? What spaces in the chart on page 210 can I and members of my family fill? What can our congregation do?

6. What connections have we observed between the oppression of the poor, bondage, anxiety, and violence in the Scriptures? in the modern world?

7. Is our Christian community a place of safety? Do children feel loved and cared for in our midst? Do we practice nonviolence in our relationships with each other?

CHAPTER 13

"Four Weddings and a Funeral"

For the beauty of the earth,
for the glory of the skies,
for the love which from our birth
over and around us lies,
Lord of all, to you we raise this
our hymn of grateful praise. . . .

For the joy of human love,
brother, sister, parent, child,
friends on earth, and friends above,
pleasures pure and undefiled.
Lord of all, to you we raise this
our hymn of grateful praise.

For your church, that evermore
lifts its holy hands above,
off'ring up on ev'ry shore
its pure sacrifice of love,
Lord of all, to you we raise this
our hymn of grateful praise.

Folliott Sandford Pierpoint (1864), alt.
Tune: Dix, Konrad Kocher (1838)

The violence discussed in the previous chapter is, of course, inextricably connected to fallen humanity's lack of love. That is obvious to Christians because we are taught to be different from the world in loving our enemies instead of hating them or wreaking vengeance on them. More subtly, however, we must recognize the many forces in U.S. society that do violence to children by causing so many of them to have to grow up without genuine love in their homes. Many of these forces are directly or indirectly related to media consumption. In addition, the most devastating aspect of media consumption is the distorted understanding of genital intimacy it creates for our offspring.

In this chapter we will consider how to raise children with godly insights into, and godly attitudes toward, their sexuality. I reserved this topic for last because all the other societal issues considered in this second part of the book are connected to this one. A culture afflicted with the idolatry of ease (as considered in Chapter 8) wants love that doesn't require any sacrifice. A society of consumerism (Chapter 9) will inevitably make genital union a consumerist recreation. This attitude is propounded, legitimized, and exploited by the media and aggravated by the proliferation of technology, which decreases skills for intimacy (Chapters 10 and 11). Violence, including sexual violence, against many children (Chapter 12) aggravates their sexual confusion and leads in turn to their violence against others.

Raising our children for sexual godliness requires careful counteraction of these destructive forces and deliberate training in the positive design of God for sexuality, in opposition to the constant false messages of the society around us. Since I have written an entire book to equip parents and pastors with tools for training young people in a godly understanding of their sexuality,[1] my main goal here is to help the Church recognize the urgency of the task and the possibility of its fulfillment if we really are a community that provides alternatives to the world around us by our "pure sacrifice of love" (as suggested in the hymn above).

We have to recognize how urgently our children need training

---

1. See Marva J. Dawn, *Sexual Character: Beyond Technique to Intimacy* (Grand Rapids: Eerdmans, 1993).

for understanding their sexuality according to God's design. They are growing up in a society in which one out of three babies are born to single moms! As documented in recent journal reports on DNA testing, medical studies are showing that up to 10 percent of all men who think they are the fathers of their children really aren't. Do we realize the disaster zone the Church's children inhabit concerning attitudes toward covenant faithfulness in sexual expression and toward family nurturing of offspring?

The Violence of Media for Our Understanding of Love

Because this book's ultimate purpose in these illustrations of an alternative Christian lifestyle is to build in our children positive character for all their behavioral choices, including their sexual choices, we must deliberately address the issues of the music to which they listen and the television programs and movies they view (and now all the sexually oriented possibilities of computer connections and other accesses to pornographic materials) that bombard them constantly with ungodly ideas about intimacy. Even programming that is not sexually explicit contributes indirectly to sexual problems, because media consumption trains young people in, and increases their demand for, instant gratification.

How can we equip our children with wisdom as preventive medicine, so that they discriminate, so that they choose carefully what they watch and listen to, so that they reject suggestions that contradict God's designs? Because the media in our culture so explicitly promote sexual values with which God's people should disagree, we must become more intentional than ever before to avoid them, discount them, contradict them, and, most important, demonstrate that God's designs are ultimately more satisfying, more truthful to who we are as human beings.

I used to speak very mildly about the dangers of television — until I started doing workshops with teenagers and saw how profoundly it affects their sexual attitudes (and until the book *Endangered Minds* demonstrated scientifically the negative effects of television viewing on human brains). How can we as a Christian family of faith tolerate such polluting of our children's lives? My theme in this book is intentionality, deliberate alternativeness. If we want to raise children for godly sexual behavior, then we must consciously form understandings and attitudes when they are young so that they have the strength of character to choose such behavior when they are older. We must diligently reject the bombardment of the media's immorality, the sexual looseness in fashion, the glib way that people talk about "sex."

In Chapter 10 I gave the example of a night in Iowa when seven out of eight shows during prime time involved blatantly immoral sexual or violent themes. I cannot imagine that parents can presume that their children could watch such programs and wind up with Christian values for their sexuality. When I think of the amount of promiscuity, adultery, fornication, flimsy clothing or downright nakedness, cheating, and abuse that is shown on television, I cannot imagine owning one in a house where there are children (or adults).

Perhaps you think I overreact. Perhaps I do. My goal is simply to ask you to think about it — and act on what you know. You may disagree with me in the end; you may think that your children only watch the Disney or Discovery channels (and are those always moral?) when they are by themselves; you may decide that the standard fare is not destructive of their faithful understanding of their sexuality — but I want to make sure that you have thought about it.

When I conduct workshops with Christian youth on sexuality, *most* of them tell me that they have never heard before what I tell them about biblical perspectives on genital involvement. "Not from your parents, or your pastor, or your youth leader, or your Sunday school teacher?" I always ask them. "No," they reply, "never from anyone." If they are bombarded by the media hundreds of times a day with bad ideas about sexuality, how much will it take for us to equip them with God's ideas?

This chapter takes its title from the movie "Four Weddings and a Funeral," very popular a few years ago, which illustrates thoroughly my point that media representations these days are extraordinarily destructive for our children's understanding of genital sexual involvement and of love — perhaps all the more destructive because so many people think of it simply as a harmless romantic comedy.

In the film, the lead characters, Charles and Carrie, meet at a wedding, briefly converse, and that evening wind up "sleeping together" — after which Carrie abruptly leaves and goes back across the ocean. To Charles's great surprise they meet again at another wedding and engage in sexual intimacies again, but Carrie becomes engaged to a rich elderly Scotsman. She asks Charles to help her pick out her wedding gown, at which time she talks about all the presents she will receive. In one scene Charles and Carrie discuss the number of persons with whom they have had sexual intercourse — and Charles is embarrassed because Carrie's list is enormously longer than his. At her wedding Carrie makes a speech telling other suitors to stick around, but Charles eventually figures he can't stay alone the rest of his life, so he makes plans to marry a woman who has appeared, chasing him, at regular intervals throughout the film. On their wedding day Carrie shows up again, announces that she is divorced, and, of course, throws Charles into turmoil. His hearing-impaired brother interrupts the ceremony at the altar on his behalf, Charles confesses that he really loves someone else, and his bride closes the scene by clobbering him. The movie ends "happily ever after" because Carrie shows up at Charles's door, and, while getting soaked in the pouring rain, they promise never to marry so that they can always love each other. Final photographic snapshots show the weddings of most of the rest of the main characters in the film and close on a picture of Carrie and Charles with their infant child, though, of course, there has been no wedding for them.

What kind of love is this? Charles and Carrie know hardly anything about each other, except that Carrie has had an extremely active "sex" life. Carrie seduces, cheats, marries only to acquire wealth, and doesn't let Charles know she is divorced until she announces it at his wedding. What kind of person can she be? But the film suggests rather strongly (as do the comments on the video box that I checked to rediscover the characters' names) that this truly is love.

The movie is hilariously funny; people all around me in the theater were laughing uproariously. I saw the film because a friend recommended it highly for its comedy, and I did laugh at most of the jokes about the various things that can go wrong with weddings. But I felt physically sick afterward because of the grotesque picture of love it gave all the young people in the audience. Are we so naive as not to recognize that a steady diet of this kind of "love" — without any contradiction or analysis from us — forms our children with really impaired ideas about genital sexuality and faithful intimacy?

The Blatancy of "Sex"

Furthermore, media representations are largely to blame for our century's loss of sweetness and genuine social intimacy in nongenital relationships with "brother, sister, parent, child, friends below, and friends above" (as the hymn above names some of the possibilities). Both psychologists and sociologists have reported the changes from the nineteenth century when people in the United States enjoyed many expressions of physical closeness. Siblings or friends could sleep in the same bed, dance together, embrace, kiss, or hold hands without necessarily seeing anything erotic or morally troubling about it. Friendship before television was both heartier and less fearful, exuberantly and innocently expressed.

Of course there were exceptions, but do we realize how much things have changed in the media? Do we just accept it blithely that fornication is publicly displayed? You might not like it that I use the word *fornication,* but I find it terribly ironic that we euphemize the offense and meanwhile continue to display it all the more blatantly. The recent winner of nine Oscars, "The English Patient," is advertised as the new "Lawrence of Arabia," as a great love story in epic proportions — but the film seemed to delight in showing nudity straight on, with breast close-ups during the love scenes.[2] Young people seem to be blasé about viewing these scenes,

2. This movie disturbed me even more because it celebrates a postmodern rejection of boundaries, such as Count Laszlo's attitude, "My [adulterous] love reigns supreme, so I don't care how many people die if I sell these maps to the Germans," or nurse Hana's achieving freedom from her burden of loved ones dying in the war by acceding to the Count's request for euthanasia. For a more thorough analysis of the film's postmodernism, see David Aaron Murray, "The English Patient Plays Casablanca," *First Things* 73 (May 1997): 10-12.

but when I work with them in discussions about godly sexuality they confess that viewing such scenes generates worry that they won't find a real-life partner as exciting, that it causes them to be overanxious to be genitally involved, or that it functions as pornography in encouraging them to view the opposite gender as an object or "commodity."

What are we allowing to happen to the Church's children when this blatancy of "sex" is a steady diet in our culture, when they are continuously fed images and ideas harmful for their souls and spirits and minds and bodies? I have met too many young people — the majority of them — who have no idea how beautiful genital union can be when it is reserved as a gift solely for one's spouse within the protection of God's design for committed, covenantal, permanent marriage. I weep for their loss, and I rage that churches fail so miserably to give them better ideas. I can't stand it that one young relative talks about "living together" as if it were just fine, and I grieve that I have been completely unsuccessful in trying to show her how trustworthy marriage is when spouses have been faithful with their whole being both before and after marriage.

What can we do? First we must develop the true social intimacy of genuine community in our churches. Then we must be specific about the Joy of God's design for sexuality. Throughout, we must resist the flagrant displays of "sex" in the media and firmly reject the media's lies about genital intimacy.

The Technological Destruction of Intimacy

All the lusts aroused by the devastating shamelessness of "sex" in the media are immensely aggravated by the desperation for social intimacy that characterizes our society. And that desperation is there because the development of our technological milieu has had a destructive effect on the social fabric in our time and has greatly reduced our skills for intimacy.[3] Jacques Ellul, the prophetic French

3. These themes are expanded in both Marva J. Dawn, *Truly the Community: Romans 12 and How to Be the Church* (former title: *The Hilarity of Community*; Grand Rapids: Eerdmans, 1992), and Dawn, *Sexual Character*.

sociologist/Christian witness, made it clear throughout his fifty-year career that the rise of the technological milieu was destroying our intimacy in these ways.[4] Furthermore, he brilliantly foresaw that one of the dangers of escalating technology and decreasing skills of intimacy is that we reverse the poles and technologize our intimacy (parents saying goodnight over the intercom instead of tucking children in, as one student reported was the family practice) and make intimate our technology (as exemplified in such ads as "reach out and touch someone," which deceives us into thinking that the telephone is as good as face-to-face conversation).

Our social fabric has changed drastically because we no longer need each other to work or play. Our tools and toys pull us away from each other. One person can put the dishes in the dishwasher, play chess with the computer, watch television, or listen to a Walkman. Auto- and snow-mobiles let us travel solo for work and sport; the car-pool lanes in Portland require only two people in a car for their use, and usually when I go to the doctor my driver and I (my visual handicaps prevent driving) are the only people in the lane. First telephones and then e-mail and faxes replaced face-to-face conversations. My friend who is a librarian doesn't talk with people anymore; she sits in her cubicle and sends messages over the modem. Airplanes and global businesses make it possible for us to fly thousands of miles away from our families and friends to pursue wealth that can acquire more technological toys; we have thousands of global acquaintances, but few really deep relationships. We could pile up an entire world wide web of examples of ways in which our technological milieu decreases the possibility for genuine vulnerability, close companionship, trusted accountability, and sacrificial intimacy.

Meanwhile all our tools and toys speed up the pace of life,

4. See especially Jacques Ellul, *The New Demons*, trans. C. Edward Hopkin (New York: Seabury Press, 1975); *The Technological Bluff*, trans. Joyce Main Hanks (Grand Rapids: Eerdmans, 1990); *The Technological Society*, trans. John Wilkinson (New York: Vintage Books, 1964); and *The Technological System*, trans. Joachim Neugroschel (New York: Continuum, 1980). For an introduction to his vast corpus, see *Sources and Trajectories: Eight Early Articles by Jacques Ellul That Set the Stage*, trans. and commentary by Marva J. Dawn (Grand Rapids: Eerdmans, 1997).

leaving us less time for the activities that create intimacy. According to a report by Fortino & Associates, U.S. citizens daily spend on average only about four or five minutes conversing with their spouse and about thirty seconds talking with their children![5] Probably you struggle in your family to create a schedule in which you can eat meals together or enjoy hobbies, sports, or vacations with your children and spouse. Congregational members have less and less time to build community with each other.

Because of these reductions in time and social fabric for intimacy, we lack the opportunity to develop basic skills. Recently I spoke at a youth convocation in Iowa where the teenagers agreed that Walkmans and other technological toys and tools hinder their development of skills for conversation — and they recognized that they felt deprived of family communication. College students at several institutions have told me that they have seen persons who e-mail each other in the same computer lab, but never talk to one another directly.

Don't misunderstand: computers and Walkmans can be very helpful tools in themselves. The problem is when they function as principalities and powers and overstep their bounds. When we use them to ameliorate our tasks (as this computer helps me write books more easily), we must also recognize that they readily begin to destroy our humanity (as when I am so engrossed that I don't immediately greet my husband coming home from school and listen to his frustrations).

The Desperation for Genuine Intimacy

All of this deprivation has led to our society's mad enslavement to the idolatry that confuses genital intimacy with the social intimacy for which persons truly long and, more deeply still, the intimacy with God for which everyone most profoundly yearns. The word *home* summarizes best all the various goals we have considered in these chapters of Part Two; people in our culture

---

5. Quentin J. Schultze, *Winning Your Kids Back from the Media* (Downers Grove, IL: InterVarsity Press, 1994), p. 43.

scramble unsuccessfully to relieve the haunting restlessness of *Sehnsucht* and hope desperately someday to feel at home. That burning longing for the other world for which we were made (as discussed in Chapter 2) is confused and provoked in our culture because so many persons have not experienced loving homes, familial support, genuine social closeness, affectionate companionship. Too many have not been the beloved of anyone who was totally committed to them as parent, spouse, friend — much less have they known that they are the beloved of God.

Besides our technological milieu, the most severe contributors to this lack of true intimacy are the idolatries discussed in the other chapters of the second part of this book. Many people betray their commitments to family and friends in the fruitless endeavor to avoid suffering. Parents find it easier to set their children in front of a television set than to read them stories or spend time playing games with them. The drive to accumulate possessions or status or wealth often prohibits lap time or conversation time with children or spouse. Diversionary amusements easily substitute for the tedium of answering a child's constant questions. Narcissistic concern about one's own rights effaces the responsibility for sacrificial attention.

Growing up and living in a milieu saturated with these idolatries, a considerable proportion of citizens in the United States are starved for genuine social closeness. This yearning for close relationships with family and friends becomes a leading factor in the rife sexual immorality of our times and, in a never-ending spiral, leads to the ridiculous overkill that instantly brands the innocent hugs and kisses of little children as sexual harassment. The pain of love-starved youngsters escalates even more as our society deprives them of the social intimacies of touch and hugs.

Since the media so lopsidedly displays genital involvement as the exclusive technique for acquiring intimacy, young people in particular who are famished for true love know no other means besides sexual intercourse as they attempt in vain to assuage their unquenchable *Sehnsucht*. Sadly, their genital unions taken out of the context of God's design are never totally gratifying, lead only to mistrust and deeper feelings of insecurity, and thus merely escalate their insatiable craving for love.

226

The True Love of God and of the Christian Community

That profound yearning for love was planted in each of us by the God who cherishes us utterly and desires by our impoverishment to woo us to himself. Beginning with Abraham, God has called a people to incarnate his love for the world through the many kinds of love that the community is called to practice responsibly and joyfully for the sake of the neighbor. Since part of the problem is that the English language uses only one word for *love,* though there are many different kinds, let us examine the various Greek terms for love to emphasize all the ways that true love can enable the Christian community to counteract our society's bad ideas about sexuality.

Most important of all is *agapé* — that intelligent, purposeful love directed to the needs of the other — which only God can bestow perfectly, but which his people can learn from God and pass on to others. If our Christian communities are truly characterized by *agapé,* we will enfold our children in constant caring that helps them know that they are the beloved both of God and of the entire congregation in which they are a cherished part. We will also act decisively to keep them from the genital confusions and pollutions of the world around them.

Philia, or friendship love, is almost becoming a lost art in our technological milieu. The ancient Greek philosophers praised it exceedingly and esteemed it as the highest form of love. Certainly in our culture there is immense need to recover its virtue and grace. *Philia* is based on mutual concerns, interests, and goals. Friends are drawn together by common hobbies, pursuits, and passions. My best friends are those with whom I can share theological conversations, music performances or practices, concern for the poor, and the work of God's kingdom. In the Church we can demonstrate to our children that friendship can trustworthily cross gender lines, that friendship in the Lord knits us in lifelong — in fact, eternal — companionship, that such relationships are deeper because we share the highest goal of serving God together. Some of my good friends, to whom I'm drawn for other reasons, do not yet know the love of God. I pray that my love and the love of the Christian community can be means by which these persons discover the Joys of following Christ.

I remember vividly many occasions of interactions between my parents and their best friends when I was a child. Many of these friends were colleagues in the profession of teaching at Lutheran schools, and some of those friendships have lasted more than fifty years. One couple were members of the congregation my parents served; they worked together with my parents on many projects and often had deep discussions about mutual concerns. Every summer they rented a lakeside cabin for a week, and our family was always invited to spend a day there with them, during which we shared great fun and wonderful memory-creating escapades.

Now I realize that these friendships were so deep because they partook of the character of love expressed by two other Greek words, *philostorgé* and *philadelphia*.[6] The first term is built from *philia* (friendship love) and *storgé*, which means family love, especially the kind of connection between a mother and her children; this word especially emphasizes the deep affection that members of the Christian community share with each other and express to each other. The second combines *philia* with *adelphos* or "brother," so it connotes brotherly or sisterly companionship. Friendships in the Church blend not only our common passions but also our kinship in Christ. We are family together because we are mutually the children of God.

Agapé, philia, storgé, philadelphia, philostorgé — these five kinds of love are severely lacking in our technicized, media-bombarded, overly aroused, fast-paced, broken-familied, homeless society. What an irresistible gift we give our children if we enfold them in all these lasting loves in our homes and in the family of the Church, so that they can reserve *eros*, genital love, for the one person to whom they become committed in a lifelong, totally intimate marriage. Moreover, in the Christian community we teach them and model that the highest role of genital union is to be a sign of the intimate faithfulness of Christ's love for his bride, the Church; thus Christian marriage symbolizes the ultimate fulfillment of our deep yearning for an even higher love.

---

6. These two Greek words, along with *agapé*, occur in verses 9 and 10 of Paul's description of the Christian community in Romans 12. For further explication, see Dawn, *Truly the Community*, pp. 139-76.

Furthermore, we give our children a great gift when we train them in the way of selfless love, grounded in the freedom of grace. As the Christian community imparts to them and nourishes in them purposefully directed love that does not require return *(agapé)*, brotherly/sisterly love *(philadelphia)*, and friendship-family love *(philostorgé)*, we empower them to reach out to the world with the true intimacy that so many long for. Because the Church dwells in the love of God, our children can be agents of love and care in a desperate world.

Nurturing Children for Sexual Character

Because the age at which children are becoming genitally active is getting lower and lower, because the percentage of teen pregnancies continues to escalate, because marriages continue to fail at a phenomenal rate, and, most important, because God has much better ideas about genital union than the world teaches, members of the Christian community must be extraordinarily specific in training their children to understand the beauty and genuine fulfillment of following God's design for genital involvement. This must be done in a positive way, explicitly emphasizing that we speak not to spoil their fun, but to deepen the true and lasting enjoyment that can be had only within a permanent commitment of marriage union.

If, as has been emphasized throughout this book, we expect our children's understanding of their lives, including their sexuality, to be different from that of the world around them, then we cannot suddenly commence teaching them when they are preteens about holding alternative values. If we want to nourish in them godly character and the desire to choose God's will over the allures of the world, it is critical that we begin when they are small to invite them into the delight of being different.

They are different, not because they are better, but because they live as citizens of the kingdom of God as a result of his forgiveness and grace. Whereas the public school "self-esteem" programs teach young people that they are special by encouraging them to look inward, we teach them their uniqueness by helping them to look upward to God's call and then outward in mission.

Having been set free by the gracious love of God, they are empowered to spend their lives for the sake of others — embracing friends, neighbors, and enemies with many kinds of love and perhaps someday cherishing a spouse with every kind of love, including unfettered, enfolding, faithful *eros*.

In my book *Sexual Character*, I use the image of a typewriter to talk about God's good design for genital sexuality. Changing the ribbons in my typewriter works best when I follow the manufacturer's instructions, because the builder knows how things are constructed and thus writes appropriate directions; in the same way, when I follow God's commands concerning my sexuality I will experience the deepest pleasure, because God, my Creator, knows how I am made and directs me accordingly. One critic of my book complained that this image is legalistic, but after contemplating her objections I am more than ever convinced that it is just the opposite, for all of God's commandments are gracious and meant for our well-being. For example, we all know that life works best if we don't kill each other, if we don't steal each other's belongings, if we keep a Sabbath day.[7] Similarly, God commands us to reserve genital involvement for our spouse not to spoil our fun, but because sexual union is the most fulfilling if it is experienced within the total protection and trust of a lifelong commitment in marriage. Consequently, we teach our children about God's wonderful designs with gladness, because they are a gift to us. Obeying God's instructions for sexual intercourse leads to our freedom, our deepest pleasure, and our most profound wholeness — that is, we live in the unity of our bodies, souls, minds, and spirits, and we live with unspoiled social relationships as well as with marital fidelity.

When I have led workshops for parents on training their children for sexual faithfulness, invariably some participants ask what to do if they themselves have made bad mistakes of engaging in genital union outside of marriage. I always inquire if they are sorry, and they always answer that if they had known what they

7. If you don't know how wonderfully healing keeping a Sabbath day is, please read Marva J. Dawn, *Keeping the Sabbath Wholly: Ceasing, Resting, Embracing, Feasting* (Grand Rapids: Eerdmans, 1989).

know now about the goodness of God's designs (but usually their churches and parents had failed to tell them) they probably would have chosen differently. That is exactly what their children need to hear. It is powerful for their offspring's positive formation if parents humbly admit that they didn't know enough about what they are telling their children now concerning genital involvement, that as a result they made choices that they profoundly regret, that their deepest wish is for their children to be spared the suffering that resulted, and that they pray fervently for their children to know more about God's designs and thereby be equipped to follow them. Parents who regret their past need not be overwhelmed with guilt and therefore unable to give their children better ideas. Instead, God's forgiveness and the forgiveness of their spouse set them free to confess their mistakes to their children, to say what they regret and why, and to image for the children what they hope for them.

In the face of our own brokenness and our society's contradictions, Christian parents cannot teach all this to their children alone. It requires the entire community for our children to be thoroughly enfolded in God's *agapé*. It takes a whole alternative society in order for young people to reject all the temptations, false messages, deceptions, and idolatries of the world around them. It demands several sets of committed marriages for our children to see the beauty of God's design. Our children need to observe scores of flourishing families and deep friendships, including cross-gender friendships, to recognize the profundity of other kinds of love. It requires numerous tellings by many people for them to claim as their own the biblical blueprint for genital union.

It takes many Christian parents to persuade the local high school to teach abstinence instead of distributing condoms; many churches need to work together to remove from elementary schools the "sex education" programs that are destructive to godly ideas. Our children need careful moral education not only in our homes but also in our congregations to learn the alternative, biblical understanding of their sexuality. They require the support of the entire Christian community to resist the ideas of society in favor of choosing behavior that flows from what they believe.

Quentin Schultze specifically stresses the value of special family activities for creating intimacy and for counteracting the

231

negative effects of media consumption and the technological milieu on the family — board games, vacations, sports, hobbies, food and talk, Christian service projects.[8] I especially recommend multiplying the effects of those activities by participating in *communities* that engage in them. One way is to vacation together at Christian camps that specialize in programs for families.

One camp at which I teach every summer has eight week-long sessions for adults and children jointly, each one focusing on different topics. The days begin with devotions all together, and each meal is prefaced with singing of prayers. Then parents have Bible study with guest lecturers in the morning, while their children are engaged in learning activities under the direction of college-aged counselors. The afternoons are filled with water and field sports, painting or other art or music classes, discussion groups, or special ventures, depending on the gifts of the week's residents. The whole family worships together with other camp guests in the evening, and late-night activities include movies with popcorn, discussions, campfires, concerts, and talent shows. Families can eat all their meals together in the common dining hall or cook their own breakfasts and suppers in cabins with kitchen facilities.[9] I have heard countless stories from people who have attended this camp or others like it concerning ways in which their family bonds have been strengthened, in which their own and their children's faith was nourished, and in which they felt encouraged to pursue the alternative life of the kingdom of God.

Bearing Children and Sexual Union

One essential aspect of our training in the Christian community must be that we reconnect for our children the link, torn apart by the proliferation of contraceptive methods, between sexual inter-

---

8. Schultze, *Winning Your Kids Back from the Media*, pp. 62-67. This book offers very helpful ideas for families to counteract media consumption; it is available in a video curriculum kit from Gospel Films and Video, P.O. Box 455, Muskegon, MI 49443, telephone 1-800-253-0413.

9. For more information on the camp I am describing contact Mt. Carmel Ministries, P.O. Box 579, Alexandria, MN 56308; telephone 320-846-2744.

course and reproduction. That link is important so that our off-spring are kept from ripping sexual union out of its context in the larger responsibility of providing a permanent marriage for the care of their own future children. This connection is also critical for them now as they learn the importance of developing their own character for the habits and skills they will need to raise godly children themselves.

Birth control has changed the questions. In the past, children were received as a gift; the conception of a child was considered the natural — actually God-given — result and purpose of sexual intercourse. Now people ask, "Do we *want* to have a child?" or "Is it convenient?" or "What method will work best to help us avoid conception?" The focus has shifted from an emphasis on the children to a new stress on the choice of the parents. The selfishness inherent in this shift in fundamental questions is indicated by the phenomenal neglect of the topic of pregnancy in many contemporary books on "sex." As Christians we raise the issues not in a negative way, to keep kids out of "sex" by making them afraid of conception, but in a wholistic and authentic way, because the genesis of a child is a holy and beautiful gift that we want our children to take seriously and to prepare for appropriately. In our era of easy abortions, the Church must carefully craft the questions again for people in our society to correlate their warfare for rights with the associated responsibilities.

And, Yes, What about Homosexuality?

Trying to reconnect for our children the nexus of genital union and reproduction forces me, finally, to add a word about homosexuality. I would rather avoid this topic, for, though I have agonized and struggled over and studied this issue more than any other moral topic, I am always uneasy with what I have to say. It is very troubling that the subject has become so volatile in churches, because the volume of discussion generated on the topic is out of all proportion to the amount of reference to it in the Scriptures. Would that our churches spent as much time rooting out materialism and consumerism, violence and the L.I.A.R. syndrome.

Because three superb pieces on the subject already exist,[10] I need only comment briefly here, though I plead with you to read what I say carefully and in its entirety. I believe that the Church has several important contributions to make to the discussions in our society about homosexuality and homosexual behavior.

First of all, the Christian community must sorrowfully say that we profoundly lament all the pain that churches have caused homosexual persons. God's mandates of love forbid the kind of judgmentalism that often characterizes discussions about sexual issues. Congregations must also repent of their double standards — for example, that homosexual behavior has been lambasted whereas divorcing couples or heterosexual couples living together outside of God's design for marriage are not admonished. Moreover, churches frequently make sexual sin the worst offense, whereas the Bible speaks far more often against greed and dishonesty, lovelessness and violence.

Second, we must warmly say that our Christian communities heartily welcome homosexual persons to dwell with us in the grace and forgiveness of God. As churches discuss the issues, both the fundamentalistic opponents of welcoming homosexuals and also some of the gay apologetes themselves argue as if sexual orientation were the foremost characteristic of a person. I have several homosexual friends with whom I have much in common; we have profound discussions and care about each other deeply as fellow Christians. We do not believe that one's sexual orientation is one's complete identity; we do believe that our primary character is our status as the beloved of God, that we are all sinners in his sight, but saints by virtue of Christ's redemption.

Third, we must clearly differentiate between homosexual per-

---

10. The best ethical work is done by New Testament scholar Richard B. Hays in *The Moral Vision of the New Testament: A Contemporary Introduction to New Testament Ethics* (San Francisco: HarperSan Francisco, 1996), pp. 379-406. Thomas E. Schmidt's *Straight and Narrow? Compassion and Clarity in the Homosexuality Debate* (Downers Grove, IL: InterVarsity Press, 1995) calmly, lucidly, and compassionately argues a strong case showing the pro-gay cause to be not only unbiblical and unreasonable, but also socially and medically highly irresponsible. See also J. Isamu Yamamoto, ed., *The Crisis of Homosexuality* (Wheaton, IL: Victor Books, 1990), and Dawn, *Sexual Character*, pp. 91-109.

sons and their behavior. The Scriptures say nothing about homosexual orientation, for, as noted sociologist David Greenberg has thoroughly explicated in Part II of his *The Construction of Homosexuality,* the idea of a permanent homosexual identity is a modern development. As Greenberg explains, this construction is due to a whole host of factors, such as mechanistic understandings of behavior, competitive capitalism, the medicalization of homosexuality, urbanization, bureaucratization, and the loss of communal guidance and friendship intimacy, as described earlier in this chapter. Greenberg concludes that any " 'essences' that structure erotic feelings" are "unstable or subject to environmental influence."[11]

Furthermore, numerous elements of our technological society intensify the development of homosexual identity — hedonism; relaxed attitudes toward divorce, premarital sex, and pornography; radical feminism that rejects heterosexual "consorting with the enemy"; cultural relativism; delegitimation of accepted authority; skepticism about values and beliefs; sociology's concern with self-identity; and gender confusions. In addition, because the typology has become so strong and so strongly positive in our society, many persons who do not belong there place themselves in the category and then, because they act on that choice, it becomes a self-fulfilling prophecy.

Basically, our culture's inability to distinguish between social and genital sexuality, its genital idolatry because of the loss of family/community social supports, and its lack of skills for intimacy have destroyed the ultimate meaning of sexual intercourse. If all these societal factors increase the possibility and tendency toward a homosexual orientation and behavior, what can the Church say to those who insist that they want a stable, permanent, same-gender love relationship that they call a marriage?

I wish I could say that the Church should affirm homosexual "marriages" or lifelong erotic partnerships between committed homosexual persons, for many people are convinced that this would be the "loving" thing to do. However, though Greenberg's

11. See David F. Greenberg, *The Construction of Homosexuality* (Chicago: University of Chicago Press, 1988).

conclusions about the "construction" of homosexual identity don't justify simplistic condemnations of homosexuals or abrogation of their basic human rights and civil liberties, his thorough research does indisputably disclose that nothing in the data authorizes a drastic change of the Church's historical position concerning homosexual acts. Thus, the fourth thing the Christian community must say, using our best exegetical and ethical skills, is that the Bible unreservedly opposes homosexual *behavior* — and so the most genuinely *loving* thing I can do is urge my homosexual friends to abstain from genital involvement.

However, because Greenberg's extensive research has demonstrated the many reasons contributing to the rise of homosexual orientation in our society, I can urge genital abstinence only if I am also willing to be the best friend possible in supporting my homosexual friends in that choice and in combating some of the negative influences that make it difficult. Our Christian communities can encourage sexual restraint only if we are all struggling together for restraint in all aspects of behavior, if we are providing modeling of chastity and faithfulness, if we are enfolding the community's young people in all the kinds of love delineated above. Furthermore, since research shows that an inordinate proportion of homosexual persons, both male and female, lost their fathers before the age of ten through death or divorce, it is essential that the men in our churches be willing to help single mothers by providing the male affection and leadership and modeling that children need.

The Church must say, gently and compassionately, that the Scriptures and almost all of Church history (until the last twenty years) univocally agree that homosexual acts manifest humanity's rebellion against God (see especially Rom. 1:18-32, together with 1 Cor. 6:9-11; 1 Tim. 1:10; Lev. 18:22; 20:13). Genesis 1 and 2 are quite clear that God's ordering involves the creation of male and female and that God's design for genital union finds its fulfillment only between persons of opposite gender and only within a marriage commitment of leaving one's family of origin and cleaving in every aspect of life to one's spouse. Romans 1, however, culminates in 2:1, which reminds us that *all* of us — take note! — are rebels against God in various ways, so in the Christian community we do not single out any particular behaviors as worthy of special condemnation. Instead, we help each other, in the deep family love of Christian friendship, to choose the alternative lifestyle of a biblical understanding of our sexuality, chastity, and fulfillment.

After his extensive study of the pertinent biblical texts and of sound hermeneutical and ethical methods to deal with them, Richard Hays, well-known professor of New Testament at Duke Divinity School, summarizes far better than I could the stance the Church should take toward homosexuals. After affirming the welcoming and supporting that I have already emphasized, he continues as follows:

> (c) *Is it Christianly appropriate for Christians who experience themselves as having a homosexual orientation to continue to participate in same-sex erotic activity?* No. . . . Unless they are able to change their orientation and enter a heterosexual marriage relationship, homosexual Christians should seek to live lives of disciplined sexual abstinence.
>
> Despite the smooth illusions perpetrated by mass culture in the United States, sexual gratification is not a sacred right, and celibacy is not a fate worse than death. . . . Surely it is a matter of some interest for Christian ethics that both Jesus and Paul lived without sexual relationships. It is also worth noting that I Corinthians 7:8-9, 25-40 commends celibacy as an option for everyone, not just for a special caste of ordained leaders. Within the church, we should work diligently to recover the dignity and value of the single life.
>
> My [homosexual] friend Gary, in his final letter to me [before he died of AIDS], wrote urgently of the imperatives of discipleship: *"Are homosexuals to be excluded from the community of faith? Certainly not. But anyone who joins such a community should know that it is a place of transformation, of discipline, of learning, and not merely a place to be comforted or indulged."* The community demands that its members pursue holiness, while it also sustains the challenging process of character formation that is necessary for Jesus' disciples. The church must be a community whose life together provides true friendship,

emotional support, and spiritual formation for everyone who comes within its circle of fellowship. The need for such support is perhaps particularly felt by unmarried people, regardless of their sexual orientation. In this respect, as in so many others, the church can fulfill its vocation only by living as a counter-community in the world.

(d) *Should the church sanction and bless homosexual unions?* No. The church should continue to teach — as it always has — that there are two possible ways for God's human sexual creatures to live well-ordered lives of faithful discipleship: heterosexual marriage and sexual abstinence.

(e) *Does this mean that persons of homosexual orientation are subject to a blanket imposition of celibacy in a way qualitatively different from persons of heterosexual orientation?* Here a nuanced answer must be given. While Paul regarded celibacy as a charisma, he did not therefore suppose that those lacking the charisma were free to indulge their sexual desires outside marriage. Heterosexually oriented persons are also called to abstinence from sex unless they marry (I Cor. 7:8-9). The only difference — admittedly a salient one — in the case of homosexually oriented persons is that they do not have the option of homosexual "marriage." So where does that leave them? It leaves them in precisely the same situation as the heterosexual who would like to marry but cannot find an appropriate partner (and there are many such), summoned to a difficult, costly obedience, while "groaning" for the "redemption of our bodies" (Rom. 8:23). Anyone who does not recognize this as a description of authentic Christian existence has never struggled seriously with the imperatives of the gospel, which challenge and frustrate our "natural" impulses in countless ways.[12]

I have quoted Hays at such length, first of all, because his exegetical groundwork, which is too lengthy to duplicate here, is the most thoroughly faithful to the biblical texts of all the commentators I have read on ethical issues. In addition, his well-founded conclusions are gracious in dealing with the complexity

12. Hays, *The Moral Vision of the New Testament,* pp. 401-2.

of the issues. Furthermore, his call to "authentic Christian existence" summarizes my goal for all of this book — that in every issue of life and work, members of the parallel Christian community would support each other in, and train our children for, the struggles of living against our human nature and for the alternative will of God.

But let us also stress the Joy, for a life of obedience to God's design is certainly ultimately more fulfilling than any sexual rebellion, whether we are homosexual or heterosexual — and I write that as a person who discovered, by God's grace and with the support of many Christian friends, that many long and arduous years of choosing celibacy were worth it, even if they had not culminated in the delight of marrying Myron. We who are God's people invite our children not just to burdens and struggles, but to the bliss of sexual abstinence or faithfulness, chastity no matter what our situation, and fellowship with Christ and our friends in the family of Christian love.

Finally, the Christian community must say that the issues are not yet resolved for all time; we can give no definitive answers to all the issues. Because we are fallible human beings, because Scripture contains so little on the subject, because many homosexual persons claim that they experience grace in the midst of their committed relationships, the Church must always be ready to listen, to consider again, to seek the Holy Spirit's guidance afresh on the matter. Never, however, dare we let the sexual idolatry of our society pull us away from being the alternative people God called us to be.

The Christian Community's Gift to the World

Last year, at a large youth convocation, several hundred young people from the Dakotas, Saskatchewan, Wyoming, and Montana totally surprised me by leaping to their feet and cheering when I suggested that they lead their high schools in making genital abstinence the "in" thing. I urged them to make commitments to each other in their youth groups so that they would have support in standing against the tide of the society around them.

239

What would happen if all the teenagers in the Church pledged to be faithful to God (and to a possible future spouse) with sexual chastity and the correlative development of deep and intimate friendships? What a gift that would be to the world around them!

When I have spoken on sexual issues at public schools, I have discovered that young people in our society are looking for better answers, for lasting relationships, for a lover they can trust, for unbroken family life, for true friendships and genuine intimacy. Let us equip the young people in our Christian communities with a vision of how they can demonstrate to the world the delight of choosing God's alternative. Let us help them realize that they minister to all their fellow members in the community, young and old, when they fulfill their responsibility to be part of the Church's modeling. May we all recognize that God's people respond to a haunting need in the world by resisting society's looseness about "sex" and by demonstrating instead the goodness of a deliberate choice to wait for sexual fulfillment until marriage and the Joy of always dwelling in the many kinds of love God creates for us in the community that incarnates his presence.

For further reflection, discussion, transformation, and practice:

1. In what ways are the violence and sexual confusion of our culture related? How much has that affected the geographical community in which I live? What can I do in my neighborhood to offset these evil influences?

2. What movies or television programs awakened in me an awareness of how destructive society's depictions of "sex" are for the moral formation of my children? What have I done or what could I do to offset those effects?

3. In what ways has the technicization of society affected the intimacy of my family? of my Christian community? What limits do I want to set to counteract these negative effects? What can I do positively to frame the social fabric, to increase the time, and

to develop in our family and Christian community the skills for genuine intimacy?

4. How have I seen the desperation for social intimacy about which this chapter speaks? Which persons whom I know have confused genital intimacy with the social intimacy for which they truly yearned? What were the results? How can I help them sort out that confusion and find the social love they need?

5. How does knowing the many different kinds of love help me to keep *eros* reserved for its rightful place? How can I help my children learn many kinds of love? Does my Christian community incarnate God's love well? Do we care about each other in the Body of Christ with *agapé, philia, storgé, philadelphia,* and *philo-storgé?*

6. How well does my Christian community deal with issues of homosexuality? Do I have any homosexual friends? Have I listened to them well, been compassionate about their pain, studied Scripture with them, discussed their feelings with an open mind? How can I be supportive of them in the choice for sexual abstinence?

7. How well does my Christian community teach its children about God's design for genital sexuality? How could the parents in our congregation work together to support each other in training our children for faithfulness and chastity?

CHAPTER 14

Epilogue:
No, It's Not a Lost Cause If . . .

Dios de la esperanza, danos gozo y paz!
Al mundo en crisis, habla tu verdad.
Dios de la justicia, mándanos tu luz,
luz y esperanza en la oscuridad.
Oremos por la paz,
cantemos de tu amor.
Luchemos por la paz,
fieles a Ti, Señor.

(God of hope, give us joy and peace!
To the world in crisis, speak your truth.
God of justice, send to us your light,
light and hope in the gloom.
Let us pray for peace,
let us sing of your love.
Let us struggle for peace,
faithful to You, Lord.)[1]

1. I have added my own English rendering of the original Spanish to the following English version contained in the hymnal because this rendering is more direct and poignant. The original Spanish emphasizes so well the note of hope in the midst of struggle and gloom that this final chapter intends to sound.

May the God of hope go with us ev'ry day,
filling all our lives with love and joy and peace.
May the God of justice speed us on our way,
bringing light and hope to ev'ry land and race.
Praying, let us work for peace,
singing, share our joy with all.
Working for a world that's new,
faithful when we hear God's call.

Alvin Schutmaat (1984)
Tune: Argentine folk melody

Is it really possible in this post-Christian United States at this time in history to raise children who love God and choose to live according to the beliefs and ethics of the kingdom of God? In the midst of our "gloom" over the issues raised in this book, can we find the "light and hope" of God? Can we work "for a world that is new," especially for the sake of our children? Unequivocally, I believe that we can because Jesus Christ is Lord of his Church and of the cosmos. He has promised that he will always be with us and that no one can snatch us out of the Father's hand. The God of hope is present in our world to prepare us for his kingdom.

But I believe that it takes great effort and deliberate action — praying, singing, struggling — to equip our children to counteract the many societal forces that would pull them away from the One who is, both for them and for us, the Way, the Truth, and the Life. I believe that it takes an entire community, faithful to God's Word, for our children to be immersed in, to welcome, and to respond to the life of discipleship.

We Are Made for Another World

Without doubt, all my descriptions of the Christian community in this book are ideal — but they are not blind optimism, for they summarize the biblical vision of God's calling of a "peculiar" people. All the needs and false goals, the alluring and the repressive techniques of the contemporary society around us remind us that, both as individuals and together as corporate bodies, we must truly be the Church, genuine communities that offer the alternatives of Christ our Head to the world. The vocation of God's people — genuine Church-being — includes recognizing that our deepest longing (our *Sehnsucht*) finds its source in the creation of God, rejecting the world's idolatries in favor of relationship with the one true God and with the Christian community, and offering the presence of God incarnated in our life together in ways that draw our children and our neighbors into hope and a home, a foretaste of the world for which we were all made.

Raising genuinely Christian children in a culture that chooses many idolatries to try to assuage or repress its restless hunger is NOT a lost cause IF the Church stands as an alternative community, incarnating — though imperfectly now — the kingdom of God for which everyone most deeply yearns. We must help our children to understand that the materialistic consumerism, desire for ease, craving for entertainment, passivity, violence, and sexual immorality of the society around us all arise out of vain attempts to quench life's deepest thirst. We must equip them with skills to resist the deceptions, to remember the truth that God alone will satisfy their *Sehnsucht*, to reach out with love to neighbors searching for the Living Water of eternal life.

The Word of that World

As an alternative society, the Christian community draws its ethics from the Hebrew Scriptures and New Testament writings that make up the Bible. Tradition, experience, reason — these all provide hermeneutical lenses that help us to study the Scriptures, and we look to those narratives together as a global community throughout time under the guidance of the Holy Spirit. The Bible paints for us the vision of the other world for which we are made, and in our life together the community indwells that vision and practices it.

Raising genuinely Christian children in a culture that rejects

244

as oppressive any comprehensive meta-narrative is NOT a lost cause IF the Church stands as an alternative community formed by the meta-narrative of God's Revelation to humankind. We must help our children to understand the biblical narrative as the over-arching account of God's universal love for humankind, of his creation, provision for our salvation, and promise of eternal Joy with him. We must equip them with skills for studying that Word and with an eager passion to let it form their life.

The People Who Belong to that World

As a parallel and alternative society, the Christian community is both in the world and not of it. It benefits the world, but its life is characterized by more intimate fellowship, mutual support, accountability, character formation, love for enemies and strangers, ministry, and spiritual growth than our society custo-marily displays. Members of the Christian community do not consider themselves any better than others in the world; they simply know that they are forgiven sinners and that their freedom and empowerment for life come from the grace and indwelling of the triune God.

Raising genuinely Christian children in an individualistic, nar-cissistic culture is NOT a lost cause IF the Church stands as an alternative community, genuinely loving each other with *agapé, philia, storgé, philostorgé,* and *philadelphia* and mutually seeking to form in each other the character of the kingdom of God. We must enfold our children in true community life, in the offering of gifts and service that is our glad response to God's overwhelming grace. We must equip them with a vision for the mission of their own lives and hold them accountable for their part in the tasks of the community.

Worship as a Foretaste of that World

The one thing that the Christian community can do that no one else can do is worship the triune God. Our worship services give a foretaste of the feast to come. They provide an encounter with God and teach us about his character, his interventions in the world, and his will for our lives. They form our character by what we learn and what we sing and offer. They connect us as a community without any barriers and give us a vision for the eternal Church throughout space and time. The beauty and truth and goodness in worship's music, art, proclamation, architecture, fragrance, taste, and movement haunt us with echoes of the eternal, so they whet our appetite for heavenly glory, justice, and righteousness in the presence of God.

Raising genuinely Christian children in an overly entertained and self-centered culture is NOT a lost cause IF the Church stands as an alternative community, worshiping God with integrity, depth, excellence, and faithfulness. We must teach our children what worship is, practice its habits with them, train them in its gestures. We must help them understand that worship is not a matter of our preferences or consumerism, but our offering to God in response to his invitation to come into his presence in Word and sacrament and community.

Pastors and Parents Who Belong to that World

Pastors are not solely responsible for the spiritual life of a congregation, just as parents are not the only ones accountable for the moral formation of their children. The entire Christian community shares in the task of nurturing our offspring; every member of the congregation is called to participate in the fostering of Christian growth. It is critical, however, that pastors and parents themselves be spiritually growing in order to fulfill their essential vocations in the lives of the Church's children. *The* most important gift that pastors and parents give to the community's youngsters is their modeling of a disciplined, joyous, fervent relationship with God.

Raising genuinely Christian children in a culture lacking pastoral and parental care and discipline is NOT a lost cause IF the Church stands as an alternative community, equipping all the members to assist in the nurturing of children and supporting the pastors and parents in their specific roles. As spiritual and biological parents, we must help our children know that the most important thing in life is their relationship with God and must faithfully teach them how to pray, study, worship, and obey. We must equip our offspring with skills by which to live as if they were already dwelling in the world for which they were created.

The Ethics of that World

The moral guidelines of the Christian community are formed by the Revelation of God and followed by a people committed to being *in* the world to serve it, but not *of* it to follow its idolatries. In a culture grasping for ease and comfort we are willing to suffer for the sake of our neighbor and the purposes of God. In a culture amassing possessions and endlessly consuming not only things but people, we are called to generosity and selflessness, vulnerability and powerlessness. In a culture awash in entertainments that dehumanize, tempt, stultify, overload with useless information, brainwash, and form people to be greedy, violent, immoral, and unresponsive, we search for wisdom and truth, for beauty and goodness. In a culture overarmed and underloved, we pass on the *agapé* of God. In a culture rife with uncovenanted *eros,* we choose chastity and faithfulness, the design of God for true love.

Raising genuinely Christian children in a culture that chooses many idolatries to try to assuage or to repress its restless hunger is NOT a lost cause IF the Church stands as an alternative community with the ethics of the kingdom of God, formed by the modeling of Jesus in the freedom created by his work of salvation on our behalf, and empowered by the Holy Spirit of promise. We must help our children see that the choice to live as God's people is the most fulfilling and Joy-full option. We must enfold them in an entire community making that same choice so that they are supported in the difficulty and disciplines of being the parallel society.

247

Children Who Belong to that World

And what does it mean for the children growing up in the alternative, parallel community, which incarnates, though imperfectly now, the kingdom of God for which everyone most deeply yearns? Jesus tells us most clearly when he says,

> Blessed are the poor in spirit, for theirs is the kingdom of heaven.
> Blessed are those who mourn, for they will be comforted.
> Blessed are the meek, for they will inherit the earth.
> Blessed are those who hunger and thirst for righteousness, for they will be filled.
> Blessed are the merciful, for they will receive mercy.
> Blessed are the pure in heart, for they will see God.
> Blessed are the peacemakers, for they will be called children of God.
> Blessed are those who are persecuted for righteousness' sake, for theirs is the kingdom of heaven. (Matt. 5:3-10)

How blessed it is for our children who delight in this description of their discipleship, who trust God to form them in this way, who are yielded to God's mighty work in and through their lives!

Raising genuinely Christian children in a post-Christian culture is NOT a lost cause IF the Church stands as an alternative community, alert to the perils of the times and place in which we now live and awake to the presence of God in our midst to form us as his beloved people. From a human perspective the genuine moral formation of children might seem like a lost cause these days, but we in the parallel society know that our Savior Jesus Christ, who has triumphed over the principalities and powers that would lead our children astray, is Lord of the cosmos and the Head of his Body, the Church!

248

For further reflection, discussion, transformation, and practice:

1. What is the most important thing I have learned from this book? How has it changed my life or how have I begun to put it into practice?

2. What is the most important thing I have learned for the sake of the Christian community to which I belong? How have I helped my community to know it and/or live it?

3. What is the most important thing I have learned in this book for the sake of my children? How have I talked with them about it or tried to help them understand it and live it?

4. What does it mean to me now that the Christian community is an alternative society? How does that affect my daily life? my worship life? my vocation? my family life?

5. How can I use what I have learned in this book to help other Christian parents in my community? How do I need them to help me?

6. What aspects of the world around me make me feel sometimes that it is a lost cause trying to raise children to be godly in this society? How does the vision of the kingdom of God at work in the Christian community give me courage to face this daunting task?

7. What has given me the greatest encouragement and Joy in reading this book? How can I pass that on to others in my Christian community? How is this Joy a foretaste of the world for which we were created and for which we most deeply long?

For Further Reading

General Works

Allen, Diogenes. *Christian Belief in a Postmodern World: The Full Wealth of Conviction.* Louisville: Westminster/John Knox Press, 1989.

Arnold, J. Christoph. *A Little Child Shall Lead Them.* Farmington, PA: The Plough Publishing House, 1997.

Bass, Dorothy C., ed. *Practicing Our Faith: A Way of Life for a Searching People.* San Francisco: Jossey-Bass, 1997.

Bellah, Robert N. "The Triumph of Capitalism — or the Rise of Market Totalitarianism?" *New Oxford Review* 57, no. 2 (March 1991): 8-15.

Bellah, Robert N., et al. *The Good Society.* New York: Alfred A. Knopf, 1991.

Brownlee, Shannon. "The Case for Frivolity." *U.S. News and World Report* 122, no. 4 (3 February 1997): 45, 48-49.

"The Bruderhof and Hollywood." *The Plough* 38 (Spring 1994): 25.

Clapp, Rodney. *Families at the Crossroads: Beyond Traditional and Modern Options.* Downers Grove, IL: InterVarsity Press, 1993.

———. *A Peculiar People: The Church as Culture in a Post-Christian Society.* Downers Grove, IL: InterVarsity Press, 1996.

Coupland, Douglas. *Generation X: Tales for an Accelerated Culture.* New York: St. Martin's Press, 1991.

Dawn, Marva J. *Joy in Our Weakness: A Gift of Hope from the Book of Revelation.* St. Louis: Concordia Publishing House, 1994.

———. *Keeping the Sabbath Wholly: Ceasing, Resting, Embracing, Feasting.* Grand Rapids: Eerdmans, 1989.

———. "Practical Theology for a Post-Modern Society." *Ung Teologi* [Oslo, Norway] 4 (1996).

———. *Reaching Out without Dumbing Down: A Theology of Worship for the Turn-of-the-Century Culture.* Grand Rapids: Eerdmans, 1995.

———. *Sexual Character: Beyond Technique to Intimacy.* Grand Rapids: Eerdmans, 1993.

———. *To Walk and Not Faint: A Month of Meditations on Isaiah 40.* Grand Rapids: Eerdmans, 1997.

———. *Truly the Community: Romans 12 and How to Be the Church.* (Former title: *The Hilarity of Community.*) Grand Rapids: Eerdmans, 1992.

———. "What the Bible *Really* Says about War." *The Other Side* 29, no. 2 (March-April 1993).

———. "Worship for Postmodern Times." *Cross Accent* 5A, no. 9 (January 1997): 6-10.

Douglas, Susan. "Remote Control: How to Raise a Media Skeptic." *Utne Reader* 79 (January-February 1997): 78-79.

Ellul, Jacques. *The New Demons.* Translated by C. Edward Hopkin. New York: Seabury Press, 1975.

———. *Prayer and Modern Man.* Translated by C. Edward Hopkin. New York: Seabury Press, 1970.

———. *Sources and Trajectories: Eight Early Articles by Jacques Ellul That Set the Stage.* Translation and commentary by Marva J. Dawn. Grand Rapids: Eerdmans, 1997.

———. *The Subversion of Christianity.* Translated by Geoffrey W. Bromiley. Grand Rapids: Eerdmans, 1986.

———. *The Technological Bluff.* Translated by Joyce Main Hanks. Grand Rapids: Eerdmans, 1990.

———. *The Technological Society.* Translated by John Wilkinson. New York: Vintage Books, 1964.

———. *The Technological System.* Translated by Joachim Neugroschel. New York: Continuum, 1980.

Erdman, Chris William. *Beyond Chaos: Living the Christian Family in a World Like Ours.* Grand Rapids: Eerdmans, 1996.

Ford, Kevin Graham. *Jesus for a New Generation: Putting the Gospel in the Language of Xers.* Downers Grove, IL: Inter-Varsity Press, 1995.

Greenberg, David F. *The Construction of Homosexuality.* Chicago: University of Chicago Press, 1988.

Grenz, Stanley J. *A Primer on Postmodernism.* Grand Rapids: Eerdmans, 1996.

Hauerwas, Stanley. *A Community of Character: Toward a Constructive Christian Social Ethic.* Notre Dame: University of Notre Dame Press, 1981.

————, and William H. Willimon. *Resident Aliens.* Nashville: Abingdon, 1989.

Hays, Richard B. *The Moral Vision of the New Testament: A Contemporary Introduction to New Testament Ethics.* San Francisco: HarperSanFrancisco, 1996.

Healy, Jane M. *Endangered Minds: Why Our Children Don't Think.* New York: Simon and Schuster, 1990.

"How to Media-Proof Your Life." *Utne Reader* 79 (January-February 1997): 73.

Hunsberger, George R. "Sizing Up the Shape of the Church." In *The Church Between Gospel and Culture: The Emerging Mission in North America,* pp. 333-46. Edited by George R. Hunsberger and Craig Van Gelder. Grand Rapids: Eerdmans, 1996.

————, and Craig Van Gelder, eds. *The Church Between Gospel and Culture: The Emerging Mission in North America.* Grand Rapids: Eerdmans, 1996.

Jackson, Wes. "On Cultural Capacity." In *Wendell Berry,* pp. 68-70. Edited by Paul Merchant. American Authors Series. Lewiston, ID: Confluence Press, 1991.

Johnson, Benton; Dean R. Hoge; and Donald A. Luidens. "Mainline Churches: The Real Reason for Decline." *First Things* 31 (March 1993): 13-18.

————. *Vanishing Boundaries: The Religion of Mainline Protestant Baby Boomers.* Louisville: Westminster/John Knox, 1994.

Kenneson, Philip D., and James L. Street. *Selling Out the Church:*

The Dangers of Church Marketing. Nashville: Abingdon, 1997.

Lasch, Christopher. *The Culture of Narcissism: American Life in an Age of Diminishing Expectations*. New York: W. W. Norton, 1978.

Leeseberg-Lange, Tom. "Crosstalk: What Music Will Lutheran Children Inherit?" *Cross Accent* 5A, no. 9 (January 1997): 4.

Liedke, Gerhard. "Das Christliche Verständnis von Frieden." In *Christen im Streit um den Frieden: Beiträge zu einer neuen Friedensethik* [*Christians in the Debate about Peace: Contributions toward a New Peace Ethic*], pp. 29-35. Edited by Wolfgang Brinkel, Burkhardt Scheffler, and Martin Wächter. Freiburg: Dreisam-Verlag, 1982.

Mains, Karen Burton. *Making Sunday Special*. Waco, TX: Word Books, 1987.

Marino, Gordon D. "In the Drug Culture." *Christian Century* 114, no. 1 (1-8 January 1997): 5-6.

Merchant, Paul. "Introduction." In *Wendell Berry*. Edited by Paul Merchant. American Authors Series. Lewiston, ID: Confluence Press, 1991.

Middleton, J. Richard, and Brian J. Walsh. *Truth Is Stranger Than It Used to Be*. Downers Grove, IL: InterVarsity Press, 1995.

Niebuhr, H. Richard. *Christ and Culture*. New York: Harper and Row, 1951.

Phillips, Timothy R., and Dennis L. Okhold, eds. *Christian Apologetics in the Postmodern World*. Downers Grove, IL: InterVarsity Press, 1995.

————. *The Nature of Confession: Evangelicals and Postliberals in Conversation*. Downers Grove, IL: InterVarsity Press, 1996.

Popenoe, David. *Life Without Father*. New York: The Free Press of Simon and Schuster, 1996.

Postman, Neil. *Amusing Ourselves to Death: Public Discourse in the Age of Show Business*. New York: Viking Penguin, 1985.

Roof, Wade Clark. *A Generation of Seekers: The Spiritual Journeys of the Baby Boom Generation*. San Francisco: HarperCollins Publishers, 1993.

Sampson, Philip; Vinay Samuel; and Chris Sugden, eds. *Faith and Modernity*. Oxford: Regnum Books, 1994.

Sass, Louis A. *Madness and Modernism: Insanity in the Light of Modern Art, Literature, and Thought*. New York: Basic Books, 1992.

Schmidt, Thomas E. *Straight and Narrow? Compassion and Clarity in the Homosexuality Debate*. Downers Grove, IL: InterVarsity Press, 1995.

Schultze, Quentin J. *Winning Your Kids Back from the Media*. Downers Grove, IL: InterVarsity Press, 1994.

Singer, Dorothy and Jerome. *The House of Make-Believe*. Cambridge, MA: Harvard University Press.

Stewart, Sonja M., and Jerome W. Berryman. *Young Children and Worship*. Louisville: Westminster/John Knox Press, 1989.

Torvend, Samuel, ed. *The Catechumenate: A Lutheran Primer*. Minneapolis: Augsburg-Fortress, 1997.

Weinreb, Mindy. "A Question a Day: A Written Conversation with Wendell Berry." In *Wendell Berry*, pp. 27-43. Edited by Paul Merchant. American Authors Series. Lewiston, ID: Confluence Press, 1991.

Whitman, David. "I'm OK, You're Not." *U.S. News and World Report* 121, no. 24 (16 December 1996): 24-30.

Wright, N. T. *The New Testament and the People of God*. Minneapolis: Fortress, 1992.

Wuthnow, Robert. *Sharing the Journey*. New York: Free Press, 1994.

Zimmerman, Martha. *Celebrate the Christian Year*. Minneapolis: Bethany House Publishers, 1993.

————. *Celebrate the Feasts*. Minneapolis: Bethany House Publishers, 1981.

Books for Children

Banks, Sara H. *Remember My Name*. Niwot, CO: Roberts Rinehart Publishers, 1990.

Drucker, Olga Levy. *Kindertransport*. New York: Henry Holt and Company, 1992.

Holland, Isabelle. *The Journey Home*. New York: Scholastic, 1990.

Lawson, Robert. *The Great Wheel*. New York: Walker Publishing Co., 1957, 1985.

Leitnor, Isabella. *The Big Lie: A True Story.* New York: Scholastic, 1992.

Lewis, C. S. *The Lion, the Witch and the Wardrobe.* New York: HarperCollins, 1994. Other books in the Narnia series in the HarperCollins Trophy edition are *The Magician's Nephew, The Horse and His Boy, Prince Caspian, The Voyage of the Dawn Treader, The Silver Chair,* and *The Last Battle.*

Lowry, Lois. *Number the Stars.* New York: Dell Publishing, 1989.

MacLachlan, Patricia. *Sarah, Plain and Tall.* New York: Harper and Row, 1985.

————. *Skylark.* New York: HarperCollins, 1994.

Morpurgo, Michael. *Waiting for Anya.* New York: Puffin Books, 1990.

Sachs, Marilyn. *A Pocket Full of Seeds.* New York: Puffin Books, 1973.

Schnur, Steven. *The Shadow Children.* New York: William Morrow, 1994.

Vos, Ida. *Anna Is Still Here.* Translated by Terese Edelstein and Inez Smidt. New York: Viking Penguin Books, 1986.

Yolen, Jane. *The Devil's Arithmetic.* New York: Viking Penguin Books, 1988.

Permissions